THE UTTERMOST PART

OTHER BOOKS BY THE AUTHOR

Though None Go With Me Rendezvous in Paris
Though One Go With Me Scotland Journey
The Region Beyond Enlarge My Coast
From Dan to Beersheba and Beyond

THE UTTERMOST PART

Barry Blackstone

RESOURCE *Publications* · Eugene, Oregon

THE UTTERMOST PART

Copyright © 2015 Barry Blackstone. All rights reserved. Except for brief quotations in critical publications or reviews, no part of this book may be reproduced in any manner without prior written permission from the publisher. Write: Permissions. Wipf and Stock Publishers, 199 W. 8th Ave., Suite 3, Eugene, OR 97401.

Resource Publications
An Imprint of Wipf and Stock Publishers
199 W. 8th Ave., Suite 3
Eugene, OR 97401

www.wipfandstock.com

ISBN 13: 978-1-4982-3159-6

Manufactured in the U.S.A.   07/17/2015

DEDICATION

I dedicate this series of memories to the students of Kerala Baptist Bible College that I have had the honor of teaching over the years. It is my desire that as they go into the uttermost part of their county they will find our time together profitable in their service to our Lord and Saviour, Jesus Christ.

ACKNOWLEDGEMENTS

I would not have gotten this book project finished if not for the editing and compiling my dear sister Sylvia did. I thank her deeply for sharing in this attempt in highlighting the plight of the persecuted church in India.

CONTENTS

Introduction: *The Uttermost Part* | Acts 1:8 | 1
Prelude: My Indian Bucket List | Psalms 37:4 | 3

1. A Trip into the Uttermost Part of the Earth | Psalms 2:8 | 5
2. The House Church at Perumbramavu | Colossians 4:15 | 8
3. The Campus Church at Kerala Baptist Bible College | I Timothy 4:12 | 11
4. The Bible as History | I Timothy 2:1-2 | 14
5. An Israeli Journey in India | I John 1:1 | 17
6. Prison Epistles | Philemon 1 | 20
7. My Prophet's Chamber | II Kings 4:10 | 23
8. The Mountains of Munnar | Psalms 65:6 | 26
9. Shadows at Green Shades | Psalms 121:5 | 29
10. Cooling Mountain Breezes | Psalms 104:3 | 32
11. Wild Goats on Anamudi Mountain | Deuteronomy 14:5 | 35
12. Wild Flower of the Uttermost | Song of Solomon 2:12 | 38
13. Out of the Mountains | Isaiah 37:24 | 41
14. Manipur Gospel Team | Mark 16:15 | 44
15. PowerPoint Presentations | Matthew 28:20 | 47
16. When All Nations Gather around God's Throne | Revelation 7:9 | 50
17. The New Mercy Children's Christian Home | Matthew 19:14-15 | 54
18. Thunder and Lighting: Wind and Rain | Psalms 77:17-18 | 57

CONTENTS

19. Writing Songs by Candlelight | Psalms 40:3 | 60
20. A Second Testimonial | II Corinthians 1:12 | 64
21. I Saw the Cross | Galatians 6:14 | 67
22. Marie: The Oldest Believer | Philemon 9 | 71
23. A Coffee Table Book to Treasure | Revelation 10:10 | 74
24. Stillness in the Midst of a Storm | Psalms 139:18 | 77
25. Death in Threes | Revelation 14:13 | 80
26. Three Weeks as a College Professor | II Timothy 2:2 | 83
27. What It Takes to be a Good Sunday School Teacher | Ephesians 4:11-12 | 86
28. Rainy Days and Sundays in Kerala | Proverbs 27:15 | 89
29. I'll Fly Away in the Morning | Job 20:8 | 92
30. Seeing India from the Air | Psalms 65:8 | 95
31. Sideways on a Scooter | Galatians 3:28 | 98
32. A Wealthy Place: Bengal and Ana | Psalms 66:12 | 101
33. The Beggar at Nandankanan | Luke 16:20 | 104
34. Blessed by a Buddhist Priest at Dhaul | Exodus 32:29 | 107
35. The Wonder of Orissa | Psalms 105:5 | 110
36. Night Train to Titiagarh | Psalms 16:7 | 114
37. Thomas of India | Luke 6:13-16 | 117
38. Orissa is Burning | Matthew 13:21 | 120
39. Getting Your Scars | II Timothy 3:12 | 123
40. Car Ride through Kalahandi | I Samuel 27:1 | 126
41. Cando Forest through Eight Stick Valley | Psalms 50:10 | 130
42. Surprising Ranjan | Jeremiah 51:41 | 133
43. Hannah's Dedication | John 10:22 | 136
44. Preachers of Phulabani | II Timothy 4:2 | 139
45. Our Days are Like Passing Shadows | Psalms 144:4 | 142

CONTENTS

46. Hindu Highlights | Deuteronomy 32:17 | 145

47. A Historic Persecution | Matthew 10:23 | 148

48. Promised Deliverance | II Timothy 3:11 | 151

49. Pastor Love and his Preacher Boys | Titus 1:5 | 154

50. Nana the Doorkeeper | I Corinthians 12:22 | 157

51. Six House Churches in Eight Hours | Philemon 2 | 161

52. Sunset and Sunrise in Orissa | Psalms 50:1 | 164

53. Three Fisher-boys at Atri Stream | John 21:3 | 167

54. A Persecuted Land | Matthew 23:34 | 170

55. Happy in Persecution | Matthew 5:11 | 173

56. Two New Names in Glory | Revelation 21:27 | 176

57. Singing Your Way through Persecution | Psalms 7 | 180

58. A Cross-less Life? | Luke 14:27 | 183

59. A Taste of Home in Hyderabad | I Peter 2:3 | 186

60. Traveling to My Indian Home | Acts 21:6 | 189

61. Campus Pastor for a Day | Jeremiah 17:16 | 192

62. The Lost Church of Gondapather | Ezekiel 34:16 | 195

63. Final Exams and Israeli Memories | Proverbs 10:7 | 198

64. Stranded by Hurricane Sandy | Isaiah 28:2 | 201

65. Why 48 Extra Hours? | II Chronicles 21:19 | 205

66. Going Home Another Way | I Kings 18:6 | 208

Postlude: My Indian Prayer List | Philippians 4:6 | 212

Conclusion: The Uttermost Ultimatum | Hebrews 7:25 | 216

INTRODUCTION
THE UTTERMOST PART

ACTS 1:8 "But ye shall receive power, after that the Holy Ghost is come upon you: and ye shall be witnesses unto me both in Jerusalem, and in all Judaea, and in Samaria, and unto THE UTTERMOST PART of the earth."

I AM SITTING IN front of my laptop computer thinking of a far-off and distant place that has captured my heart. A few short months ago, I returned from my thirtieth short-term mission's trip in forty years. This one took me back to India for a fourth time to a place that in any definition of the word would be considered an uttermost place. I traveled from my home on the coast of Maine to a remote village in central Orissa, India. The journey had covered nearly eleven thousand miles by car, plane, and train. After I got there, I felt the excitement I experienced in 1972 when I visited a similar place in the great outback of Western Australia during my first mission trip abroad, a place called Warburton. I recorded this spiritual adventure in a book called *The Region Beyond*. Once again I felt I had helped fulfill Christ's commission to "go ye into all the world, and preach the gospel to every creature." (Mark 16:15) Once again I felt I had been to the uttermost part of the earth" or what the New English Bible calls, in Acts 13:48, "earth's farthest bounds!"

Few Christians ever get to go to such places, and fewer Christian know anything about this last instruction of Jesus. We all start in Jerusalem, or, at least, our own kind of Jerusalem. For me that was a small village in Northern Maine called Perham, a truly out-of-the-way place, as all uttermost places are! Most of us have reached Judaea and Samaria, or at least surrounding counties and countries bordering our Jerusalem. For me, that was the county of Aroostook and the States of Maine and New Hampshire and the Canadian provinces of Quebec and New Brunswick. Twenty-five of my short-term mission's trips have been to Canada, the country next door. I have given most of my life to three-quarters of the Great Commission (Jerusalem, Judaea, and Samaria), but for forty years and more, my heart has always been drawn to the uttermost part, the final quarter of the Great Commission.

The Lord knows that my heart was willing to give my life to the uttermost part, whatever part that was, and I suppose those living in India or Australia may consider the towns of Maine to be uttermost places. I originally wanted to give my early life to the aboriginal people of Australia and the uttermost places of the Gibson Desert, but the Good Lord in His wise providence directed me back to New England where I have given forty years of my life to small-town pastorates in the uttermost counties of Aroostook, Washington, actually on an island off the coast of Maine, and Hancock. Ever since that first taste of the uttermost, I have desired to return to such a place. In 2006, the Lord opened the door for me to experience again the uttermost in a small village in Kerala, India called Edayappara. This spiritual adventure was recorded in my book called *Though None Go With Me*. Four years later, I again traveled to an uttermost village in Andrah Pardesh, India called Kanekel. This spiritual adventure I recorded in *Enlarge My Coast*. So now it is time for me to share with you what took place on this my fourth expedition to the uttermost part of the earth.

This part is called Dangul. I traveled there to visit a group of persecuted believers I had first met in 2006 and 2010. I promised if the Lord opened the door, I would visit them in their uttermost village. Before you are the spectacular stories, the sweet saints, and the spiritual statutes I experienced on this my latest journey into the uttermost part, one of the places the Heavenly Father promised His Son Jesus Christ.

> "Ask of me, and I shall give *thee* the heathen *for* thine inheritance, and the uttermost parts of the earth *for* thy possession." (Psalms 2:8)

It excites me to think that I have been to some of these parts, and from these parts, I have heard the songs Isaiah speaks about in his prophecy, "From the uttermost part of the earth have we heard songs, *even* glory to the righteous" (Isaiah 24:16).

It is my desire that this book will stir those who read it to venture into the uttermost parts, for until we finish this precept of the Commission, the Lord will not return. "And this gospel of the kingdom shall be preached in all the world for a witness unto all nations; and then shall the end come." (Matthew 24:14)

PRELUDE

MY INDIAN BUCKET LIST

> Psalms 37:4 "Delight thyself also in the Lord; and *HE GIVETH THEE THE DESIRES OF THINE HEART.*"

I WROTE THIS AFTER my third trip to India, but little did I know that within three years, most of this Indian bucket list would be completed on my fourth trip into the uttermost part.

Another Indian adventure was over (March of 2010), but my desires for India were far from over. I had hardly gotten back home from my third trip to the subcontinent when new dreams and desires for a fourth trip to India began to formulate in my mind. This fourth trip would be completed in November of 2012.

I have always been one to put my desires on paper. I have in my desk drawer a small blue notebook that contains my earnest expectations and my hopes for a variety of aspirations in my old age. (Philippians 2:20) Despite reaching sixty years of age a few weeks ago, I still want to experience India again, to enlarge my coast into other regions of this fabled land. As I close the pages on this trip, let me share with you what I would like to write about in another India book called *The Uttermost Part*. Here is my Indian bucket list:

1. To see the completion of the new Mercy Children's Christian Home. Work on this orphanage would double the capacity of the home, began in 2010 while I was there. (The major structure was finished in June of 2012, and I got to conduct the very first spiritual service in the new complex in October of 2012.)

2. To be able to teach again at Kerala Baptist Bible College and share with the students my Israel experiences through film and Power-Point. (I was able to do just that through fifty classes on the Prison Epistles, the Historical Books of the Old Testament, and my Powerpoint Lessons from Israel.)

3. To be able to visit my pastor friends in Orissa and to see the Church in Bhubaneswar, the capital of Orissa, and Dangul, the only church

building that has been rebuild since the devastating persecution of 2008. (A six-day trip that took me to both places and more is at the heart of this book.)

This last desire, to visit the persecuted in Orissa, has been on my heart for seven years, but because of the persecution in the region, Shibu believes it is too dangerous for me to go. I did get an encouraging e-mail from Shibu just a few days before I wrote this. For the first time since I made my request, some positive changes have taken place in Orissa concerning the persecution. Nearly a hundred families in the fellowship of churches in Orissa were forced out of their homes in 2008 and half of them have taken up residence in the capital, while the other half have stayed in Phulbani. The Hindus in the area are saying that a repeat of 2008 will not happen again. Shibu gives these four reasons:

"One, they have been able to bring only a small group of people back to Hinduism. Two, most of the people who had lost everything now have better and newer homes, and they are more committed to Christ than before. Three, the Hindus got a very bad reputation over the persecution of the Christians. Four, that attack forced the government to give better protection to the Christians. Christians are happy about this and have become bolder with their faith!"

This change might just open the door for my desired visit to Orissa in the future. (The door was opened, and I was able to enlarge my coast even further into the heart of India.) Dr. A. T. Pierson once wrote, "Saints have never yet reached the limit to the possibilities of prayer. Whatever has been attained or achieved has touched but the fringe of the garment of a prayer-hearing God. We honor the riches both of His power and love only by large demands." (Psalms 37:4)

Phillips Brooks says, "Pray not for crutches, but for wings!" I pray for the wings to take me back to India again. That prayer was answer in the autumn of 2012; and now I can share this spiritual adventure with you to the uttermost part of Orissa, India!

1

A TRIP INTO THE UTTERMOST PART OF THE EARTH

Psalms 2:8 "Ask of me, and I shall give thee the heathen for thine inheritance, and *THE UTTERMOST PARTS OF THE EARTH* for thy possession."

AT THE AGE OF twenty-one, I made my first trip into one of earth's uttermost places. It was a remote missionary settlement on the border of the Gibson Desert of Western Australia. The soul-tingling thrill of planting one's feet on God's holy ground of the uttermost against the edge of the unknown ignited a passion in my brain that has never left me. And now I was going again. It was September 27, 2012, and I was in a car with my wife heading for the Portland Jetport in Southern Maine for a flight to New York, then on to Kuwait City, and finally to Kochi, India. Since that first uttermost part adventure, over forty years have passed. I have ventured into other similar places in Canada, Israel, and India, but I knew before I boarded a JetBlue flight to JFK Airport this trip would be unique and special. Perhaps it was the anticipation of knowing I was going into a hostile land, or the soul stirring reality I would be coming face to face with a persecuted people in a persecuted land. I had read all my Christian life of such people and places, but now I was on a quest to experience that honored and respected trail myself, if only for a few days and a few fleeting hours.

Above and beyond the sheer adventure of getting there, (thirty-seven hours alone just from Ellsworth to Edayappara), there was deep within my soul an intimate love of the people of India, the pristine, tropical land of the subcontinent, and the splendor of the elephants and other marvelous creatures that inhabit this fabled country. Unlike other short-term missionaries who see India as just impoverished, dirty, overpopulated, pagan, and hot, I view India as a magnificent environment in which to move and live with awe and amazement. I have yet to fear anything in or of India, and the uttermost places I have visited have only been soul satisfying and spirit stirring in every sense.

I have written about this imperial land in three previous books: *Though None Go With Me, Though One Go With Me,* and *Enlarge My Coast.* In all three books, I have tried through word pictures to describe the people that have tempted me to return and explore more of their land and the landowners that have sparked this wonderful romantic affection for the uttermost places in India. Deep within this desire is the actual reason why I have such a drive to go. What does it mean to go? Going into the uttermost puts a certain strain on one's physical strength and stamina. I would discover on this trip just how different this trip is in one's 50s versus one's 60s. It is not easy to leave climate and culture and cuisine because there is nothing familiar or similar in the uttermost compared to back home. It calls for a spiritual fortitude, a moral discipline, and a Christian certainty of mind and muscle to push through the obstacles and pitfalls that will hinder reaching your goal. Two of these would be a place called Dangul and a young man named Ranjan.

Often a trip like mine begins with a rather tedious trail through some major airports of the world. This leads you through thick crowds, security checks and delays that are only endured because of what you know will be found at the end of the trail. Bit by bit the hours tick by with increased awareness that you are nearing the end of the first leg of your long journey. Your vista widens, distant views keep you focused, and the advantage of flying versus sailing makes you glad you live in the twenty-first century rather than the nineteenth century. In time, the path breaks as you near the western coast of Kerala. A coastal plain comes into view and, after a day and a half and losing ten and a half hours, you land at Kerala's newest airport. You were here in 2006 when it was a backwater, primitive airfield at best. Now it is as modern as any United States airport. You realize the modern world has come to Southern India, but you also know this isn't where you will be staying. This is only the edge of the uttermost. You are heading for a place just as you left it, still unspoiled by the grasp of modern man. This destination will take a three-hour car ride. Finally, after a long trip and countless miles, you see it: your home-away-from-home, a world of great stillness, your second uttermost place, now as familiar as your American town, a world punctuated only by peaceful sounds, crying blackbirds, and friendly words spoken in a language you can't speak but understand perfectly.

There is stimulation, an uplifting of one's spirit, an all-engulfing excitement that energizes your soul in such a place as Edayappara. I have spent enough time in this rural village of central Kerala for that place to have changed me. When I returned from this uttermost place the first time, my parishioners in Ellsworth thought they had gotten a new pastor. I had tasted of the uttermost and learned that it is a place that will change your perspective, your priorities, and your pastorate. I left as a pastor in a spiritual rut and returned spiritually energized and eager again to take the reins of responsibility of a local church. Going into the uttermost place with God is the greatest experience of my Christian life second only to a visit to the Holy Land and walking the Bible. There are many Christians who think they can get such a charge in the comfort-zone places of their lives. You must get outside your comfort-zone to get such a Spirit-filled surge. You will not get this thrill in one bold leap of faith or one weekend in some spiritual retreat. It is not that simple. *You must get-away, go-away, and be-away from everything you know, who you know, where you are known to breakaway to really experience the 'uttermost'.* As I settled into my familiar India, I could only anticipate that before this trip was finished, I would leave my uttermost place for another uttermost place. A place I had claimed the promise of Psalms 2:8 over.

2

THE HOUSE CHURCH AT PERUMBRAMAVU

Colossians 4:15 "Salute the brethren which are in Laodicea, and Nymphas, AND THE CHURCH WHICH IS IN HIS HOUSE."

I ARRIVED IN INDIA at 5:30 A.M. on Saturday morning, September 29, 2012. Waiting for me at the Kochi Airport was my dear friend Shibu Simon and his nephew, Sijin. Sijin (Jose) would be my driver for most of my Kerala trips and a fitting replacement for Binu, the young man who had been my driver on my three previous trips to India's most southern state. Binu was now working in Kuwait, and before I returned to the States, he would call me to say hello. The sixty-five mile road from Kochi to Edayappara was filled with familiar sights and sightings. The switchbacks and corners were as numerous as I remembered from 2006, and, before I finished my India adventure, I would travel this road six times.

My first day in Edayappara was filled with unpacking and taking a three-hour afternoon nap. Jetlag and little sleep and the calming joy of just not moving gave me a marvelous rest. I played cricket with Joshua Simon and his two friends in the Simon's front yard, ate a supper of chicken fingers, French fries and tomatoes, and enjoyed an evening Thanksgiving service. I was promised, during my last visit to India, that on my return they would not greet me with a traditional welcome service. I needed no service at all, but they changed it to a Thanksgiving service. What a blessing it was! The kids from the orphanage, the young adults from the college, my pastor friends from the IGBC and my professor friends from KBBC were there. I have never been to a place that has made me feel so welcomed. Heavenly! I had a chance to share a few words, and I summarized my feels on my return to Edayappara with these classic words from the pen of Paul, "Thanks be unto God for His unspeakable gift!" (II Corinthians 9:15)

I went to sleep that night dreaming of the uttermost places I would visit during the next month of my life. I felt like a missionary again. A great feeling for me!

My first day of ministry in India began early at 4:00 A.M. I was still on Maine time, so I was up well before dawn at 6:00 A.M. praying and planning and preparing for my first Sunday of being an Indian Pastor. I had two services on my schedule, and both of them would be firsts for me. Ever since I first went to India, I have tried to make the rounds, to visit the various ministries of the IGBC. Since I was last in Kerala, a twentieth church had been added to the association of churches in the organization. I would visit that church for their morning worship service. Because of the diversity in the student body at KBBC and because most of the students at the college were from other states in India and each state had its own language, it was decided that it was best to create a campus church at KBBC versus making the students attend Kangazha Baptist Church where the students could not participate fully because of the language barrier. That evening I would preach my first message at the new College Church on the campus of KBBC. There were more firsts but only the beginning of a series of firsts I would experience on this trip to the uttermost.

After eating breakfast with Shibu's family, I was picked up by Shaju for the ten-mile trip to Perumbramavu. I would refer to it as the Peru Church, and I think you see why! This was the hometown of my very good friend Joy Thomas, the director of the Orissa Outreach. I was excited to visit Joy's town because I had heard him say during my other visits to Kerala that someday he would get a church going in Perumbramavu. While planting churches in Orissa, Joy still had a burden for home, as we all need to have. So many in missions work to the uttermost forget that unless Jerusalem is reached we have missed this important instruction in the Great Commission. Shaju and I were on our way to Joy's mother's home with two of her grandchildren. Joy was leading us with his motorcycle for he would stay the afternoon to visit with his mother before leaving for Orissa to prepare for my coming at the end of the month. This house church was well established with its own pastor, Matthew Thankachan.

The journey east of Edayappara took us through the typical curvy roads, climbing hills, and quiet villages. Sunday in Kerala is a slow day. Having one of the largest Christian populations in all of India, we met many people heading for the churches located along the way. Perumbramavu was a quarry town located high on a hill, as are most of the IGBC churches, a fitting testimony of Matthew 5:14. Small homes were scattered here and there on the side of the hills that provided a livelihood for the people in the region. We drove as far as we could on a dirt-side road, parking in the front yard of a Hindu neighbor. Unlike Orissa, there seems to be no hostility in the two communities in Kerala. I was greeted warmly by Joy's mother. A side room had been built on the end of her home to accommodate the church of about thirty people. I was the first American to visit the church, so Shaju and I received the full welcome of flowers and Malay. That morning I spoke on "The Key to Being a Good House Church: Obedience in Obscurity" based on Colossians 4:15. After Shaju gave an invitation, one hand was seen. Later I discovered it was a young man named Lijoy who wanted to rededicate his life to the Lord. The trip was already worth the time, expense, and sacrifice.

After the service, Joy walked me further up the hill to see the huge stone quarry. Most of the men of the church, including Joy's brother, worked in the quarry. Massive amounts of stones had already been taken from the hill that left deep holes in the hillsides surrounding the village. Some of these holes were filled with water; others were still being excavated. Most of the stones were broken-up by hand, and all the stones taken away were loaded by hand. Because of the heat, a quarry worker's day begins at 4:00 A.M. and finishes around noon or whenever the trucks are loaded. In that time, teams of three men load ten trucks of rocks for 1500 rupees or $30 that is split between them. Talking to some of the men, I only heard how they made good money! I was reminded just how *hard Christian Indians* work to make a living, but, in their living, they do not neglect the Lord's house even if that House is in somebody's home.

Before I would leave India, I would visit six more house churches. Each time I did I was reminded that in my early ministry of starting a church in Pembroke, New Hampshire, I spent nearly a year pastoring a house church. There is something intimate about worshipping each Sunday in somebody's home. The Pembroke Bible Fellowship didn't meet in a room added onto the side of a home like at the Thomas' house at Perumbramavu. We met in the basement of the Trombley home. It took me back to the beginning of the Church of Christ when the gathering places for the Church were the homes of the saints. Maybe it is time to realize the value of such places of worship, whether on a Sunday or any other day of the week.

3

THE CAMPUS CHURCH AT KERALA BAPTIST BIBLE COLLEGE

> I Timothy 4:12 *"LET NO MAN DESPISE THEY YOUTH*; but be thou an example of the believers, in word, in conversation, in charity, in spirit, in faith, in purity."

I AM JUST A few months away from ending my fortieth year in the pastorate. I stand amazed at the time that has passed when I recall how determined I was to be a missionary to the uttermost part of Australia. I see now that the Lord knew best, that I was really a pastor at heart not a missionary at all. Yet in the pastorate, I have been able to pastor young people and older people that have gone to the uttermost parts all over the world. Right now my small church on the coast of Maine has a very unique record ongoing. Ever since I have been pastor of the Emmanuel Baptist Church, this church has had someone go to minister to an uttermost part of the earth as a short-term or long-term missionary sometime during the calendar year in every year since 1991. Let me share some of the places my flock has gone.

1. Alma Babson-Korea-1991
2. Jan Smith-Korea-1992
3. Nora Kent-Eastern Europe-1993
4. Sherry Clark-Washington County-1994
5. Lindsay Milne-Washington County-1995
6. Marnie Blackstone-Washington County-1996
7. Marnie Blackstone-Nigeria-1997
8. Andy Burns-China-1998
9. Hillary Summerville-Canada-1999
10. Becky Foster-Honduraus-2000
11. Alison Chamberland-Chile-2001

12. Aaron Frost-Washington County-2002
13. Marnie Blackstone-Slovikia-2003
14. Danielle Page-China-2004
15. Alison Chamberland-Mexico-2005
16. Peter Weaver-Guatemela-2006
17. Marnie Blackstone-India-2007
18. Marnie Blackstone-India-2008
19. Alison Chamberland-China-2009
20. Russ Coffin-India-2010
21. Bud and Donna Clark-Alaska-2011
22. Christina Sobel-Dominican Republic-2012
23. Alison Chamberland-China-2013

Needless to say, I know how to minister to people who have a desire to reach people in the out-of-the-way places on this planet. They are just like the young adults I preached to on that first Sunday night back to India.

My last time directly ministering at KBBC was in 2006. No former students remained and only a few of the staff of 2006 remained. I had seen the student body grow from eighteen to sixty-seven. Sixty-seven new young people to challenge, to instruct, and to exhort. That first night, I expanded my influence into nine states of India, uttermost places that I might never see, but hope to visit. At the writing of this chapter I have been to four of these states: Kerala, Tamil Nadu, Andrah Pradesh, and Orissa. But like the young people of Emmanuel Baptist, I have pastored to reach the world, now I would have a chance to do the same in India. Over the next month I would be their teacher, preacher, and mentor, and I was determined to impress on them the important responsibility to reach into the uttermost parts of their states of Kerala, Tamil Nadu, Karnataka, Andrah Pradesh, Orissa, Chhattisgarh, Manipur, Nagaland, and Assam.

Professor during the week and pastor during the weekend, Raju Sagar turned his pulpit over to me six times (five evening services and one morning service) while I was in Kerala. As with most of the professors at KBBC, Raju wears many hats: Men's Retreat Director, Dean of Students, Registrar of the College, and chaplain. A native of Orissa, Ragu is married to a lovely lady named Rejani, and they have a son Rejoice. He graduated from South India Baptist Bible College and Seminary with three degrees and is currently working on his Master's degree. Sagar has been teaching at KBBC for eight years; he had come the year before I made my first trip to Kerala. A close friend to my daughter Marnie, Ragu and I have also developed a deep spiritual friendship in two areas: the students of KBBC and his home state of Orissa. That first night was filled with singing. How the students of KBBC love to sing! "Wonderful Words of Life" was fitting for my message "Send the Light". Because English is the only common denominator between the nine states represented at KBBC. An old English hymnal, *Living Hymns*, donated by a church from the United States is their primary source for hymns and spiritual songs. After a special number from one of the young men sung in his native tongue, I preached on "The Bible is": the soldier's sword, the laborer's lamp, the teacher's truth, the saint's soap, and the sower's seed. Because I could preach in English, I had a good forty minutes to expound on their need to be well versed in the Bible before they ventured out with the Gospel of Jesus Christ into the uttermost places in their country.

Over the next few weeks I was able to exhort them with a concept that helped me when I took my first steps into the uttermost places: the instruction to Timothy by Paul in the text printed at the start of this chapter. Ministry requires a godly pattern in six areas: word (our speech), conversation (our behavior), charity (our love), spirit (our relationship with God), faith (our trust), and purity (our bodily temperance). As I have tried to instill in the young people of my churches over the years, I was trying to implant in the hearts of the students of KBBC this same pattern. These are the Christian characteristics that serve you well in the uttermost parts of God's creation.

4

THE BIBLE AS HISTORY

I Timothy 2:1-2 "This is a true saying, if a man desire the office of a bishop, he desireth a good work. A bishop then must be blameless, the husband of one wife, vigilant, sober, of good behavior, given to hospitality, *APT TO TEACH*."

ON OCTOBER 1, 2012, I began my second stint as a college professor at Kerala Baptist Bible College. Long before I desired to be a bishop, I desired to be a teacher. It was my intent to serve my country as a soldier then return to school and get my teaching degree in history. Ever since I started reading about historical events, I saw teaching as an honorable profession. Mrs. Cole, my high school history teacher, was my mentor and encourager to follow this line of work. Interestingly, she saw my potential and during my senior year allowed me to teach my fellow classmates my favorite historical topic at the time, the Second World War. For a week, I was the teacher-in-training, and she mentored me. I not only fell in love all over again with history, but I also fell in love for the first time with teaching. It was a love of soul and mind, and that love affair has lasted now for nearly forty-five years. So when the Good Lord called me into His service, I was already apt to teach.

Whether teaching kindergarteners the tabernacle or adults the book of Malachi, I enjoy teaching whenever, wherever and whatever I can. So it is not surprising when Shibu Simon, the president of Kerala Baptist Bible College, asked me to return and teach three classes at his school I jumped at the chance. I had desired for years to teach at a college level and that dream came true in 2006 when I traveled to KBBC to teach for a month the Books of the Thessalonians, the Book of Acts, the Minor Prophets, the Book of the Revelation, and the Parables of the Kingdom. It was a thrill beyond explanation and only gave me a greater thirst to do it again. I taught fifty classes in 2006, and I would return to teach fifty more classes in 2012. This time my subjects would be The Bible as History, a survey of the historical books of the Old Testament, the Prison Epistles, a survey of the Books of Ephesians, Philippians, Colossians, and Philemon, and a sharing of the classes I took during my daughter's and my 2010 trip to Israel through Dallas Theological Seminary. Unbeknownst to me, when I first arrived I was told that I would also be able to teach an evening school on the Tabernacle.

My days at KBBC started with the second period, 9:25-10:15 AM. My first class was with the Junior Class of twelve students with names like Ashok Kumar Kalum, Presentith Basumatary, and Salim Aind Munda. The first obstacle for me has always been the name barrier. If I stayed the whole school year, I would never be able to pronounce the students' names correctly. This is something I have always envied in my daughter, a gifted teacher that has no problems with the language barrier or name barrier. So what I learned in 2006 was to give each student a nickname that was in some way connected with his given name. So Presentith Basumatary became known to me as simply Present. It would be to this class I would teach my understanding of The Bible as History, the blending together of my two most favorite subjects. Needless to say, for the three weeks I taught that course I was in a history and Bible teacher's heaven. Here is the introduction I shared with them on that first day:

Here are THREE REASONS why we should study the historical books of the Old Testament.

1. *BECAUSE THEY ARE INSPIRED.* II Timothy 3:15-17. All teachings about the Bible, ANY PART OF THE BIBLE, must start, in my opinion, with this belief. I believe what the Bible says about itself. A) It is *Holy* Scripture (II Timothy 3:15). The word holy means to be set apart. As God is set apart unto holiness, so is the Word of God. The Bible is a book set apart from all other (history) books. B) It is *all* Scripture (II Timothy 3:16). Without exception, all of it, including the historical books of the Old Testament. All books, all chapters, all verses, all words, all stories are included as well. Once you remove one letter into the category of unbelief, then the rest falls. C) It is *inspired* Scripture (II Timothy 3:16). The word inspired means *God-breathed*. We are not saying just the thoughts are of God, but the very words are from God (Thus Saith The Lord). It is *human in penmanship, but divine in authorship.*

2. *BECAUSE THEY ARE INERRANT.* Titus 1:2. Inspired therefore inerrant. We have concluded that they are God's words not Joshua's words. If they are God's words then they are honest and true and *without error*; therefore trustworthy. They can be totally, absolutely

believed because they come from a God that cannot lie. The omniscient God, the all-knowing God which includes *foreknowledge, forth knowledge,* and *full-knowledge* (Psalms 139:1-6) makes the Scriptures authentic and authoritative whether you're speaking about *Geology* (Genesis 1:1), *Archeology* (Joshua 2:1), *Geography* (Luke 19:28), *Biology* (I Corinthians 15:39), *Prophecy* (II Peter 1:20-21), *Anthropology* (Genesis 1:27), *Astronomy* (I Corinthians 15:41), or *HISTORY.*

3. *BECAUSE THEY ARE INFALLIBLE.* Matthew 5:18. Distinctly, decisively, definitely the Word of God contains *God's Truth*, without falsehood or error. God's facts are divine facts; God's descriptions are divine descriptions, God's dates are divine dates; they will all stand the test of time and critics, even if it takes time for mankind to catch up to God's history. It is *pointedly, precisely,* and *powerfully* the Word of God (Hebrews 4:12), and we can use it to tell others of the thoughts and intents of the mind of God (Titus 2:1, 7, 8). I believe this precept in the Proverbs of Solomon says it best: *"Every word of God is pure: He is a shield unto them that put their trust in Him."* (Proverbs 30:5) What is true of Him is true of His word! [/NL 1–3]

It is time to discover what God wanted to teach us from the historical books of the Old Testament. "For whatsoever things were written aforetime were written for our learning . . . " (Romans 15:4).

What a joy it is to share with others your passion for the Word of God even if that Word is the historical accounts of the great events of ancient Israel. History is just another way God has used to reveal Himself to us.

5

AN ISRAELI JOURNEY IN INDIA

I John 1:1 "That which was from the beginning, WHICH WE HAVE HEARD, WHICH WE HAVE SEEN WITH OUR EYES, WHICH WE HAVE LOOKED UPON, AND OUR HANDS HAVE HANDLED, of the Word of life."

AFTER MY FIRST PERIOD of teaching with the juniors of KBBC, I immediately went into a chapel (10:20-11:00 A.M.) service with all the students of KBBC. Another one of the reasons Shibu wanted me to return to Kerala was to share the thrilling adventure I had two years before in Israel. Realizing that few if any of his students would ever get a trip to Israel, he wanted me to share what I saw and heard and touched in Jesus' land. I would do that through PowerPoint presentations during the daily chapel meetings. This is how I introduced the series of lectures I would give over the next four weeks.

For me there is no other Biblical verse that can express in a few lines what happened on Israel Study Program BE903A sponsored by Dallas Theological Seminary from May 10-30, 2010 than the verse I have printed at the beginning of this chapter. I began to read the Bible when I first learned to read. I was taught the Biblical stories long before I started school or before I could read. To say my life has been wrapped up in the pages of God's Holy Word would be an understatement. I had read it, memorized it, meditated upon it, studied it, preached and taught it for decades, but one aspect of my Biblical training was lacking, visualization. I had yet to see it, touch it, handle it, walk it, smell it, but that is what happened when I joined the Dallas Field Study team to Israel in the spring of 2010.

In the summer of 2009, my daughter Marnie began to send me information about this trip. I still can feel the excitement I felt when I read things like this:

"Picture yourself climbing through Hezekiah's ancient tunnel as it snakes beneath the city of Jerusalem . . . reading about David slaying Goliath while standing at the spot where the event took place . . . gazing out over the Judean Wilderness were 'the voice of one crying in the wilderness' announced the coming of Jesus Christ . . . looking over the Sea of Galilee from atop a cliff and review the ministry of Jesus along its shores."

I was hooked immediately, and then I read, "This program is designed for a seminary/college-aged student. It is physically VERY strenuous and much more demanding than a normal sightseeing tour! Participants will be required to walk/hike for long hours on consecutive days, uphill, downhill, on uneven steps and over rocks. You must be able to walk 8 to 12 miles on some days. Weather conditions can be very hot!"

I was far from a college student, thirty-seven years removed. I was fifty-eight, and I couldn't ever remember walking eight to twelve miles a day, ever, NOT ONCE! I began to rethink my desire, but deep in my soul the urge to go and the desire to see the Promised Land for myself quickly overcame my fear that I couldn't do it.

I soon realized that the opportunity to see Israel up close and personal could not be compared to the walking in the hot weather I might have to endure. Nevertheless, I started to prepare for the physical aspect of this trip by walking around the lanes and back roads of my coastal community of Ellsworth. Interestingly, within three months of leaving for Israel, I would be fulfilling a planned missionary trip to India. What better place to train for the heat of Israel than the 100-degree days I would experience in India? How many people get to train for a trek through Israel in India?

On a thirty-day journey through three states in India (Kerala, Tami Nadu, and Andrah Pardesh), I prepared for the strenuous aspect of my Israel adventure. Every day in India, I experienced temperatures that reached as high as 124. The hottest we saw in Israel was 105 at the Dead Sea. After India, Israel was a piece of cake. For the one hundred miles in nineteen days we had to walk, the surrounding sights were so interesting and inspiring I didn't even notice the miles slipping by, either uphill or downhill! Just to be clear. One of my companions on the trip had a walk-a-meter, and he recorded the miles we actually walked each day. The most we ever did was seven and a half miles in one day. The warning had more teeth than the actual trip had bite.

On May 10, 2010, the study tour actually began at the Dallas/Fort Worth Airport where we meet Dr. John Hilber, his wife Charlotte, and the other members of the group for our first flight to Newark, New Jersey. My daughter did recognize a few names on the team list, but we were strangers that first day. Most were students of DTS, either at the main campus in Dallas or at one of the many extension campuses around the country. In actuality, Dallas Theological Seminary was partnering with IBEX (Israel Bible Extension) of The Master's College of Santa Clarita, California to provide the expertise for the Israel Study Program. Dr. Hilber, from the Old Testament Studies department at DTS, and his wife would be our primary travel host and hostess, but once we got to Israel we would be met by Dr. Greg Behle, a professor of the IBEX Institute located in Israel itself. He would be our primary instructor and guide for our travels throughout Israel.

We left Dallas around seven in the morning and arrived in Newark about eleven. By 2:30 P.M. we were on El AL flight #28 for an overnight flight to Tel Aviv. Israel is seven hours ahead of East Coast time. The travel was uneventful including the very strict Israeli security. We arrived on time (8:20 A.M. on May 11) at the Ben Gurion International Airport on the shores of the Mediterranean Sea. It was an amazing sight and a much deeper emotional experience than I expected to have actually being in God's country. Even the strict security didn't dampen our spirits as we make our way through immigration and customs towards our waiting bus, a bus that would take us to Jerusalem. Yes, Zion itself! My eyes were beginning to see, and I was starting to look upon the miracle of Israel. (I have also written a book on this wonderful adventure to the Promised Land called "From Dan to Beersheba and Beyond"-published by the same publishing company as this book!)

That first morning chapel at KBBC was just the beginning of reliving my Israeli experience in India. Step by step I took my India students with me as I retraced the steps of Jesus. A special spiritual journey is always thrilling, but to relive those steps with others is even more of a thrill. India had prepared me for Israel and now Israel was coming alive again in India. To see and touch and experience for oneself is one thing, but to share those sights and adventures with others is the best thing a teacher can do.

6

PRISON EPISTLES

> Philemon 1 "Paul, A PRISONER OF JESUS CHRIST, and Timothy our brother, unto Philemon, our dearly beloved, and fellow labourer."

AFTER TWO STRAIGHT HOURS of teaching, I had a break before my last class of the day (12:05-1:00 P.M.). This would be my down time during my stay at KBBC. It was the students' lunch period or another class period. They eat in shifts, but I wouldn't get lunch until after my class with the seniors. I ate every day at Shaju Simon's house, next door to the campus of KBBC, where his wife or mother prepared me a fine American meal including some interesting variations on some classic American dishes, like meatloaf with hard-boiled eggs inside! I would either spend my time between classes in Shibu's office, which had air-conditioning, reading or preparing for other meetings or classes, take a trip over to the college office to check my e-mail or write e-mails, go up to the third-story library, or simply relax and read my Bible and pray. When the hour neared one, I would climb the stairs to the second floor where Julie Simon was just finishing her women's class; I would follow her class for most of the time I was at KBBC.

The senior classes contained nineteen students, one more than the entire student body in 2006. Once again I was confronted with some interesting names like Ningthoujam Alon Singh. I simply called him Sing. Romita Devi Irungbam, I simply called her Rome. I was excited to teach these young men and women Paul's four letters written from prison. I had taught all four books before in my pastorates, but never as a group, a totally different approach had I never attempted before. This was a first after nearly forty-five years preaching the Bible and forty years teaching the Bible. I love the challenge of sharing the Bible from a different angle, and Shibu gave me that chance in October of 1012. This is the outline of how I introduced the senior of KBBC to Paul's Prison Epistles.

PRISON EPISTLES

A. Introduction

   1. Paul's four prison epistles: Ephesians, Philippians, Colossians, and Philemon.

   2. Paul, a prisoner of Jesus Christ (Philemon 1)

   3. Whenever Paul visited a town, he would check out the prison before the motel because he knew he would eventually be put in jail!

   4. Illustration: Acts 16:24 and II Corinthians 11:23

   5. When written? Somewhere between 56 and 61 A.D.

   6. Where written? Caesarea (Acts 24.27) or Rome (Acts 28:30)

   7. Why written? To continue Paul's instruction to the churches as he had been doing early in his ministry and to fulfill Paul's own instruction:

   8. "All scripture *is* given by inspiration of God, and *is* profitable for doctrine, for reproof, for correction, for instruction in righteousness: that the man of God may be perfect, throughly furnished unto all good works." (II Timothy 3:16-17)

B. Was Paul really in prison?

   1. Seven times he speaks of being in prison.

   2. Ephesians 3:1, 4:1, 6:20; Philippians 1:12,13; Colossians 1:24;

   3. Philemon 1

   4. Paul was in Nero's prisons, but he was never Nero's prisoner.

C. Whose prisoner are you?

   1. We can be a prisoner to sin - Romans 6:12.

   2. We can be a prisoner to self - James 1:14.

   3. We can be a prisoner to Satan - II Timothy 2:26.

   4. We can be a prisoner to situations - Philippians 3:13.

   5. We can be a prisoner to society - I Corinthians 15:33.

   6. We can be a prisoner to a sect - Mark 8:15.

   7. Or, we can be a prisoner to our Saviour – Ephesians 3:1

D. What does it mean to be a prisoner to Jesus Christ? Matthew 11:28-30.

   1. We must see our yoke as easy - Romans 8:18 and II Corinthians 4:17.
   2. We must see our burden as light - Philippians 4:11-12 and I Peter 4:13.
   3. We must see our prison as a rest - Romans 7:17-25 and Philippians 3: 4

Over the next three weeks, I would teach chapter by chapter through these four epistles. I can honestly say that I probably learned more than my students, but it was a thrill to think that I was preparing another generation of servants to travel to the uttermost parts. Most of the seniors were from the northeasterly states of Manipur, Nagaland, and Assam of India. I also knew very well that it was a possibility that each of them could be so challenged by their faith that prison might be in the future of anyone of them. One of the most amazing aspects of the Bible is the practicality of the Word of God to a twenty-first century student, despite the fact that it was written by a first century jailbird.

7

MY PROPHET'S CHAMBER

> II Kings 4:10 "Let us make A LITTLE CHAMBER, I pray thee, on the wall; and let us set for him there a bed, and a table, and a stool, and a candlestick: and it shall be, when he cometh to us, that he shall turn in thither."

ONE OF THE JOYS of India for me has been the Elisha experience. Are you familiar with the Biblical story that surrounds the verse you just read? Elisha was a mighty prophet of God during the days of the kings. One of his responsibilities was to travel throughout the country of Israel visiting the various villages and farms scattered in the countryside. One day he was journeying through the village of Shunem (II Kings 4:8) and found hospitality and a meal from a kind woman. After he left, the woman asked her husband if it would be possible to add a room onto their home so that the next time the prophet passed through he might also have a place to rest. The husband agreed, and the next time Elisha passed through Shunem the room was ready (II Kings 4:11). Few get to experience such provision, but I have. I still remember the day the Simon family told me of the prophet's chamber they would build in their new home for others and me.

My relationship with Shibu and Julie Simon goes back to the days of their moving to India to stay. For years they had lived in the United States, going to college and starting a family, but with the sudden death of Shibu's father, a return to India was inevitable. The move came in the fall of 2005, and I made my first visit to see them in the winter of 2006. At first, they rented a place and during that visit, I stayed with Shibu's mother and brother. It was during my second trip to India in the winter of 2007 that I was taken to the property where Shibu and Julie would build their dream home. My daughter Marnie was with me, and that year we stayed in a couple of rooms in the new administrative building at Kerala Baptist Bible College. The Simons had started construction on their new home, but it would take a couple of years to complete it. This is typical for Indian construction. Remember it took them over three years to build the new Venmony Baptist Church sanctuary and parsonage. Despite the fact the work had just begun, Marnie and I got a tour of the shell of the building while we were in Edayappara for graduation 2007. It was on the second floor that Shibu pointed out to me a room being particularly built for future guests of the ministry. By the time Marnie returned to teach at KBBC the next year, the home was still under construction, but the promise was repeated to her and she was asked to pass it on.

It wasn't until my third visit to India that I got a chance to experience my prophet's chamber. True to their word, Shibu and Julie had created a wonderful haven for travelers to their mission in Kerala. The room sets on a corner of a second story floor. It contains its own bathroom with two huge windows that look out over a neighboring field filled with banana trees, coconut trees, rubber trees, and a variety of other tropical shrubs and bushes. It also overlooks the Simon's front yard and a view of the street that connects Edayappara to Mundathanam. Just like Elisha's prophet's chamber, this room is also simply furnished. Just enough for me! It contains a bed and a table (desk) and a stool (chair-plastic) and, yes, a candlestick or two. Because the lights go out quite regularly, it is important to have a flashlight, or, as they still do in India, a candle. One of the first things Joshua, the Simon's son, delivered to me on my last arrival was a couple of candles on candlesticks to be used when the need arose. I have now stayed in this chamber twice, and each visit has been a month of wonderful rest, renewal, and revelation. I have written more hymns and choruses in that room than in any other room in my life. It would be from that room I would venture out to fulfill my obligations at KBBC and various church functions at the Kangazha Church as I did that first week in Kerala.

As often happens when traveling to minister among the variety of ministries of the IGBC, an unexpected opportunity arose. On my second day of teaching at KBBC, my schedule was changed to accommodate a meeting of the pastors, deacons, and the wives of the IGBC. It was their fall conference, and I was asked to share the keynote address. After sharing my Bible at History class with the juniors of KBBC, I rushed up the street to the Kangazha Church to share a message I called "The Virtues of Our Vocation" taken from Ephesians 4:1-2. My outline was simple. I chose four words lowliness, meekness, longsuffering, and forbearance, to define the characteristics needed today in the pastorate. I worked on this during the chapel hour at the college and my free period. This gave me enough time to deliver the address and get back to have my Prison Epistle class with the seniors. Such were my days in India. Now you see why I love my prophet's chamber. It gives me plenty of time in-between events to rest and recover and revive myself for the next events. When you add the extremely hot temperatures, between 100-120 degrees that first week, and high humidity, a cooler place with a heavy duty ceiling fan was just what was needed for a northern hemisphere body to adjust to a tropical atmosphere.

My first full day in India I preached once; my second day in India I preached twice; my third day in India I taught three times; and, on this my fourth day in India, I would teach and preach four times. After my two classes at KBBC and my keynote address at the annual fall conference of the IGBC, that evening I left my prophet's chamber about seven for my most favorite meeting of all: the Tuesday Night Pastors' Prayer Meeting at Shaju's house. This weekly prayer meeting has been ongoing for nearly fifty years. Started by Shibu and Shaju's grandfather, it was a weekly event that allowed the area pastors and professors a chance to get together and pray. I had first been invited to the meeting in 2006. Since my other times in India, I had come to cherish this prayer meeting above any other meetings I attended. I would be able to attend four of the five Tuesdays I was in India. I only missed one meeting because I was in Orissa. That first meeting in 2012 allowed me to come face to face again with eight of my closest colleagues in India: Joy, Luke, Sabo, Reggie, Shibu, Shaju, Robin, and Raju. On that first night, I shared with them "The A-C-T-S of Prayer" taken from Nehemiah's prayer (Nehemiah 1:5-7).

A prophet's chamber is certainly a place of preparation and planning and wonderful peace, but it is also a place of prayer. If you haven't read of what happened after the Shunemite built Elisha's prophet chamber, I would encourage you to read II Kings 4. In summary, shortly after Elisha's first visit, he repays the kindness of the woman by granting her request to have a baby. Years later, the boy is suddenly stricken ill while helping his father in the field. The boy is taken to the prophet's chamber, and the prophet is summoned. Elisha doesn't get there in time, and when he enters the room he finds the boy dead on his bed (II Kings 4:32). He shuts the door and the room becomes a prayer chamber. "He went in therefore, and shut the door upon them twain, and prayed unto the Lord." (II Kings 4:33) One of Elisha's greatest miracles was performed in that room with the resurrection of the boy (II Kings 4:35-37). I can honestly tell you that such has been my prophet's chamber experience. With plenty of spare time, no TV, radio, or computer, it gives one time to pray. Amen!

8

THE MOUNTAINS OF MUNNAR

> Psalms 65:6 "Which by His strength setteth fast *THE MOUNTAINS*; being girded with power."

ONE OF THE BONUSES I have enjoyed on each of my trips to India is a special day planned by Shibu Simon whereby I am treated to an adventure to some part of Kerala. For a day, I was allowed to play the tourist and bask in the topical beauty that is India's southernmost state. Each day has been a surprise, a pleasant surprise filled with amazement and wonder at the splendor and spectacular landscapes and animal life of my adopted state. In 2006, I was taken to the Periyar National Park at Thakkadi to see wild elephants and other native animals on a boat ride behind one of India's greatest dams. Included in that expedition was a chance to sit on the back one of God's greatest creations, Ana-elephant. In 2007, Marnie and I were taken to the Kodanadu Elephant Rescue Sanctuary to experience the majestic Indian elephant up close and personal, including an elephant ride, playing with young elephants, visiting baby elephants in their nursery, and actually standing underneath a giant male elephant while hanging onto his tusks! In 2010, Russ and I were taken to Kumarakom where we spent an afternoon on an Indian houseboat cruising around Venbamad, Kerala's largest lake. I knew I would probably get a similar day sometime during my stay in Kerala, but I was surprised at the end of my first week when Shibu told me to get ready, for after Friday classes at KBBC, we were heading for the mountains of Munnar.

Over the years I have relished the mountain interludes of my life. I was born in hill country, not mountain country. The tallest hill in my Aroostook Country would be barely a thousand feet. The highest mountain in the State of Maine is just a mile high. It is impressive when you travel by it because it rises sharply from a flat plain, and it is only surrounded by hills, no other mountains in the region. So it has only been when I have gone far a field that I have experienced the unusual uplift and inspiration that comes from God's majestic mountains. I had traveled into the mountains of Kerala twice before, but this time I would be journeying into Kerala's greatest mountain range and would climb her highest hill, one nearly two miles high, the highest to this point in my life. Never did I dream that such climbs would happen to me, nor did I know the solitude of mountains would have such an impact on my life. I have actually written down my mountaintop experiences in a series of devotionals I call "The Western Hills and The Holy Word". In this series of mountain observations, I have chronicled my forays into the mountains of Maine, the mountains of New Hampshire, and the mountains of Kerala. Now once again I stood ready to climb the highest hill and catch a glimpse of glory bright that can only be seen from a mountaintop.

We should not be surprised that mountains have this kind of impact on mortals like me, for was it not so often repeated that the Almighty met his men in the mountains: Noah on Ararat, Abraham on Moriah, Moses on Sinai, Elijah on Carmel, and Jesus on Hermon? I believe it is the impression of the height and the vastness of space that can be seen, not to mention the durability and everlasting nature of a mountain. Time never seems to change a mountain, just like God Himself. A trip into the high country of any state will stimulate your very soul and refresh your spirit with its sweeping views and serene vistas. The higher you get the grander and more glorious the sights, and the closer you feel to God. This is how I feel each time I venture into the mountains created by the Word of God so long ago (Hebrews 11:3). They remain impressive and inspiring, and then there are the cooler temperatures after a week in the heat and humidity (110 most days) of the foothills of Edayappara.

We left Shibu's house around 2:15 P.M. with a car full of excited tourists. Besides the Simon family, Shibu, his wife Julie, their son Joshua and daughter Abigail, there was an uncle, an aunt, and a nephew Sijin, our driver. Despite the fact we were only going to travel sixty-five miles, it would take us four and a half hours to get to our destination. Shibu decided, because of the traveling time, it would be better if we drove up on Friday, stayed the night at a bed and breakfast, giving us all of Saturday to explore before returning to Edayappara late Saturday night. Given the honored seat beside Sijin, I had a front-seat view of the scenery into the mountains at Munnar. I knew this was going to be another marvelous trip when, within a few miles, we saw our first elephant. A massive male tied up in a grove waiting his next day's job. Of course, I had to stop and get a picture. He was my thirty-sixth elephant sighting since my first in 2006. Yes, I keep count of the mountainous creatures that have thrilled me with each encounter, just like the mountains.

Modern man has, in my opinion, cut himself off from the joys and benefits of God's wild world. Locked in the mayhem of his own creation, metropolitan centers, average individuals know nothing of the calming value of trees, water, birds, flowers, hills, and fields. A God-made environment can only relieve the stress and strain of a man-made environment. I have come to believe that there was a reason God created hills and mountains and why this planet isn't flat. The hills challenge our strength, the mountains challenge our muscles, and the foothills harden our bodies, and energize our minds, quicken our spirits, and toughen our resolve and purpose. Just like the Creator-God shaped the mountains thousands of years ago, the mountains sharpen our souls and stir us into a confrontation with just how small we really are and how the grandeur of God is far above us. As we covered the slow, curving miles from Edayappara to Munnar, the valley grew smaller and smaller. The mountain ridge that contained Kerala's highest peak grew larger and larger. The switchback lane they called a road got narrower and narrower as one dead-man curve after another brought us into the high country of northeast Kerala. Darkness overtook us about seven miles short of the town of Munnar. We would have to spend the night on the slopes and wait the morning light to continue our ascent. I was pleased because in all my mountain experiences this would be the first time I actually slept at this altitude.

What a rare and special treat would be that night in the mountains of Munnar! Perhaps, the only such night in my life. In this most harmonious setting, I would experience one of those mountaintop experiences that reminded me of what the mountain men of the Bible must have experienced. With the psalmist I echoed, "Praise the Lord from the earth . . . mountains and hills . . . praise ye the Lord." (Psalms 148:7, 9, 14) In this lofty landscape, where the mountains push their ragged ridges against the edge of the sky, one of the most common emotions I experienced is the spin-chilling thrill of being in awe of God's untouched dominions, free from the advance of man's hand. I knew from the moment I arrived under the shadowing slopes of the mountains of Munnar that I would love staying here if only for twenty-four hours.

9

SHADOWS AT GREEN SHADES

Psalms 121:5 "The Lord is thy keeper: the Lord is thy SHADE upon thy right hand."

Have you ever had an experience, spent a day, and witnessed something that when it was over you thought, "That must have been a dream, did I really see that, feel that, see that?" The psalmist was right when he wrote that life is sometimes like a shadow (Psalms 144:4). James writes of the same concept this way: "For what is your life? It is even a vapour (a fog), that appeareth for a little time, and then vanisheth away." (James 4:14) This was like the mountain mist at a bed and breakfast seven miles outside of Munnar called Green Shades.

Our climb into the hill country of northeast Kerala continued late into the afternoon of October 5, 2012. One of the interesting aspects of this day off was the fact it was an answer to a prayer I had started when I first heard of this corner of Kerala. In previous conversations, Shibu, years before, had told me of this paradise his father loved above all other natural sites in Kerala. He talked about waterfalls, wild elephants, beautiful flowers, rare goats, and towering mountain peaks. I breathed a simple prayer to the Almighty, "How I would love to visit that place someday!" That day had come, and I was witnessing what had drawn Thakadiel Simon to this mountainous retreat. Besides the deep valleys and the thick forests along the winding road, there were the spectacular waterfalls. I have been a waterfall lover since childhood, but the waterfalls of my youth were small in comparison to the ones I have experienced in adulthood, including the most amazing one of all, Niagara Falls. The waterfalls of Munnar were not as large as Niagara, or as broad, but they were nevertheless awe inspiring, much like the waterfalls I have experienced in the backcountry of Northern Quebec while fishing with my father-in-law. The only difference was the sheer height from which the water fell off the granite cliffs alongside the mountain road we were climbing. It was cold, clear, pure water pouring off soaring ridges into deep gorges, roaring rivers of H_2O tumbling down massive slides of stone into a seemingly bottomless ravine. We stopped a few times to get pictures with these streams of water behind us, but my digital camera wasn't up to the task of actually capturing the might and majesty of the sites or the sights. At each turnout, there were vendors selling their wares, trying to capture the tourists that stopped for a look, but I was drawn to the music more than the merchandise. Music, you might ask? A man playing a musical instrument, taped music, a band? None of the above. It is the music of the mountain. There is an uplifting thrill that comes to the mountain traveler when he stops by a hilltop brook for a pause during a long hike upward. Rejuvenation and restoration await the soul that is ready to listen to water rushing over rock. For me, this is one of the original hymns of God. Its tune is divine; its melody from the creative hand of God Himself, and its harmony can cure the worst of days and heal the ailment known as 'valleyitus'. There is a wondrous therapy in the falling and flowing of water over mountain rock. Truly, a song from a summit that soothes a soul.

Our stops by wonderful waterfalls ended as the shadows of evening began to engulf our party of eight. Shibu had realized that we might not make Munnar by nightfall because he knew that with elephant stops and waterfall stops our window of time would run out before we arrived at our appointed destination. He had called ahead to a brand new bed and breakfast located on a side hill just south of Munnar. We were to learn that we were only the second party to stay at Green Shades, and I would be the first foreigner. The massive shadow of a high mountain ridge swallowed us as we turned into our night's resting place. The owner's wife meet us at the gate and, despite the dusk that was falling rapidly, I could see that I was entering the finest bed and breakfast I had ever stayed in my life, whether in India, Canada, Israel, England, or the good old USA. Only in the breaking of the dawn would I understand and realize just how special this stay would be.

The manager of the resort took us to our rooms in a separate building behind the owner's massive ranch style home. You might have thought you were in Texas, for I had seen that type of home there. It was like a Spanish hacienda. A red brick circular driveway led to a large front porch filled with flowerpots. If there was one flowerpot there were a hundred. The lawns along the driveway and the lawn in the middle were covered in grass, a very rare sight in India. I had only seen grass a few times in my visits to India. I knew other surprises were waiting for me as I settled into my private room and got ready for bed. The ultimate joy of that night was the fact I slept under a blanket, something I had never done in Edayappara. Once the sunset happened, it felt like the temperature dropped twenty degrees. The combination of altitude and the forest the bed and breakfast was located in helped bring the temperature down. The owner of the complex had literally built his home and the bed and breakfast in the middle of a ten-acre cardamom plantation. It appeared that he had dropped the building into the clearings, for the estate had become a part of the forest versus the forest becoming a part of the estate. I had one of the best nights of sleeping I had ever had in India, dreaming only of what I would see when I awoke.

I was up at dawn, long before my fellow travelers, but not before George, the owner. I met him as I exited my room for a walk-about. At first I thought he was one of the staff, but soon realized I would be given a grand tour by the boss himself, a man proud of what he had created in a forest plot on a high mountain slope. A two thousand foot hill soared over George's plantation, and the morning shadow was still lying heavy as the sun tried to struggle over the ridgeline. I had never seen the sun fight to gain height over a surrounding landscape before. Amid such grandeur, the massive trees seemed small against such a backdrop, but in reality stood a hundred feet high above me. They were some of the greatest trees I have ever seen in my life. One stood all night beside my room that would measure at least twenty feet around. How they had found footing and flourished in this high, harsh terrain was amazing to me. Standing tall on a mountainside, the sturdy trunks, dwarfed by the mountain, had survived untouched. It was a virgin forest in a world that has destroyed most similar places. George had created his dream home and business without changing the environment. He was a very rare fellow indeed.

I learned, as I walked with George through his creation, that he had made his money in satellite dishes and television cable. His main business was located in Munnar, but he had built his dream house and started his bed and breakfast for his wife. He had two boys: one worked for the Indian government and the other was applying to work for NASA. Despite his successful business, wonderful family, and Green Shades, he was most proud of the fact his family had been Christian since the tenth century. Through nearly a thousand years of family history, he could trace his spiritual roots. I would see his church building when we got to Munnar and pray for him and his family in his home before I left. But to my discerning spirit, it was only a shadow. Sincere, but only shades of real Christianity. There are many false shadows in this world today.

10

COOLING MOUNTAIN BREEZES

> Psalms 104:3 "...WHO WALKETH UPON THE WINGS OF THE WIND."

I WOKE, THAT SECOND Saturday in Kerala, to the sound of a gentle zephyr swaying the massive trees surrounding Green Shades. The mountain winds have a special scent when you're standing in a cardamom planation. In my mountaintop experiences, I have realized that there is no wind like a mountain wind. There is a unique, simulating energy to hill breezes that profoundly stirs your soul. The best aspect of such breezes is that they are cooler than the tropical breezes that blow through Edayappara. Because my home away from home is near the ocean, the trade winds of the Arabian Sea are hot and humid. That is why I have enjoyed every day I have spent in the mountains of Kerala.

For nearly two hours, George showed off his magnificent mansion and gorgeous grounds, and, all the while, that cooling breeze invigorated me. I had experienced the baking heat and humidity in the foothills of Kerala for a week, and I knew that within twelve hours we would start our descent back into that oppressive oven, but, for now, the winds off the slopes of Munnar's mountains cooled my blood, filled my lungs, and sharpened my senses to one of the best visual experiences I have ever had on my pilgrimage through the hills and valleys of this planet. I have learned of the beautiful regularity of wind: as the sun warms the morning air of the mountains a zephyr is created. The circulation of that wind brings such calmness and coolness to the weary traveler that making the long climb to the summit is well worth the effort. Little did I know, as we travelled on to an even higher elevation, what joy that wind would give my traveling companions and me!

After our walk-about, we had breakfast. This was a bed and breakfast wasn't it? In a back room off one of the lodges, a dining room area had been set up for us. While the Simon clan had a traditional hot and spicy breakfast, George's cook had fixed me an egg omelet and toast. What made the omelet one of the best I have ever eaten was the fresh pepper straight off a planation bush and wild honey for my toast straight from wild honey bees from the surrounding forest, another sellable product from George's woods. I tried for the first time Doze, a kind of flat bread that would have been much better with a bit of Maine maple syrup, but it was all right. The food was good and the fellowship was sweet. We all talked of the wonderful night's sleep we had experienced and the number one best virtue of the place—the cooler air, a chilly breeze that required a blanket. The Simons all agreed that it was even a bit cold, but as for this Maineaic, it was like a night at home!

Before we left Green Shades, George invited us into his home: the richest, most elegant house I have ever entered. It had the same richness that characterized the room I slept in the night before, and blowing through that mansion was the same breeze that caressed my face as I exited my room earlier that morning. The mountain breeze was beginning to bend the branches of the surrounding bushes and shrubs, and the rustling of leaves could be heard even in the house; the soothing, cool, therapeutic touch that only a mountain breeze can give! The kind of wind that enfolds your whole body, softly touching your cheeks, massaging your muscles, and leaving the surface of your flesh tingling. You know the kind, don't you? The kind of breeze that on a cool spring day makes you think that anything is possible, that you will stay forever young by one breath of such a breeze. We left Green Shades with the windows of the car open, the air-conditioner off, enjoying a mountain breeze beyond description.

Only a few corners after our departure from George's grand home, we entered tea country. We had seen a few hills covered in tea bushes before Green Shades, but after Green Shades, every hill and hilltop was covered in those beautiful manicured shrubs. Since my first sightings in 2006, I have enjoyed every vista that is tea bush covered. How do I describe the canopy that is an Indian mountain tea planation? Whole hills and down into the valleys between those hills, nothing other than these three to four foot high bushes perfectly placed so that a tea gatherer has room to walk between each bush, just wide enough to reach each leaf that needs picking. The tea hills continued until we arrived in the village of Munnar. Our first trip there was to just pass through. We would stop later, but for now our goal was beyond Munnar to the Eravikulam National Park. Just on the eastern side of town, more hills and valleys with more tea bushes, planation after planation right into the park itself. All along the way that wondrous breeze blew through the window. If the sights along the way were amazing, the smells were divine. One of my favorite drinks is tea, but I must admit the best aspect of tea isn't its taste but its smell, and the best smell is driving through a roadway surrounded by tea bushes. The pungent aroma is better than a pot of tea. My dear wife would disagree, but she has yet to witness the mountain tea bushes of Munnar.

The mountain air moving through Shibu's car that morning was sharp and clear and clean and wondrously wholesome. No pollution there! No factories or power plants belching those foul smells. Munnar was a place you could inhale deeply as the surge of a mountain updraft of tea-spiced air enters your lungs. Despite the fact that the oxygen is lower at eight thousand feet, I sensed no difference. I have never gone high enough to know what oxygen deprivation is. The air, as we climbed higher up the slopes of Anamudi, began to be more refreshing not less, more invigorating not less, more pleasant not less. To breathe deeply of a mountain breeze is tremendously freeing. It is to be fully awake, fully alive. It gives one strength and energy for the climb. There is something very arresting about a mountain wind that brings freshness to your day. It is inexhaustible and without restraint. You can breathe without worry of its limit or supply. Though invisible, it is enormously apparent that its virtues vastly outweigh it vices. Before I returned to the USA, a terrible gale named Sandy would destroy sections of the East Coast of America, but, on the day I climbed Mount Anamudi, the wind was energizing not destructive, rejuvenating not deadly, tender not bold.

We got to the bottom of Anamudi about ten in the morning along with scores of other desiring to take a bus ride to the summit. We had to wait in a long line for about half an hour for our turn, but all that time our familiar friend blew in our faces. It carried with it the same sweet scent we had enjoyed at George's place, and as we got on the bus for the ascent, the breeze got on board. With windows opened and with the steep winding road, I felt like the Psalmist. I was '"walking on the wings of the wind". As the park station grew smaller and smaller and the mountain road just a thin line in the rolling hills, the breeze grew stronger. By the time we reached the end of the road, still a thousand feet short of the mountaintop, the breeze was huffing and puffing. Even cooler than before, yet still comfortable, the now of reality struck me. The mountain air I was inhaling would only do me that day. The breeze that was refreshing me would not last beyond the moment. The surge of mountain oxygen was only for the now. I could not store it, hoard it, or bottle it; I must enjoy it and then leave it. Such are the realities of a mountain breeze and a moment in time. Relish it now, for the hot air will soon return.

11

WILD GOATS ON ANAMUDI MOUNTAIN

Deuteronomy 14:5 ". . . AND THE WILD GOAT . . . ."

As I started up the trail that wound its way across the western slopes of Kerala's highest mountain, I recalled the words of Solomon, "There be three things which are too wonderful for me, yea, four which I know not . . . ." (Proverbs 30:18) The wisest man of all time spoke of eagles (the only eagles I have seen in India have been in a zoo), serpents (I have yet to see a cobra in the wild), a ship in a storm (I am no mariner), and maids and men, of which India has plenty, but I was thinking of Neela Kurinjy, Nilgiri Thars, Anamudi, and Attukad. I had witnessed the mighty waterfalls of Attukad on the ascent to Munnar, and now I was under the brow of Anamudi as the Simon family and I walked the path upward toward the summit. Before we reached the end of the trail, a white fog would engulf its peak, and the wonder of seeing the world from the top wouldn't happen. I had to be content with witnessing its majestic ridge from below. Because the summit was outside of my reach, I started focusing my attention on another wonder of Munnar, Nilgiri Thars, the rarest mountain goat in India.

I am always thrilled to tramp a new path lined with new sights. So as we criss-crossed the high country of Anamudi ever upward, I kept a sharp lookout for the famous wild goats of Munnar. It was a really good day for a hike of exploration. That wondrous breeze was keeping us cool, and despite the gathering fog on the mountaintop, the visibility up to the top and down to the bottom was crystal clear. As I topped the crest of another level of the trail, my breath was taken away when I realized just how high I was. I had passed my all-time record. I have a picture in my office of my daughter and me on the top of Mount Washington in New Hampshire. Of course, we drove to the top and walked only the last few feet. We are standing on a pile of rock next to a marker that read: Mt. Washington Summit - 6,288 feet. I was now well over two thousand feet higher than that, and I knew that well over another one thousand feet would be required to reach the summit of Anamudi. Stopping to catch my breath, I am not a professional mountain climber by any stretch of the imagination; I stood near a stunted shrub when suddenly a distant movement high up the slope caught my attention. Some sort of animal was moving under the overhang of a massive cliff protruding from the side of Anamudi, but what creature?

Silently I eyed the movement for some recognition. My natural eyes couldn't pick up anything distinguishable, so I got out my digital camera and zoomed in to see if the artificial eye could see what the natural eye couldn't. Through the viewfinder at the back of the camera, I carefully scanned the rock face. At first it seemed devoid of life until a fellow hiker shouted, "There they are!" I refocused my attention to the spot he was pointing and, sure enough, there masterfully camouflaged against the gray side of Anamudi was my first wild goat of Kerala. Within moments I found a second goat similar in size walking along the steep slope, as easily as if it was walking on level ground. Their traction was incredible; why they didn't slip and fall on the wet rock is unknown to me. It's a God-given ability that defies man's understanding. If they were the only two goats I saw that day I would have been content, but added delight was to follow me all the way to the end of the trail and all the way back to the bus.

Fortunately, the amount of visitors to the mountain had taken the fear of man out of this group of wild mountain goats. So it was possible to stalk the herd easily from our path. We were not permitted to exit the trail, but the goats were permitted to come close. What a rare and special treat this was for me! I have always loved watching wildlife in the wild, much more so than in a cage. Few and far between have been my visits to a zoo, for I prefer sightings just as I was enjoying them on Anamudi. Often my encounters with wildlife have been fleeting, a glimpse here, a glance there, but on our hour long hike we met the Nilgiri Thars up close and personal fifteen times. When you consider that only two thousand remain in the wild, this is amazing! For most of my special animal encounters in the wild, the dark shadowy shape is momentary against the backdrop of a tree, a stream, or a forest road, but that late morning ascent brought me at times within ten feet of a wild goat. Often the goat would stay put for minutes grazing on the grass near the trail. I got some marvelous pictures, but the photographs in my head are still the most vivid.

I spent a total of ninety minutes on the slopes of Anamudi in the company of the wild goats. They were heavy, well fed, and flourishing on their rugged ridges where their only enemy is a leopard-like cat, of which we saw none. Needless to say, these goats are protected animals in Kerala.

Their coats are grayish-brown, which allow them to blend into their environment perfectly. At first they were hard to spot, but once I got used to their shape and size, I could see them everywhere. We found them most often near the water sources along the trail. These small mountain springs flow periodically out of the side of granite split in the rock. After a few minutes and a few photographs at the top, we headed down off Anamudi. Beyond was a car road which led to a settlement of native people that lived on or near the top of the mountain, a road we were not allowed to go on. On the way down, we saw more wild goats, and the best sighting was left to the end. Rounding a bend in the trail, Shibu said, "Barry, look over your shoulder!" And sure enough, standing on a large boulder was a medium size Thars. One of my prized pictures of that trip is a photograph Shibu took of me and a Nilgiri Thars in the background. This had been a tranquil, thrilling day in the mountains, the hills all draped in clouds with a soft, fragrant breeze blowing through the stunted shrubs lining a steep mountain path. The gentle interlude with fifteen wild goats gave me the feeling of gracious thanksgiving to the Maker of the horned Nilgiri Thars for allowing me to interact with this rare part of His creation!

As we waited for the bus to take us back to the valley, I treated my companions to an ice cream. There was a tourist center at the end of the bus route. You didn't think that man hasn't found a way to make money even in this pristine place, did you? Though cooler, a hike up and down a steep 1000 feet was warming, to say the least. I sat back and took one more look into the harmonious world of the Nilgiri Thars, and how they had adapted to the high altitude, the exposed environment, and the rarified air of their world. And now I know firsthand why 'the wild goat' is not an abominable thing to God (Deuteronomy 14:3-5). Amen. And sometimes when the Good Lord takes you to the uttermost part, He shows you His handiwork of creation and the amazing detail He wrought even in the uttermost!

12

WILD FLOWERS OF THE UTTERMOST

> Song of Solomon 2:12 – "THE FLOWERS APPEAR ON THE EARTH..."

IN THE LOFTY LANDSCAPES where the mountains of Munnar push their rough ridges against the edge of the sky, one of the most amazing transformations I have ever heard about takes place on the slopes of Anamudi. As I was enjoying the sweet taste of an ice cream bar awaiting a bus ride off Anamudi, Shibu told me the story of Neela Kurinjy. Incidentally, we all eat our ice cream in honor of my daughter Marnie who would have loved to be with us. It was after such adventures that Marnie and I always rewarded ourselves with an ice cream cone, as we did at the Eiffel Tower in Paris and Hezekiah's Tunnel in Jerusalem. But, let's go on to Shibu's story of Neela Kurinjy.

Eight years before Shibu took me to Eravikulam National Park, he had taken his wife Julie and their young son Joshua to witness one of the rare flowerings of nature. The Neela Kurinjy is a violet-like flower that only appears on the hillsides of Eravikulam once every fourteen years. Did you get the time frame? Once every fourteen years, a purple swath of flowers spreads like a colorful quilt up and down the slopes of the hills of the park. For only a few short weeks in the year of their resurrection does this violet of flowering glory appear as a mantle of wilderness wildflowers. What is it that tells the Neela Kurinjy it is time to blossom and bloom in the high country of Munnar? Or should I ask Whom? The closest I came to this marvelous event was a few poster-size photographs hung on posts along the trail we climb. I knew I would have to return in 2018 to witness this spectacular myself. A picture and a description by my host wouldn't be enough to fully explain this rare marvel of God's creative power and continual influence.

If you believe like I do, it was on the third day of creation that the Almighty God created the Neela Kurinjy. It would be different than most flowering plants. Its rebirth wouldn't happen every spring; it would hibernate for fourteen years between re-blooming. It would survive the worldwide flood and would be limited to the barren soil and open ground on stony slopes in the mountainous terrain of Northeast Kerala, India, so steep that they are almost vertical. High in the mountains, it would thrive despite the high terrain and shallow soil. With deep roots, it would anchor itself to the side of mountains accessible only to mountain goats and mountain leopards. Few at first would even know it was there until mankind got a taste for tea, discovering that the higher the tea bushes the better the tea. One of the items I brought back from India was a sample of the world's highest grown tea for my tea-loving wife. While cultivating the hills around Munnar, the first residents discovered a rare visual treat that happened only once in a decade and nearly a half. Why is it when man witnesses such miracles of nature they fail to acknowledge God? Year after year the Neela Kurinjy patiently waits its appointed time. Season after season it calmly waits its time of budding. Generation after generation its purple flower cloaks the high hills of Munnar to the gladness and glory of those who get to experience this transformation in a bleak and nearly barren land. It becomes a violet carpet flung openly and freely over the hills by the hand of God.

If one looks beyond the impressive granite slopes and the magnificent Nilgiri Thars, the land of the Neela Kurinjy is not noteworthy. There was very little color on the hills the morning I spent on Anamudi. Granted, far below you could make out the green and yellow hue of the tea plantations. This coloring is a sign that the tea bush needs picking. But, high above, even too high for tea, there was little color at all. One of the reasons the wild goat was so hard to see was it was the same color as the surrounding terrain. Bland at best, I would call it. My first trip to Eravikulam was certainly for the goats and the mountain and, yes, maybe the cooler air, but if I ever get a chance to return it will be to witness the spectacular appearance of Neela Kurinjy. It was, I believe, God's way of putting a little color into a drab environment.

I must admit as we slowly wound our way down the treacherous roadway, I focused on Shibu's story rather than my fear of the roadway. Without a doubt it was the most dangerous road I had ever been on. The only way to explain it is to say it was like a bus on a rollercoaster. In my mind, I tried to imagine the territory I was driving through covered with this beautiful purple flower. Off in the distance, I could see another one of the gorgeous waterfalls that periodically pop up, and within a few minutes, we were low enough for tea bushes again. Looking back over my shoulder, I took one final look at Anamudi and its greyish silhouette resting in the clouds, touching the sky. What would millions, if not billions of small violet flowers do to the landscape? Even when we finally disembarked from our flying rollercoaster, I couldn't get the image of the mountain draped in purple out of my thoughts.

While Sijin got the car, I wandered through the local market looking for a treat. My eyes fell on a carrot farmer who was selling his vegetables just outside the entrance of the park. For twenty cents (ten rupees), I bought a bunch of tiny carrots and ate them as I waited. They were great, good and fresh, but my mind and eyes turned upward once again to the story of Neela Kurinjy, God's flower that is only found in the uttermost part. It was there on the side of a road under the shadow of Kerala's highest hill, I understood the lesson of Neela Kurinjy. "Bloom where you are planted!"

This old adage sounds simple enough, but how many of us actually live its precept? People have romantically repeated this concept for years, especially us preachers. But when it comes to the practical application, few behave like the Neela Kurinjy. The problem is that most of us are more like Neela than we care to admit. Who of us has not felt like we too have been abandoned for years on end with no productivity in sight? Rarely do we shine in the spotlight and more rare in the limelight! I am troubled by the modern preachers, charismatic pastors, and hyper-evangelists that proclaim that God's miracles bloom and blossom daily, instantaneous, ours for the asking. They rant and rage at their congregations telling them they ought to claim their rights and receive their prosperity, now! Instead, I believe the Almighty would have us look around and quietly notice the Neela Kurinjy. There, in the patient, perseverance of that plant is the miracle we need to seek. On a gaunt granite mountainside, He has planted one of the most beautiful bouquets in all the earth. There He has turned rain and sunshine and soil into one of the most spectacular, natural events that ever happens, and most of the time He is the only one that sees it. A mountaintop flower of the finest purple pushes its lovely bloom through the rocky soil on a remote hillside meadow. No man's hand has any part in such a spectacle. O, to see such a sight and remember " . . . .that even Solomon in all his glory was not arrayed like one of these." (Matthew 6:29) And " . . . ye are of more value than many sparrows," (Matthew 10:31) How much more valuable are we than the Neela Kurinjy? Bloom where and when your Creator says and be content with His time and timing.

13

OUT OF THE MOUNTAINS

Isaiah 37:24 " . . . I COME UP TO THE HEIGHT OF THE MOUNTAINS . . . "

ONE OF THE REALITIES of hiking in high country is what goes up must come down. I had stood on the highest summit in my life and witnessed wondrous animal life and amazing scenery, but now I was slowly working my way back, from sky edge to sea edge. From above the timberline to below the ridgeline, the Simon car was descending into the village of Munnar as the afternoon of our Saturday retreat continued. Our goal was to do some shopping in the business district of Munnar before having lunch and an evening return to Edayappara.

Sijin parked the car in a very busy section of downtown Munnar, a typical India village with scores of people, plenty of autos, and small shops lining every available space. India is all about small businesses, and there were plenty to visit in Munnar. I was constantly looking for George's office, but never found it. Instead, we found a spice shop where I checked off all the spices and tea on Coleen's wish list. My mother-in-law Opal wanted a candy bowl, and in a shop next to the spices shop, I found her a rosewood bowl. Also in that shop I found a rosewood rolling pin for my wife. She loves to cook and rolling pins are a favorite kitchen gadget of hers. I asked if they might have a carving of a mountain goat to add to my carvings of elephants, but they didn't. I was disappointed that in Thars country no one had carved the image of the rare goat in wood, for at least a tourist like me! I also picked up a map of the area for my journal and, as a treat, a couple of bags of Lays potato chips. I am addicted to potato chips, and it was a rare treat in India to say the least. As we wandered through the bazaar, Joshua and I found a place that sold soda, and I bought a bottle for each of us. I can honestly say it was one of the best tasting sodas in a while for me. I am not much of a soda drinker, but a taste of home in a strange land is special. I was also looking for scarves for the ladies in my life, and in a back alley, Julie found a shop that had plenty, but not the size my wife and mother-in-law desired. I did find a beautiful blue and cream colored one for my favorite daughter Marnie for Christmas; she loves Christmas presents from India.

After an hour's walk up the mountain and an hour or so walking the streets of Munnar, we all decided we were hungry. George's breakfast had worn off. It was nearly two in the afternoon when we arrived at Silvertips. I know it sounds like a seafood and steak place, (I could only wish!), but it was your typical India restaurant with plenty of hot, spicy food. I did find chicken fingers and French fries on the menu, so I was content. I bought lunch for eight people, and it only cost me $35. By the time we left the restaurant it was raining, and our trip out of the mountains of Munnar began. It would take us five hours to retrace the sixty-five miles back home, but the descent was just as spectacular as the ascent. We would make six stops on the road home, a very typical journey in India:

1. At a roadside vegetable stand to pick up some carrots
2. At a nursery to buy some flowering plants for Julie's garden
3. At a village market to buy bananas and oranges
4. At a rubber tree grove to take pictures of my second elephant of the trip
5. At a secluded place so the boys could go to the bathroom
6. At a bakery for some Sunday treats and a few cashews for me

As I came out of Shangri-La, I enjoyed the view of looking down just as much as I enjoyed the view of looking up. It was the same road, the same scenery, but the world looks much different depending on the angle of your view. On the way up into the mountains, I was focusing on the waterfalls we saw, but as we descended most of the falls were behind us. This time I was focused more on the cliffs and bluffs of the hills we passed. Periodically we passed a section of mountain that had been converted to a tea planation, but most of the time it was a rocky cliff or a tree-covered bluff that caught my eye. There was also occasionally a home situated on the outcropping, some poor shacks at best, but sometimes beautiful houses; the view must have been beyond description. Tucked in a woody land surrounded by granite, the placement defied explanation, yet there it was. As I watched these places go by, I reflected on how our lives are like a mountain road. The first half of our life is an ascent, a wonderment of everything new, but a time come when we crest the summit and start down the other side of life. We come to the place Solomon reached when there is nothing new under the sun for us (Ecclesiastes 1:10). We have seen it before, we have traveled the road before, and for some we stop looking and sleep through the rest of the trip. I have learned that even when you retrace your steps and travel the same road again, there are new sights to see: things you missed the first time, the renewed influence of people, the special impact of the natural world, and the care and affection of family and friends that change your vision and perspective of what is important in the last mile of the way.

Granted, the cliffs and bluffs of life are not always the same, some are barren, some rocky and dangerous, but sometimes as you round that next corner of life there is a vista you have never seen: some God-made, some man-made, but beautiful to behold. Part of the pleasure is sharing these experiences with others. To say, "Look at that" and have someone there to see it too. For me, the biggest thrill of the descent out of the mountains that day was the late afternoon sighting of another elephant with two huge tusks. It was a glance at first with a shout for Bijou to stop. Our driver finally got the car stopped about a hundred yards beyond the male Ana. I quickly disembarked my ride and worked my way back to get a better look. Some would say I had seen elephants like that one before, but I hadn't seen that elephant before! Sad is the state of mind that says I have seen that before, experienced that before, and tasted of that before. Despite being similar, they are not the same. The sunrise you saw yesterday will not be the same sunrise you see today. Granted, this was my thirty-seventh elephant sighting in my India trips, but each was unique and special. I have seen the same elephant more than once, but under different lighting, timing, and circumstance making it different in many ways than those before. When will we realize that each event of life is a gift of God to encourage, inspire, help, instruct, or simply please us?

As my day in the mountains of Munnar came to a close, I witnessed again the beauty of an Indian elephant as he ate his fill of banana leaves under a fading sun. Another marvelous day in India was coming to a close, another unforgettable week in Kerala was coming to an end, and here I was as free as a bird standing beside a rural road taking in the glory of God's creative power. This ascent and descent out of the mountains of Munnar was a reflection of God's grace and goodness to me His child. May we all relish each day He grants, and may we look closely for a new blessing even when we have traveled that way before, climbed the same mountain trail, and retraced our steps only to find a different elephant along our way.

14

MANIPAR GOSPEL TEAM

Mark 16:15 "And he said unto them, Go ye into all the world, and preach the GOSPEL to every creature."

MY SECOND SUNDAY IN Kerala started with no power. This outage took away my ceiling fan and lasted for four hours. The cool day air of Munnar had been replaced with the hot night air of Edayappara. When I say the power was out, even Shibu's backup battery in the house had gone dry by morning. I woke in the middle of the night with the change of sound. When on general power, the bedroom fan whirls at a higher rate than when the auxiliary power comes on. Shibu had warned me that his battery was getting weaker and would have to be replaced eventually, and now would only last about an hour at best. And so it was I woke to a hot, stuffy bedroom that first morning back in Edayappara. Nevertheless, I had a good night's rest getting to bed about 9:30 after our exciting day and a half in the mountains of Munnar. While I waited for the power to return, I got my journal updated and prepared for my two messages for that day: "Our Singing God" (Zephaniah 3:17) for the folks at the Edaikkapuzha Baptist Church and "Examples of the Believers" (I Timothy 4:12) for the students at the College Church.

The cold shower felt good as I got decked out in my Sunday best, a white shirt and black pants, the garb of an Indian pastor. During the week I wore sandals, but on Sunday I always wore my black shoes. The power finally came on around eight. I had breakfast about nine and was off to Edaikkapuzha about ten. This would be my third visit to Pastor K.J. Thomas' church where he is the senior pastor. As usual the fellowship was sweet, the music was inspiring, and the hospitality was heavenly. Located only three miles from Edayappara, the church building was one of the first built after Kangazha, a site Shibu helped clear as a teenager and helped build as a young adult. Now he was taking me back to rejoice with the saints of Edai, my name for the assembly. As president of the organization, I especially enjoyed Pastor Thomas, a friend from my first visit in 2006. Despite the fact he can't speak English and I can't speak

Malayalam, we have always seem to communicate our feelings to each other. We were back to Shibu's by one in the afternoon where Julie had a nice lunch of peas, potatoes, chicken fingers, and the carrots we had bought in the mountains. I thought to myself, am I really in India?

After lunch I had a rare opportunity to have a cherished afternoon nap. I experience them in the States, but not so often in my trips to India. But on that Sunday, I needed a rest and got it. I was finding that the heat was getting to me much more than on previous trips. My age, I suppose. I woke to a phone call from my dear wife informing me that Eddie, my cat, was now sleeping with her each night (a family joke). It would also be our last verbal communication for a while because Coleen was heading to Texas to visit our daughter Marnie. She also told me our soldier son Scott was on the road from Fairbanks to Valdez with a military load, his first trip on icy roads. Winter comes to Alaska early! After Coleen hung up, I prepared two new sermons: "Those That Passed By" (Mark 15:29) and "Every Good and Perfect Gift" (James 1:17). I had already prepared twenty-five sermons and songs in just nine days! A snack of fresh papaya from one of Shibu's trees finished my afternoon activities before I headed for the college and my second Sunday being their guest pastor.

The event of the evening was not my message on "Being an Example of the Believer" or my singing to the student a favorite gospel song, "Ten Thousand Years", nor the special numbers from the men's quartet and the ladies' trio, but the introduction to the student body of the members of the 2013 Manipur Gospel Team and the passing out of their promotional calendars to raise support for the missionary project. The group would be led by two professors, Joel Valte and Sabu Andrews. The team was made up of KBBC students: Ashem Newme, C. H. Asa, D. Standhope, Ipungwangbe Newme, Rajen Teron, Vijay Kumar, Jesulkambe Zeme, Danile Sanelie, Chujangmei R., Romita Devi Irungbam, T. Rachel, and T. Luckyson. The calendar had two pictures of the campus at KBBC on the top and a group picture of the team in the middle. Under their photograph were these words from Acts 5:42:

"Ceased not to teach and preach Jesus Christ!"

And then the 2013 calendar with these words below: In aid for fundraiser for vacation ministries. The team needed to rise between 30,000 and 35,000 rupees to cover the cost of the month-long trip throughout the State of Manipur, India's most northeasterly state. Located on the border of Burma, this small state is equal in position to the State of Maine in the United States. I thought it was only fitting to support the mission with my prayers and funds. I bought ten calendars at thirty rupees a piece to share with my prayer warriors back home. Between gifts I had been given for such needs as I found and my own resources, I gave Shibu half the money needed for the trip considering that 30,000 rupees is only $600! I told Shibu to wait until after the students' fund-raising was over and then give them the funds, so they learn how best to trust in the Lord. What amazes me still in missions in India is how little money it takes to accomplish the task. Fifteen people for a month, travel expenses, food expenses, and all other expenses, and it only cost between $600 and $700; we could barely kept one person sustained for a week in an American project!

Before my days in India were over, I would be able to minister to all the members of the Manipur Gospel Team. I learned from Sabu that the plans for the team were simple. Day by day, village by village (over thirty were already scheduled), the team would enter remote towns, set up a meeting in a public place and through Gospel songs and a Gospel message try to win as many people as they could to Christ. Most of the team members were seniors, and this would be their final activity at KBBC. Can you imagine giving the month after your graduation to seeking souls instead of seeking a job? The young people of KBBC understand that our number one job as a Christian is winning souls to the cause of Christ. Most would do it full-time if they could, but financial support isn't always available, so many of them work to witness! Maybe that is why I respect the Indian Christians so much. They understand more clearly than do most American Christians that Christ's commission to go to every creature with the Gospel is each Christian's responsibility; whether in Manipur or in Maine, the instruction is the same. Even before I preached to the students that Sunday evening, they were already demonstrating an example of the believer we all should exhibit in our corner of the world, our uttermost part!

15

POWERPOINT PRESENTATIONS

> Matthew 28:20 "TEACHING THEM to observe all things whatsoever I have commanded you: and, lo, I am with you always, even to the end of the world. Amen."

I STARTED MY SECOND week of teaching at KBBC with the anticipation of a new class. Shibu asked if I would teach an evening school class for all students that wished to attend. I told him that I had brought along a series of PowerPoint presentations I had recently put together. Teaching by PowerPoint was a new method for me. Most of my Bible teaching life had been the traditional lecture format. I had years before started to use handouts to illustrate or add to the lessons being presented, but using a computer was really new. I had only bought my first laptop the year before, so the novelty of using it as a teaching tool was experimental. I had a computer since 1980, but the old Apple II GS was a dinosaur and by 2011 an antique. I have always come kicking and screaming into the electronic age, but as soon as I realized the benefits for teaching (especially kids) with a computer through a PowerPoint presentation I was hooked. Development of programs to share the Word of God came quickly after I finally took the plunge. I had brought a few on a flash drive, another great advancement, if the opportunity arose, and on the first night of my second week at KBBC it did!

My other classes were going well as I continued teaching the Juniors about II Samuel and the Seniors about Ephesians 5. In chapel I had started the southern part of our Israel trip, now the only question was which lesson I would download on Shibu's computer to teach my first evening school class. The day was brutally hot; it hit 120 by midafternoon. I was having a hard time thinking through my options. I had also brought handout materials for the various lessons, and I would have to run them off, so I needed to act quickly. It was then I realized I had an opportunity to share my most favorite Old Testament study in India. Ever since I started studying in a series format, I have put together over two hundred twenty to date. The very first was on the Tabernacle, the greatest portrait of Jesus Christ in the Old Testament. I taught it several time over the years to adults as well as children, but I had just finished a new presentation using PowerPoint before I left for India. What was new about this presentation of the tabernacle was the additional material and pictures I was able to add after an Israeli experience in 2010. Just north of the seaport of Eilat is Timnah, a desert place where a full-scale model of the wilderness tabernacle has been constructed. To see the tabernacle in its natural setting and to walk through its parts only added to my love of the symbolism, an analogy of Christ as our Tabernacle. I would take the opportunity to teach it to the students at KBBC. A chance to teach them just how God loves to dwell with His people, demonstrated in the most dramatic way by sending His only begotten Son to dwell among us. I still remember when I first realized the magnitude of Colossians 2:16-17:

> "Let no man therefore judge you in meat, or in drink, or in respect of an holyday, or of a new moon, or of the Sabbath days: WHICH ARE A SHADOW OF THINGS TO COME; BUT THE BODY IS OF CHRIST!"

What was written about in the Old Testament was just a shadow; the real substance would be revealed in Jesus. That is why I have come to believe that anything that has to do with the Levitical Worship System is merely a representation of Christ. God told Moses to build the tabernacle exactly after the pattern He gave him. Why? Paul explained it best when he wrote this in Hebrews 8:5:

> "Who serve unto the example and shadow of heavenly things, as Moses was admonished of God when he was about to make the tabernacle: for, See, saith He, that thou make all things according to the pattern shewed to thee on the mount."

Why so careful with the manufacture of a tent? Because it was more than a tent. It was the shadow and pattern and example of the coming of God's Son. John would use the same word as tabernacle when he wrote in John 1:14:

"And the Word was made flesh, and dwelt (TABERNACLED) among us . . . "

I wanted the future missionaries and pastors and evangelist and pastors' wives to realize that no matter how far they roam and no matter where they go their Heavenly Father would journey with them just as Jehovah did with the children of Israel from Egypt to Canaan.

After my last class, I rushed over to Shaju's for a wonderful lunch of fried onions, fried chicken, sliced potatoes, bananas and milk, and for dessert a strawberry shake. Wow! Then I went back to the office to have my tabernacle handouts run off. I was then off to Shibu's office to download my Tabernacle PowerPoint. By mid-afternoon I was back to the prophet's chamber at Shibu's for a little R and R until evening. Again I felt the heat and tried to rest, but my mind was too excited about Evening School. As I write this remembrance of India, I have just passed a milestone in connection to my Evening Schools. I started teaching special Bible classes during week-day evenings back in the 1970s. It was a way for me to share the extra materials I was studying. In my last two churches, I have offered the opportunity for my parishioners to study God's Word in depth. Just ten days ago I conducted my one-thousandth evening school class. Over thirty-three years, I have conducted forty-five different studies on subjects varying from Biblical Geography to the Signs of the Times; from the Book of Jeremiah to the Book of Hebrews; from specialty topics like The Levitical Law and the Lord to Old Testament Typology; from doctrinal lessons on the Diabolical Devices of the Devil to the Fundamental of the Faith; from practical discussions on Decisions Determine Destinies to Disciplining Deacons. I have taught through sixteen books of the Bible during this extra time, and of the one thousand classes nine have been conducted in India. I did six in 2006 and I would do three on the Tabernacle in 2012; extra times with the KBBC students in God's Precious Word!

While some pastors and Bible teachers are seeking fewer opportunities to share God's Word, I am always looking for another chance, a different way or day. Most of my evening school classes over the years have happened on a Tuesday night but any night is a good night to share the Bible, to learn something new about the Scriptures, to study a passage of the Holy Word that hasn't been explored before. That Monday night in October in 2012, I was given another occasion to do what Jesus commanded His followers to do: "Teaching them to observe all things whatsoever I have commanded you . . . ." The end of the world is near and we have yet to teach all.

16

WHEN ALL NATIONS GATHER AROUND GOD'S THRONE

> Revelations 7:9 "After this I beheld, and, lo, a great multitude, which no man could number, of all nations, and kindred, and people, and tongues, STOOD BEFORE THE THRONE, and before the Lamb, clothed with white robes, and palms in their hands."

MONDAY FLOWED INTO TUESDAY and Tuesday into Wednesday with a calm regularity that I love. I love routine; I love a predictable schedule; I love when my days are filled with service to my Lord and King, and at KBBC I was in Heaven. Rare was the day now that I didn't get four chances to teach or preach because, besides my normal daily classes, there seemed to be a nightly opportunity to share more of the same. On my second week as professor at Kerala Baptist Bible College, Monday night was filled with my first evening school on the Old Testament Tabernacle as a picture of Christ; my Tuesday night was at the weekly pastors' prayer meeting at Shaju's sharing a lesson on Abraham's Adoration: praying for others (Genesis 15:2-3), and then I was informed that my Wednesday night would be spent in a very unusual way, at the Annual KBBC Cultural Night Celebration at Bethany School.

Once a year the college allows the students to share songs, stories, customs, dances, and any other aspects of their unique cultures with each other and any others that would like to attend. Remember, the student body of KBBC now comes from nine different states of India. Each state is like a different country with a different language and certainly different cultural heritages. It was the School's way to teach the students that there can be unity in diversity and that God loves all the races, all the nations, and all the tongues. I was excited to be able to experience the 2012 version of this annual event. I had never before been in a meeting where so many distinct dialects were spoken, and I was asked to give the keynote address in my native tongue, so now there would be ten people groups represented in the celebration!

In the days leading up to the Wednesday night program, I decided that I wanted to share with the students, staff, and visitors the heavenly event still to take place. I have for years pondered the amazing reality of Revelation 5:9 and Revelation 7:9, the day when all the redeemed from every nation and people will be gathered around the Throne of God and the Lamb of God. To think that ten of those represented groups would be gathered at the assembly hall of the Bethany English School at one time was profound for me. Up to that point in my life maybe five would have been the most for me in one place, so for me this was a unique experience I wanted to relish and remember. I decided to share a pre-prepared message with the group titled "Abraham's Connection to His and Other Cultures" (Genesis 13:18). My goal was to show that God has always loved all people groups, despite the fact that He was the one that forced mankind into diverse language groups (Genesis 11:1-9). God split us up, and one day God will bring us back together. What a day that will be when we gather to hear all the tongues as one praising and honoring the God of us all!

In the past, on such occasions as this, I have attempted to write a song to highlight and underline the rarity and specialty of the event. I wanted not only to share God's Word, but also to share a word on this being just a foretaste of glory divine when we all would gather again under the unique diversity that we are as human beings, but the grand unity we have under Christ. I chose the wonderful music of Ralph Hudson that was originally written for William Clark's classic church hymn, "Blessed Be The Name", but I changed the theme and title to "When All Nations Shall Gather Around God's Throne".

> When the nations gather around God's Throne, to proclaim Him all in all.
> There will be one from every land, on this terrestrial ball.
>
> The purpose for this gathering, to crown Jesus Lord of Lords.
> There will be peace and unity, no clashing of any swords.
>
> From every kindred, from every tribe, they will come from far and wide.
> To bow before the mighty God, forever with Him to abide.
>
> From Kerala's hills to Andhra's plains, to Manipur's tribal farms.

Gather them with the Gospel truth, with an outreach of
 loving arms.

From India's distant and populous states, from Nagaland to
 Karnataka.
Reach them all before Christ comes, and don't forget Orissa!

CHORUS
Gather all the lands, Gather all the tongues, and gather for
 God's only Son.
Gather all the nations, Gather all the nations, and gather them
 one by one.

What a joy it was that night to share with the congregation the joys of this true, this coming day, this memorial meeting! Mrs. Charles Cowman has pictured this great gathering in her bestselling devotional, *Springs in the Valley*, with these words:

"What a scene of unimaginable grandeur that will be, when at last all nations are gathered to His feet! That will include representatives from all the European States, from Iceland in the far north to Greece in the south, and from Portugal in the west to hidden saints of God in the Soviet Russia in the east. There will be many from Algeria, Morocco, and the Atlas mountains; from Egypt and the Nile Valley, from the sandy deserts and the mountains of the Sahara; from the Caliber, the Congo, and the Zambezi rivers; from the uplands of South Africa. There will be gathered to Christ many from Palestine, Transjordan, and Arabia; INDIA WILL CONTRIBUTE HER MILLIONS; and even the closed lands like Nepal, Sikkim, and Tibet. Christ will gather His own. From the islands of the Dutch East Indies they will come-Java, Sumatra, Bali, Celebes, Lombok, Sumbawa, Borneo, and the rest, and will be gathered at the feet of the Redeemer. From the teeming millions of Central Asia, from China, Japan, Korea, Manchukuo, and Mongolia, there will be an immense home-going to the Saviour. From the myriad islands of the Pacific, the people of Polynesia and Melanesia will be gathered to the Lord who redeemed them. From Australia and New Zealand there will be multitudes that will join in the glad song of praise. From every republic of Central, South, and North America, and from the West Indies islands-Cuba, Haiti, Jamaica, Porto Rico, and the Lesser Antilles, they will come. From the far-off forests and lakes of Canada there will be a similar home-going.

Whether the tongues be those of the white race, or of the red, or of the black, the gathering to Christ will be overwhelmingly splendid!" Amen and Amen!

17

THE NEW MERCY CHILDREN'S CHRISTIAN HOME

> Matthew 19:14-15 "But Jesus said, SUFFER LITTLE CHILDREN, AND FORBID THEM NOT, TO COME TO ME: for of such is the kingdom of heaven. And He laid His hands on them, and departed thence."

ONE OF MY FIRST loves in India was the children of the orphanage started by the Simon family very early in their ministry in Edayappara. During my four stays near this Christian home, I have taken numerous opportunities to visit the residents of that group home in obedience of James' great admonition:

"Pure religion and undefiled before God and the Father is this, TO VISIT THE FATHERLESS and widows in their affection, and to keep himself unspotted from the world." (James 1:27)

Shibu told me that over the time of the ministry there have been nearly one hundred helped through this mission. Over the years the kids have changed, but the purpose of the home has stayed the same: to offer a safe and peaceable place for the children of school age to find Christ. Besides shelter, food, clothes, schooling, and a trade, the orphanage team members have taught the children about Christ through daily devotions and personal instruction from Pastor Lukose and his dear wife Mary. It has been my privilege and honor to have conducted a number of devotionals myself. Each visit, I have been invited to the home to share with the children, as I did on a very special Friday night that ended my second week in Kerala.

In this chapter, I would like to share a tremendous answer to prayer in my ongoing supplications for the Mercy Children's Christian Home. During my first visit in 2006, I was burdened for the orphanage because of the lack of space. Nearly thirty children were crammed into a small space. The girls were housed in a small two-story house just up the road from the Kangazha Church. The boys were housed in a smaller place next to that house that doubled as the residence of the house parents, the Lukose family. Packed in like sardines where the only sleeping area was a hard concrete floor, the boys laid out thin mats each night on which to sleep. Shibu had dreams of building a larger place, but the funds were not there. He had even had an engineer draw up the plans for an expansion. My first year there he gave me a copy of the plans, and I began to help him pray for the funds necessary for the expansion. One of the thrills of my return was with the knowledge that our six-year prayer was almost answered. When I left in 2010, the new construction was just months away from beginning, so it was with a deep sense of fulfillment that I drove into the new Mercy Children's Christian Home driveway to see for myself what God had provided since my last visit. It would be my deepest honor to conduct the first devotion time ever held in the new director's residence of the new facility. My joy was boundless as I entered the new home that could now house up to fifty neglected or abused orphans of Kerala.

Paid for by the loving gifts of numerous Americans like my wife and me, the new three-story orphanage was wonderfully large. The first room I visited was the boys' room where each lad had a bed, a place to keep his things, and a desk and chair for study. Most of the kids attended the local school, but a few attended Bethany. I found the same with the girls' room. The new dining hall was spacious, and the bathroom facilities were modern and numerous. The eating place in the old orphanage was very lacking, as were the toilet facilities. What the plans accomplished was an additional building attached to the original two-story house. Adding additional space on the back side of the residence created a third floor, and plenty of space for more dorm rooms, bathrooms, study halls, and even a place for a nursery. Up to this time in the history of the orphanage, they could only take kids of school age, but now other options of ministry were open. They even had room to create a separate wing that would allow young people that wanted to learn the ins and outs of orphanage work to come and stay on site while they were instructed in orphanage management. As we walked through the cavernous rooms, I could see that the ministry to underprivileged kids of Kerala would have a great facility to accomplish the ministry Jesus gave His followers in the verses I have printed above. Before I left, I would be able to contribute my part in the work through the Word.

The service of dedication in the new residence of Luke and Mary was filled with children singing, reciting scripture, repeating the Books of the Bible, and sharing in the monthly birthday party. Once a month, every month since the home opened, they have celebrated the birthdays of the children in the home with a party on the month of their birth. This was the third that I had attended over the years. The last time I was on site for the celebration I had Russ Coffin with me. We had actually gone shopping for a pair of dresses for the twins of the home. Those twins were still there the night I shared a message on "The Lesson of the Least" taken from Jesus' great challenge of Matthew 25:40. I also got to see Joyce, now seventeen, the only young person still there since I first visited the home in 2006. About ready to graduate, Joyce has been the face of the home for me. It was good to see her again, probably for the last time this side of heaven. Her sweet smile, pleasant personality, and gracious charm had only matured. She had become another staff member in the helping of the new children in the adjustment to new surroundings and a different way of life. Following the service, we had a party of sweet treats made by the resident cook, an elderly lady who did all the cooking for the kids, and the staff in a kitchen off the back of the home. It was during our fellowship I met Kannon, the orphanage cat, another new member to the new Mercy Christian Children's Home.

One of the realities of the uttermost part is that the children there need Christ as much as the adults. So often, especially in places like India, children are the overlooked segment of the population. That is why I am so excited every time I go to Kerala and see that there are still those that see the worth of a child's soul. Shibu told me that only one of the new children hadn't as yet accepted Christ as Saviour. He told me of an event that had taken place at the Annual Conference in January that highlighted the importance of Mercy's mission. A young couple come to the conference and approached Shibu. They asked if he remembered them, but he couldn't place them. They told their story of how each of them as small children had spent some years in the orphanage, but not together. It was only after they both had left the home did they meet, but their common connection to Mercy brought on a love affair. Now they were married and serving the Lord together. A child won early to Christ has a lifetime to serve Him, an adult only the remaining days, how many that might be. I praise the Lord He called me at seven, and though I never lived in an orphanage, I was brought up in a Christian home, just like the children of Mercy!

18

THUNDER AND LIGHTING: WIND AND RAIN

> Psalms 77:17-18 "The clouds POURED OUT WATER: the skies sent out a sound: thine arrows also went abroad. The voice of Thy THUNDER was in the heaven: the LIGHTNINGS lightened the world: the earth trembled and shook (WIND)."

WHEN I READ THE Psalmist's account of a thunder and lightning storm, I said to myself, "He must have experienced what I witnessed in Kerala!" I am no stranger to the strength and spectacle of such storms. As a child I witnessed my share on the family farm in Northern Maine during the hot, humid months of July and August. I have always enjoyed watching the grandeur of such upheavals from the safety of a hay barn, the cab of a pickup truck, or a milking shed door. I thought over the years I had seen and witnessed the best of the best that nature could deliver, until I experienced the fury of a Kerala monsoon. Some might call them the worst of the worst, but for me these storms are marvelous and wondrous to behold. I had been in India ninety-four days before I saw my first real storm. Up until October 11, 2012, I had seen it rain just three times in my four trips to Kerala. It only rained once in my first trip of forty days. It never rained in my second trip of fourteen days. I witnessed only two light showers on my third trip of twenty-eight days. By the time my first real storm arrived, I had been in India twelve hot, humid, 100-degree days and then it happened, twelve consecutive days of torrential afternoon downpours with a side order of lightning and thunder and gales. I was going to experience my first monsoon. What a pure, perfect God-given storm!

I had wondered when the late season storms of India would arrive in Kerala. I had been warned that I was going to India in monsoon season, unlike my other three trips which took place either in January, February, or March, the dry season in Kerala. Kerala, unlike Maine, has but two season, wet and dry. One of the joys for me in Maine is the four distinct and descriptive seasons: clearly defined, perfectly patterned, and amazingly predictable. Located in the tropical south of India, Kerala is governed by the trade winds that bring in moisture off the Arabian Sea. Twice a year, June and July, October and November, the rains come; much needed rains, despite their severity and strength. I never saw it rain until I witnessed the water of Kerala. I never saw the wind blow until I felt the tremble and shake of Kerala. I never witnessed lighting until I saw the arrows of Kerala. I never heard thunder until I heard the sound of Kerala. I am honest when I tell you that, for me, it was one of the top five natural experiences I have ever had in my life - to see the mighty combination of thunder and lightning, wind and rain.

During the days leading up to this amazing stretch of weather, the severe heat of the twelve-hour Kerala day caused gigantic cumulus clouds to build up over the tropical landscape of Edayappara. Out of these huge canopies of white thunderheads intense electrical energy began to form. If I had known what I was looking at during those preliminary days, I would have been ready for what was to follow. Wrapped up in teaching at KBBC, preaching in the area churches, participating in special events, I was paying more attention to what was happening on the ground than in the atmosphere. Granted, I was enjoying the cooler days, lower 100s and upper 90s, instead of the 110-120, with the cloud cover each afternoon. The conditions for the monsoon were building, but I wasn't noticing, until that afternoon from my bedroom windows I heard the rumble, saw the flash, and felt a gust of wind enter the room. I was still unmoved until I heard the splash of water on the windowsill. It was then I took notice of the four elements of nature coming together creating a classic tropical storm.

Edayappara is hill country, which only magnified the display that took place outside the prophet's chamber at the Simon house on Mundathanam Road. Moving to the window, I watched the gigantic streaks of light flash across the upland hills north of the village. Seconds after the flash came those distinct sounds of thunder rolling through the narrow valleys. Over the next two weeks, this awesome display of divine invention would last several hours, starting between three and four, and sometimes lasting to well after dark. It was at dusk the real beauty of the storm came to light. The celestial fireworks were a thousand times better than any man-made light show I have ever witnessed. Even those new modern laser shows don't compare to what I watched out the Simon's windows. As the lightning flashed, the thunder rolled into the area like a freight train rumbling over an unstable track. The haunting sound reverberated over the hills, echoed in the valleys, and boomed against the forest trees like a military barrage. When lightning is close, the thunder happens almost instantaneously, shaking your world, like riding a train, a concussion, like standing beside a high-powered rifle when shot.

I watched in awe as lightning bolt after lightning bolt lit up the area even in the full daylight of a late afternoon. Fingers of fire appeared between the tall coconut trees that line the ridge above the Simon house, as the deluge of water came down in sheets. It seemed to me the order was lightning, thunder, wind, then rain. It seemed when the rain began the wind stopped, or was the downpour so strong it could cut through the wind? Instead of a driving storm with horizontal rain, as we often get on the coast of Maine, Kerala's storms are vertical in nature. I was mesmerized by the spectacle before me. Later I would learn that my hosts are terrified of these storms, but like every other aspect of India I found nothing to fear. Oh, I know one can be hit by lighting, die under a falling tree, or get washed away in a flash flood, but for me none of these possibilities entered my thoughts. I only wanted to watch, listen, feel, and touch the monsoon storm. That first afternoon I was out playing in the front yard with Joshua and Abigail, dancing in the puddles formed by the deluge. Granted, we did wait until the thunder and lightning had passed us by. I do know something about dancing with lightning!

One of the first joys I recognized from such a storm was the drop in temperature. It felt like we were back in Munnar; the garden thermometer in Julie's circle had dropped to 90 degrees. Sometimes the rain would last an hour, sometimes hours. How much rain fell, I know not. There is no rain gauge in Julie's garden, but usually before the rain stopped the Simon's front yard was a swimming pool. The ground would drink it in quickly, but vast amounts of liquid were deposited in a very short time. The lightning and thunder would move off to other regions, and the wind would calm down as the rain slowed down. Is there any wonder that within the pages of Holy Writ our God is sometimes see in a storm? We should not be surprised that the images of a thunder and lightning storm produce a divine revelation in the mind of the Scripture writers! As the children of Israel looked toward the hills of the Sinai and caught a glimpse of Almighty God for the first time, this is how their chronicler recorded the scene: "And it came to pass on the third day in the morning, that there were thunders and lightning, and a thick cloud upon the mount, and the voice of a trumpet exceeding loud; so that all the people that was in the camp trembled." (Exodus 19:16) I heard that voice and saw that sight in Kerala, but I did not tremble because, unlike Israel, I know that God and His name is Jesus Christ!

19

WRITING SONGS BY CANDLELIGHT

Psalms 40:3 "And He hath put A NEW SONG IN MY MOUTH, even praise unto our God: many shall see it, and fear, and shall trust in the Lord."

OFTEN WITH THE STORMS of Kerala, the expected power outages will soon follow. Sometimes when the power goes out, I will lie on my bed and rest, while at other times I will stay at my desk and finish a sermon or write a new song by candlelight.

I am a songwriter, a converter of hymns and choruses. I am not musical, so I have to borrow an old tune to make my prose lyrical. Over the years I have been given on occasion, like the Psalmist, a new song, but rare are those conversions unless I am in India. My mind and my heart seem to be open to music there more than at home, when it comes to inspirational song writing. Over the years I have written one hundred seventy songs, eighty-three hymns and eighty-seven choruses. Of those one hundred and seventy, one hundred and fourteen of them have been composed in India.

During my stay in 2012, I complied fourteen hymns and eleven choruses. All the choruses were in my largest series of choruses based on the childhood chorus, "Only a Boy Named David". Over the years I have written thirty-four versions of this chorus using other Biblical characters as my focus: Daniel, Jesus, Moses, Abraham, Joshua, Mary, Peter, and many other familiar Bible personalities. My purpose for these conversions was to use the method that helped me most in my boyhood when it came to understanding a Bible story or learning a Bible verse. That method is song. I have always been able to memorize something in the Bible better through a chorus than just repetition or pure memorization. While in India I added Naboth, Nehemiah, Cornelius, Luke, Andrew, Tabitha, Samuel, Jacob, Esther, Naaman, and Ruth to that collection.

One night as the two small candles flickered in the light breeze coming through the prophet's chamber window, I also wrote this song based on the church hymn "I Am Resolved" written by Palmer Hartsough. I borrowed J. H. Fillmore's melody for my hymn, "I Am A Christian".

> I am a Christian no longer a captive, held by Satan's snare
> Things that once drew me, things that once kept me, now it is all "Beware".
>
> I am a Christian called by my Saviour, to live a glorious life
> Things are much better; things are much sweeter, even in the midst of strife.
>
> I am a Christian walking with Jesus, each step hand in hand.
> No matter the trial, no matter the testing, we can always withstand.
>
> I am a Christian heading to glory, through Earth's darkest night.
> Times getting harder, saints getting weaker, the future is always bright.
>
> I am a Christian waiting the rapture; I know my Lord is near.
> Eye on the clouds, ear on the trumpet sound, what then can I ever fear?
>
> CHORUS:
> I will praise the Lord; praise Him every day (Praise Him every day)
> Jesus, thank you, Jesus, is all I have to say.

That night I also wrote this, based on W. A. Ogden's hymn and tune to "He Is Able To Deliver Thee" with my theme being "Tis The Grandest Song".

> Tis the grandest song thru the ages sung
> Tis the grandest song for a human tongue
> Tis the grandest song that the church ever sung
> Our Jesus always loves us.
>
> Tis the grandest song in the east or west
> Tis the grandest song of the pure and best
> Tis the grandest song that will give you rest
> Our Jesus always loves us.

Tis the grandest song on the coast of Maine
Tis the grandest song with an Indian refrain
Tis the grandest song with a heavenly strain
Our Jesus always loves us.

Tis the grandest song in the earth or sky
Tis the grandest song with the angels on high
This the grandest song with a mighty why?
Our Jesus always loves us.

Tis the grandest song on a distant shore
Tis the grandest song with the rich or poor
Tis the grandest song, there will be no more
Our Jesus always loves us.

CHORUS:
He loved us from the beginning.
He loved us from the beginning.
He loved us from the beginning.
Through sinners we, His children to be.
Our Jesus always loves us.

Then this final candlelight song adapted from the classic church hymn "Be Still My Soul" by Katharine von Schlegel and music by Jean Sibelius, to "Will You Now Live?"

Will you now live as one who rests in Jesus?
Who walks with God each hour of the day?
Who knows that if the path becomes too rugged
That he can call, can call without delay?
And God will be ever nearer,
He is a Friend, a Friend no dearer!

Will you now live in peace and joy and freedom?
And know the love of Christ the crucified?
And then proclaim His message to the nations,
Until the day that you are glorified?
And then to know His grace, His grace in dying,
To know a place where there is no crying!

Will you now live in the example of the Saviour?
As one who knows that he is heaven-bound?
That in this life we must always please our Master,

For in His grace His mercy can be found.
Our pilgrim way is hard and often long,
But He will, gladly, gladly give a song!

20

A SECOND TESTIMONIAL

> II Corinthians 1:12 "For our rejoicing is this, THE TESTIMONY OF OUR CONSCIENCE, that in simplicity and godly sincerity, not with fleshly wisdom, but by grace of God, we have had our conversation in the world, and more abundantly to you-ward."

My third week in Kerala began with a one-service day, but what a service it was! One of the joys I brought back from my first stay in India was the experience I had at the monthly Thanksgiving Testimonial Service of the Independent Gospel Baptist Churches of Kerala. While we in America celebrate Thanksgiving once a year, these churches celebrate Thanksgiving once a month through a testimonial service at one of the churches in the association. My first experience with an Indian Thanksgiving took place in the small, hill church at Kunnam in 2006; six years later I would relish the happiness of a second Indian testimonial.

I didn't have to travel far for my second taste of a testimonial service, Indian style, because the meeting would take place at the Kangazha Church on Saturday morning on October 13 at 10:00 A.M. After another great night of sleeping, the monsoon had brought cooler temperatures and less humidity, I was ready to share in the praise with the Kerala people. Because I had shared in the testimonial before, I pretty much knew what to expect. As before, I was asked to give the keynote address and share the first testimony. After a delightful breakfast of chicken sausage, English toast, and grape juice, Shibu and I talked of the unique monthly service of the IGBC. Started years before by his dad, the testimonial, as it was called, had become one of the most popular meetings of the churches of Kerala. It gave the people a chance in a public forum to share the blessings the Good Lord had bestowed on them. I was so impressed with the concept in 2006 that I brought the method and style back to my church on the coast of Maine. At first I tried to do a monthly service, but over the years it has happened bi-annually, Easter Night and Thanksgiving Eve.

This was the order of service for the October Testimonial Meeting at Kangazha:

A SECOND TESTIMONIAL

1. Opening prayer by Pastor Chacho
2. Two congregational songs lead by Pastor Robin
3. Responsive reading of Psalms 103
4. Prayer by retired Pastor Joseph
5. Congregational prayers by three in the group
6. Welcome by the pastor of the Church, Pastor P. C. Mathi
7. One congregational song led by Pastor Matthew
8. October leader, opening remarks, Pastor Matthew Kutty
9. Introduction of the keynote speaker by Pastor Kutty
10. My message and testimony. I spoke on "How Sowing Spiritual Seeds Will Result In A Harvest Of Spiritual Testimonies" from Galatians 6:7-8 and II Corinthians 9:6. Shibu did the translation of my message as well as the words to the hymn, "Count Your Blessings" which I sang at the end of my sermon for my testimony.
11. Pastor C. S. Matthews then opened up to the congregation a chance to testify, starting with the women, and the official testimony part of the meeting began.
12. The woman started their part of the testimonial with a group song.
13. Over the next sixty-five minutes, one hundred and one women (the first lady up was Joyce from the orphanage) stood to their feet to give praise to God for some blessing in their lives. Because they spoke Malayalam, I didn't understand a word, but the emotion and tone expressed the simplicity and Godly sincerity that Paul writes about in the verse that started this chapter. Of those hundred women, I only recognized Joyce, Sophy (one of my junior students), Julie (Shibu's wife), Pastor Aby's wife, Sindhu (one of my senior students), Annamma, and Julie (Shaju's wife).
14. The men started their part of the testimonial with a group song.
15. Over the next sixty-five minutes, forty-six men stood to their feet and gave testimony to the great things God had done in their lives. I certainly recognized more of them: Kutty, Thomas, Shibu, Shaju, Robin, Ragen, Regi, George, Luke, John, Aby, Sawgee, and many, many more. My heart was especially touched when the five little

boys in the front row stood as one and individually gave praise to God!
16. Pastor C.S. Matthews ended the testimonial time with a prayer for the offering.
17. Shibu gave the benediction.
18. Pastor P.C. Mathi invited everybody to stay for lunch, which would be served at Bethany School and then prayed over the meal.

The service started at ten in the morning, but the last prayer wasn't lifted up until two in the afternoon. When you consider this was done on a Saturday in high humidity in a non-air conditioned building with most of the people seating on a hard concrete floor, it is exceptional to say the least!

One of the blessings in the uttermost is the songs of the righteous (Isaiah 24:16) and the glory to the righteous! I counted them one by one, just like the song says, and when I reached one hundred forty-eight I stopped. Was there ever a time that you participated in a service where one hundred forty-eight individuals stood to their feet and one by one gave praise to God? In 2006 I listened through one hundred five people praising God in a three-hour service. The only two I have experienced this side of eternity. Isn't that what eternity will be, a testimonial service? In the years I have been hosting such meetings at my Ellsworth Church, thirteen in seven years, the most I have had out was twenty-six, and the most time one hundred minutes! We have lost our desire to praise God in America. And yet, this is one of the fundamental instructions of God's Word. Take time to read the last five psalms in the Book of Psalms (Psalms 146-150). Each song begins and ends with "Praise ye the Lord"! These psalms will not only tell you what you can praise God for, but with what you can praise God for. These songs tell us who praises God and who should praise God. This section of songs ends with these convicting words:

"Let everything that hath breathe praise the Lord. Praise ye the Lord." (Psalms 150:6)

When was the last time you participated in a testimonial service? When was the last time you gave a public testimony? Even when you can't find a church that has one that is no excuse not to have one!

21

I SAW THE CROSS

> Galatians 6:14 "But God forbid that I should glory, SAVE IN THE CROSS of our Lord Jesus Christ, by whom the world is crucified unto me, and I unto the world."

AFTER MY SECOND TESTIMONIAL service in India, I experienced one of the most enjoyable encounters I have ever had in the ministry of Christ, home or abroad!

I had now been at Kerala Baptist Bible College for over two weeks, and my interaction with the students had reached a familiarity that allowed us to be very comfortable with one another. I have always been amazed at the trust of these people with a total stranger, how they opened their homes, classrooms, lives, and, yes, their hearts. I had taken great pleasure in previous trips in teaching the students at KBBC some western hymns. They already sang the classics like "The Old Rugged Cross", and "How Great Thou Art", but the minute I realized they loved to sing I opened up their musical library to songs unfamiliar to them. My first year at KBBC during every Friday chapel, I taught them old church hymns and choruses I had learned as a child. Though I didn't do that in my second tour at KBBC, I did use hymns, and songs, and spiritual choruses to illustrate precepts I was trying to teach them in class. I would periodically burst out in song in the middle of a lesson. I have become known as the singing professor at KBBC. I also enjoyed listening to them sing, whether before chapel or at one of the church services I attended. Normally an event at KBBC wouldn't be complete without a special number from the ladies' singing group, the men's singing group, or a solo, duet or trio from one or more of the students. One of the first songs I enjoyed when I got to India was a southern gospel number by five male students. Their melody was wonderful, and their harmony was sweet to listen to. Immediately a thought came to my mind, and after that first service, I approached them with "Do I have a song for you!"

Our first practice took place the Saturday afternoon after the testimonial service and luncheon. We met in the professor's lounge at the school, and I taught them Hank Williams, Jr.'s classic gospel song, "I Saw The Light".

> I wandered so aimless, life filled with sin.
> I wouldn't let my dear Saviour in.
> Then Jesus came like a stranger in the night.
> Praise the Lord, I saw the Light.
> I saw the Light, I saw the Light.
> No more darkness, no more night.
> Now I'm so happy, no sorrow in sight.
> Praise the Lord, I saw the Light.
>
> Just like a blind man, I wandered alone.
> Worries and fears I claimed for my own.
> Then like the blind man that God gave back his sight.
> Praise the Lord, I saw the Light.
> I saw the Light, I saw the Light.
> No more darkness, no more night.
> Now I'm so happy, no sorrow in sight.
> Praise the Lord, I saw the Light.
>
> I was a fool to wander and stray.
> For straight is the gate and narrow the way.
> Now I have traded the wrong for the right.
> Praise the Lord, I saw the Light.
> I saw the Light, I saw the Light.
> No more darkness, no more night.
> Now I'm so happy, no sorrow in sight.
> Praise the Lord, I saw the Light.

We practiced nearly an hour that afternoon, going over and over again through the unfamiliar tune and words. We were halfway through the session when I realized it was them teaching me not me teaching them. Oh, I taught them the words, but they taught me the music, which would sing each part, and, to my surprise, I had been taken into their group. When the song was performed, I would be part of the group.

Kamminlal Chongloi - Manipur

Akashito Wotsa - Manipur

Solomon Rongpar - Assam

Daniel Swu - Nagaland

Ashem Newme - Nagaland

Barry Blackstone - Maine

I have always had aspirations to sing in a male quartet, but little did I know I would do it in India. In my last chapel, I stood with these five young singers and sang "I Saw The Light". One of my treasured souvenirs from my 2012 India trip is a digital recording of our rendition of that southern gospel classic. I play it every once and awhile and relive the day I joined an Indian singing group to sing an American song. The second blessing that came out of that practice was I went back to the prophet's chamber at the Simon house and wrote my own version of the song. Using Hank's melody, I changed the focus of the song to "I Saw The Cross" and wrote this.

> CHORUS:
> I (you) saw the cross; I (you) saw the cross,
> No more sadness, no more loss.
> Now (you're) I am heaven-bound, My (your) Saviour to see.
> Praise the Lord; I (you) saw the cross.
>
> I was a lost man wandering in sin,
> Then in the distance a pardon to win.
> There on a hilltop my debts were paid,
> Praise the Lord I saw the Cross.
>
> Fell at His feet, confessed every wrong,
> Then in my heart came this message and song.
> Jesus took my hand and lifted me up.
> Praise the Lord I saw the Cross.
>
> Now I am walking in SonLight and grace,
> Each day brings me closer to His face.
> How can I praise Him, thank Him for His love?
> Praise the Lord I saw the Cross.
>
> Dear friend of mine are you wandering in sin?
> Turn to the Saviour, He'll let you in.
> Forgiveness is yours at the foot of the cross.
> Praise the Lord, you saw the Cross.

Paul taught us that there should always be a song in our heart when he wrote, "Speaking to yourselves in psalms and hymns and spiritual songs, singing and making melody in your heart to the Lord." (Ephesians 5:19) He also taught us that singing is a teaching tool when he wrote, "Let the word of Christ dwell in you richly in all wisdom; teaching and admonishing one another in psalms and hymns and spiritual songs, singing with grace in your hearts to the Lord." (Colossians 3:16) I feel I did both at KBBC in October 2012!

22

MARIE: THE OLDEST BELIEVER

> Philemon 9 "Yet for love's sake I rather beseech thee, being such a one as PAUL THE AGED, and now also a prisoner of Jesus Christ."

My third Sunday in India brought another opportunity to visit some old friends at a familiar church, Kunnam. Since I last attended a church service at this secluded sanctuary in the hills of Kerala, they had gotten a new pastor. The old pastor of 2006, K. T. Philip, had retired and Pastor Robin, one of my dear pastor friends, had taken over. I had known since my arrival in India this Sunday service was on my schedule, and I was looking forward to the revisit.

I woke that Sunday morning to the sounds of the Muslim call to prayer, a new noise for me in Edayappara. When I first visited Edayappara in 2006, the community was primarily Christian. There was no Hindu temple or Islamic mosque in town. On my walks around town, I had counted at least half-dozen Christian assemblies, from Salvation Army to Church of India to Pentecostal to Anglican, and within a mile of Shibu's house was the largest Catholic Church in the region. However, since my last visit in 2010, a group of Muslims had move in just a few hundred yards from the Simon home and had started a house mosque. It was their call I heard early that morning. I also heard something else, the sound of the power coming back on. I slept through another night without a fan, but that was fine because with the arrival of the monsoon rains it was much cooler. I woke in the middle of the night and had to pull the covers over me, not cold, but cooler. Combined with the human voices were the animals' sounds that echoed through the tropical trees during a typical Kerala morning sunrise: roosters crowing, cows mooing, dogs barking, and ravens cawing.

After a fine breakfast of Indian flat-bread, on which I put some Maine Blueberry honey and Canadian Maple Syrup I had brought with me, and grapefruit juice, I got ready for the forty-five minute ride to Kunnam. It was during breakfast that Shibu changed my morning message from a salvation theme to a "getting back to the work" theme. I felt like Jude when he wrote,

> "Beloved, when I gave all diligence to write unto you of the common salvation, it was needful for me to write unto you, and exhort you that ye should earnestly contend for the faith which was once delivered unto the saints." (Jude 3)

Sometimes the saints need to be rebuked before the sinners need to be convicted. That morning I shared a message I called "Get Back to Work, Believer" based on the story of Elijah in I Kings 19:11-18. It was Shibu's Sunday to take me, and the whole family joined us, including Julie who was going so that she could promote a Ladies Retreat she was organizing for the women of the churches in November. Shibu was true to his word, and the local church, not as a visitor but as a member, greeted me. I certainly felt like I was among family and friends as we worshiped together that morning and into the afternoon of October 14, 2012. It was a two-hour service, but with travel time and fellowship time, the trip took us four and a half hours.

As I sat waiting for the service to start, Pastor Robin showed me a couple of pictures of my daughter Marnie that I had never seen. Pastor Robin is one of the original members of the Heavenly Singers, the singing group of the IGBC. During Marnie's visit in 2008, she had picked up the language so quickly that she was asked to sing with the group in Malayalam. Robin showed me a couple of photographs of Marnie singing with the Heavenly Singers. I also got to meet Robin's new son, Jabez (I Chronicles 4:19-10). However, the thrill of the morning service was kept to the end. As has been my custom since I first visited the churches of the IGBC, the last event on the schedule for me was a group picture of the church families. I have in my picture collection from India a church family photograph of every church assembly. I would ask at the end of the service if we all could gather outside the building, weather permitting. Sometimes the pictures have been taken inside, more often because of darkness. But on that fine morning with the monsoon rains still hours away, remember they only came late in the afternoon and into the evening, we gathered on the front steps of the church sanctuary. Most Kerala church buildings have a small porch on the front of the facility. It was there we would take the 2012 photo of the Kunnam Church. Let us never forget that the Church is the people, and it would be there I would meet Marie again.

Longevity is not necessarily a characteristic of Kerala people. Most die relatively young, and few are the individuals that live into their nineties, but Marie has. If you could see the picture portrait of my Kunnam photograph, you would see me kneeling beside a tiny woman of ninety-three. I was told she is the oldest member of the organization, not just the Kunnam Church, but the entire IGBC association of churches. Weak and worn, Marie now stands barely four feet tall. If she weighs eighty pounds, I would be surprised. Bent over with age, her petite body felt fragile in my hug. She reminded me of the little lady Jesus healed after eighteen years of being bowed together (Luke 13:11-17). She was Marie the aged, but she was still in church on a Sunday morning. Standing beside me in her pure, white sari with a smile as broad as the Indian Ocean, Marie exhibited all the characteristic of a persevering saint, an enduring believer, a worshipping Christian. When her age could have been an excuse to stay home, she found more joy at church. We are all without excuse when saints like Marie are still alive. Just yesterday I visited such a saint in Ellsworth, Maine. Alice Clark, who was ninety-six years young on February 24, 2013, and confided to a nursing home, still painfully walks her way from the end of the hall to the dining room each and every time I conduct a service at Courtland Living Center. Her sister Maxine, who is ninety-three, still attends the church I pastor, the oldest member of our church. Blessed with great health, Maxine Braley still lives alone, drives her own car, and attends all services of the Church. When the Church door is opened, I can count on Maxine being one of the first ones through the door.

 Whether in Maine or Kerala, I have for most of my life known the aged saints who have shown me that the " . . . . forsaking the assembling of ourselves together, as the manner of some is . . . " (Hebrews 10:25) is without excuse. Oh, I still hear excuse after excuse, but whenever I do I am reminded of the aged believers in the uttermost parts. By their very presence, they are "earnestly contending for the faith once delivered to the saints". (Jude 3) Oh, that a few more thirty-three-year olds or twenty-three-year olds would develop the habit of consistent church attendance, so that if they ever reach ninety-three, they still will be found in the House of God on the Lord's Day, like Marie and Maxine! Two aged saints who live two continents apart yet still live the same exemplary life: still at the work, still worshipping, still encouraging an aging preacher by their attention to his preaching.

23

A COFFEE TABLE BOOK TO TREASURE

> Revelation 10:10 "AND I TOOK THE LITTLE BOOK OUT OF THE..."

I STARTED MY LAST full week teaching at KBBC with a now predictable routine. In my junior class on the historical books of the Old Testament, I had arrived at the Book of Ezra. During the daily chapel service, I started sharing with the students the adventures my daughter and I had in Northern Israel. In my senior class on the prison epistles, I was in the third chapter of Philippians, and that evening I would be sharing a lesson with the children at Mercy Christian Children's Home. It is often when routine settles in that the Dear Lord shakes you up with something totally unexpected and surprising: an unspeakable, unimaginable find from a roaming book salesman.

I exited the second floor classroom door to a narrow balcony that runs the entire length of the educational building on the campus of Kerala Baptist Bible College a little after 1:00 P.M. on October 15, 2012. To my surprise, the entire student body was congregating in the outdoor lobby next to the girls' dormitory. I was shocked because normally all the students would be heading for the dining hall for lunch. Rarely did anything distract the students from food; how they love to eat! At first I didn't quite understand what was happening until one of the students from my Prison Epistles class informed me that the bookseller was here. I asked, "What bookseller?" I was told that nearly every month this man came by the college with a number of boxes full of old English theological books and other spiritual books. He got the books through his English and American contacts, and then went around to various Bible colleges in Kerala trying to sell them to the students. I had a suspicion that the books were donated and this was the man's livelihood? Because I had never been in Kerala when this event happened, I hadn't yet experienced this side of campus life. As a matter of fact, two other Christian booksellers with their wares, knock-offs of classic Christian works printed in India whereby making them dirt-cheap, would come by before my time in India was up, but unknown to me, this bookseller had a treasure for me!

I climbed down the stairs thinking at first that I certainly wouldn't find anything interesting. As I was walking by on my way to lunch at Shaju's house, my interest in old books surged within me as I saw the tables filled with box after box. I am still one that loves to read from a book, not a Kindle or any other reading device created by modern man. What was in those boxes? What was in those boxes? I just had to know, so I joined my students in pawing through the stacks of musty volumes. The books smelled like they had been stored in a damp place for a very long time. The minute I got into the middle of the fray that stale, moldy smell came to my nose and that damp, trite taste to my mouth. You know the kind that comes when you enter a basement with a water problem. Despite the strong odor, I searched on through old Bible commentaries, dictionaries, atlases, biographies, and spiritual books on a variety of topics. Many I had seen or read before; a few I had already in my library. I was about ready to head for lunch when a thin, blue book caught my eye, or should I say the picture on the dust-cover of that thin, blue book caught my eye. I thought I recognized the photograph, so I picked up the musty book to see what it was about. The picture was of a desert scene with a small grove of trees, an oasis, tucked in a small valley. It looked like Israel; sure enough the title of the book was *High Above The Holy Land* by Tim Dowley. The minute I opened up the cover I knew I had found a rare treasure; one I must have no matter the cost! Fortunately, it would cost me less than five dollars.

Ever since my first, and hopefully not my last, trip to Israel, I have been about all-things-Israel. I have written and published (From Dan to Beersheba and Beyond-Resource Publishers-an imprint of Wipf and Stock Publishers) my own book on the trip. I have collected anything and everything I have come across since the trip that would remind me of that trip, but was I surprised to find something in India! This was the last place I suspected to find something that would help remember the once-in-a-lifetime trip again and again. As I leafed through the sixty pages, the photos amazed me. The book measured 13 by 10 inches and contained thirty large aerial photographs, coffee book style, of various sites located in Israel, some famous and some not so famous, like that stretch of desert on the front cover. What became fascinating to me was that just about every picture was of a place that I had visited in May of 2010. The very first picture on the inside cover was of a group of young people riding donkeys on a hill, and I would swear it looked exactly like the hill at Wadi Kelt overlooking Saint George Monastery where I rode a donkey down a hill. The next picture was of Mount Hermon and the surrounding lowlands, a place we had bused through on our northern tour. Embedded within the larger pictures were smaller photographs of relevant sites associated with the master picture: with Hermon, a picture of the archaeological excavation at Hazor and the Herodium theatre at Caesarea, two other places we had visited. The pictures were so clear I could trace the footsteps I had taken over those historical, Biblical sites!

The work was the brainchild of two photographers, Sonia Halliday and Laura Lushington, and was simple in its concept. They had hired an Israeli pilot to fly them over Israel, yes, all of Israel. Remember, Israel is only two hundred sixty miles from north to south and at its widest only seventy miles. Their toughest job was getting permission from the Israeli government for the fly-over, but when they did the rest was a piece of cake. After the pictures were taken, Tim Dowley added the simple text explaining the picture and a book of personal beauty was created. The more I flipped through it the more excited I got as I flew over Tel Arad, one of my favorite sites in the Negev. I could clearly see the trail we hiked to the hilltop fortress. It is in ruins today, but the outline of the massive two-tower gate and the interior could be clearly seen. Then it was off to Tel Jericho where I walked the ancient ruins from one end to the other. Some say Jericho is the oldest city site in the world. The aerial picture allowed me to revisit that thrilling stroll. The next page took me back to Beth Shan and the greatest archaeological site we visited in our three weeks in Israel. The massive old city overlooking the modern new city of Jesus' day was a highlight of our northern tour. Megiddo was next, including a picture of the impressive water tunnel, followed by an amazing picture of the Dead Sea, where Marnie and I floated. Qumran's important caves were next, and then Nazareth highlighted by the massive Church of the Annunciation. Bethlehem was underlined by another church, the Church of the Nativity recognized by its famous bell tower and Saint Jerome's grotto next door. A Jordan River photograph was next, and while I didn't recognize the section, my numerous crossings of the sacred stream were brought back to life. The picture of the recognizable synagogue of Capernaum brought back the morning Marnie and I walked through the ruins, and then a Sea of Galilee photograph that vividly brought back the three days we traveled around and over the Middle East's most famous lake.

Picture after picture from Masada to Jerusalem to Avdat reinforced the memories of that spectacular adventure in a vista of photographs that made me feel like I had returned!

24

STILLNESS IN THE MIDST OF A STORM

> Psalms 139:18 " . . . WHEN I AWAKE, I AM STILL WITH THEE."

OCTOBER 16, 2012 WAS an important day in my India adventures. That day was the one-hundredth day I had lived and ministered in the great subcontinent. It was also another day of what was now a weeklong event they call monsoon storms, that daily deluge of water and wind, thunder and lightning that defies any description. It is an event you must experience to fully understand, whether you can explain it or not.

On the afternoon of this memory, I had taken a nap after another busy morning at Kerala Baptist Bible College. I was beginning to realize that this trip would require more rest time than the other journeys. I had the time, so I took the opportunities given me to relax and rest in the sanctuary provided for me in the Simon home. After a peaceful and pleasant nap, I woke to another raging storm outside my bedroom windows. Lightning was flashing through the room, and the thunder shook the furniture. Meanwhile, the wind was roaring and that now all-to-familiar waterfall rain was drenching the landscape. It is at such times when the utter stillness and quiet grandeur of God speaks strongest in my soul, when the encroaching clamor and modern noises of human invention are silenced, and the still, small voice of God can be heard in the midst of a storm.

Let us be honest; stillness is not an adjective that describes this age. Stillness has been shattered by an invasion of modern sounds that has tried to silence God Himself. The scream of modern gadgets, the roar of vehicle engines, the thunder of construction equipment, the chatter of conversations, the blast of horns and whistles and buzzers have all contributed to destroy the pristine stillness that can only be found sometimes in the midst of a storm. One has to go farther and farther afield to find secluded stillness. Perhaps that is why I love Edayappara so much. Oh, there are the buses and motorcycles and trucks and cars that periodically race by with their noise, but there is also that profound stillness at times when Edayappara is quiet because this simple village in Kerala has yet to be ravished by the ruthless grip of civilization. Tranquility and quietness and stillness are still possible even in the midst of a storm.

You might be surprised by my next few observations on Edayappara, but they are true of the one hundred days I have lived there. I have yet to witness a fly-over by any aircraft. I have yet to hear a chain-saw. I have yet to hear a fire engine or police car siren. I have yet to hear an all-terrain vehicle. I have yet to hear a rifle or a gunshot. In Edayappara an unusual stillness prevails most of the time. Despite being a populous town, the tropical forest that surrounds and pervades the village seems to absorb most noises. The clamor of the crowd is only witnessed in a few places. I have walked to the two local bus stops on occasion to see a score of people at most, and there you might hear the babel. Certainly when the students of KBBC get all together in the dining hall or in chapel, you might for a while hear loud talking, but again that is rare. But when the sun begins to set, and a storm is building in the west, the village of Edayappara seems to go silent, especially in the midst of a storm.

You may hear few human sounds in a storm, but it amazes me how the animal and bird kingdom also go silent and still. I have written before of the continual and constant sounds of the forest. I observed that the animals of Edayappara were the first to warn of an impending storm. Sometimes an hour before the downpour and terrible thunder would descend on our little village, the dogs would start barking louder and the birds would be flying around frantically seeking shelter. I watched one man come into his backyard and lead his mooing cow back to the shelter of his home. Everyone and everything seemed to sense the storm and when it finally came the dogs stopped barking, the birds stopped chirping, and the cows stopped mooing, as if to acknowledge that one is to be still in the midst of a storm.

For me, finding stillness in the midst of a storm is recognizing the God of the storm. Was that not the reason Jesus could say, "Peace, be still"? (Mark 4:39) Each storm, every storm is under the control of God. I feel it is God's way of forcing us at times to stop, quiet our lives and "Be still, and know that I am God: I will be exalted among the heathen, I will be exalted in the earth (India)." (Psalms 46:10) In the canyons of concrete we call cities, mankind has built structures that seemingly can shut out most storms. Cliff-dwellers in the highest iron mountains we call high-rises are mostly unaffected, but occasionally God will even get their attention, like the super-storm Sandy that put an explanation mark at the end of my trip. Why does God continue to send such storms? I think He is still trying to communicate to the world that He hasn't gone anywhere and that He still wants to be exalted, recognized, and known. There is a strong solace in the Spirit of God that can only be seen and felt in the midst of s storm.

In a book by a favorite author Phillip Keller, I found these words he quoted from an old poem. They were new to me, and Keller didn't name the author or the prose, but they speak volumes to me of the truth I am trying to underline in this chapter.

> "All the earth is in constant change.
> Even these majestic mountains weather away.
> The granite rocks are worn down by water.
> The giant valleys grow ever deeper.
> No tree, no shrub, no flower endures.
> The clouds come and go. So, too, night and day.
> The birds take wing. The insects perish.
> Even the bear, the buck and the chattering chipmunk
> Are here but a breath in time.
> All is change. All is passing. All is perishing.
> Be still and know I am God.
> Only I endure. Only I remain. Only I change not!"

One might ask how one can find stillness in the midst of a storm where nothing is still. The trees are swaying in the gusty breeze. The air is filled with a rushing liquid that seems to create its own roar. The area is bombarded every few seconds with a thunder that could wake the dead, if possible. Where is the stillness one asks? The stillness is not found in the storm, but in the midst of the storm, the heart of the storm, in the very presence of God. (Matthew 18:19, Revelation 1:13)

The cooling breeze slowly quieted down as the hours passed. The storm could be heard in the distance, but around the Simon house stillness engulfed the yard. The solace was heavenly, the peace divine as the storm passed and another encounter with my Father came to an end. In stillness, God touched my soul with a revelation that remains and is now recorded.

25

DEATH IN THREES

> Revelation 14:13 "And I heard a voice from heaven saying unto me, Write, BLESSED ARE THE DEAD WHICH DIE IN THE LORD FROM HENCEFORTH: yea, saith the Spirit, that they may rest from their labours; and their works do follow them."

My one-hundredth day in India will also be remembered for another reason: a reality that I wouldn't fully understand until the next few days, the truth of death in threes.

I have been a pastor long enough to know that death is a part of the pastorate. Because of the uncertainty of death, no man knowing the time or the hour, there is one clear certainty that seems to repeat itself over and over again. I don't know where I first heard or first began to observe on my own the uncanny precept I call death in threes. If you hear or know of the passing of someone, within a few days you will hear or know of at least two more. I have been noticing this pattern since the earliest days in my ministry. I was blessed in my childhood and young adulthood to know of few deaths. I come from a family of exceptional longevity, both on my father and mother's side. My mother's mother lived into her mid-90s, and mother is nearly ninety herself. Nineties are not an unusual life expectancy with my father's family. My father will enter his ninetieth year in August, while his mother lived into her one-hundredth year. Needless to say, I went to few funerals in my boyhood and the only important funeral of that era, my grandfather Barton, I was too young to go, or so was the philosophy of the 1950s! The 1970s changed everything for me in the category of death. Starting with my grandfather Blackstone's death in 1975, I began to witness the passing of individuals in threes, and India 2012 would not be an exception to the rule. Even in the uttermost, people die in threes, even when you're not there.

A hint of trouble began as I was walking from the college chapel to the college office. I met President Simon heading for his office at the end of the dormitory/classroom building, the first structure you come to when you drive on campus. His only words to me were, "I think someone has died." Shibu had been on the Internet checking his e-mail when he noticed I had gotten a few messages with death in the description. My mind began to go over the possible candidates as I walked the final fifty yards to the administration building and climbed the steps to the second story office. Who could have died? I first went through my family, but nobody was sick-unto-death when I left. My mother's brother and sisters were old, but none critically unhealthy. Immediately my mind turned to my flock, but once again nobody was critical when I left. If they had been, I might not have left. Next I went over my friends, people that were close to me but neither a part of my flock or my family. Once again I came up empty as I entered the computer room of the IGBC office to check my e-mail. Who had died?

The first surprise as I scrolled down through the listings was an unexpected e-mail from a lady of the church at home. I opened the e-mail and this is what I read:

"Shibu and Julie . . . . We are truly so thankful that Pastor could be with you for this period of time. We truly do miss Pastor so much . . . the Lord has blessed with some wonderful 'fill-ins' while he is away, but they could never, ever take his place. Please give him our love and we KNOW THAT IT MUST BE TERRIBLY HARD ON HIM BEING SO FAR AWAY AS HE HEARS OF A GREAT SAINT OF THE LORD, PRISCILLA, PASSING AWAY IN OUR CHURCH . . . but we know the Lord doesn't make mistakes and God took her home at this particular time. It was such a joy to have her at church this last Sunday morning and she was so happy and excited to be there. Gave many of us an opportunity to give her a hug and chat with her. Little did we know that would be our last time to visit with her here on this earth. Please be in prayer for the family . . . extremely hard on them without their Pastor but we are all trying to do our part to help where we can. Love to all your family, Donna Clark"

Priscilla? Priscilla? I kept repeating her name over and over in my head, but not because I was surprised. I had visited Priscilla Bowden on her deathbed more times than any other individual I had ever pastored. Priscilla had been a sickly person throughout the twenty-one years I had been her pastor. Priscilla had one of the earliest open-heart operations every attempted in the State of Maine in the early 60s. As a matter of fact, just the year before they had celebrated that fifty-year milestone in medicine with a big party that brought together the surgical team and the patients. Priscilla and the lead doctor were the only individuals still alive from those early days. To say Priscilla had a hard life health-wise would be an understatement. Early in the 2012, it appeared Priscilla wouldn't make it to Easter when I got a call from her only son Greg telling me that he was rushing his mother to Boston, and he didn't think she would be alive when they arrived. Yet, as so often before, Priscilla rallied and recovered to spend a carefree summer with her family, even planting her flower garden and going on a camping trip with her husband Allen, her grandson Ross, and daughter Miriam. When I left for India, Priscilla was as good as she had been in years. So what happened?

Donna had assumed that my wife had already e-mailed me about Priscilla's home going, but before I heard from Coleen, I had another e-mail from my daughter Marnie in Texas which read: "Hey Bubby (Marnie's name for me). This is Mar. Just wanted to let you know that Priscilla passed away tonight at 10:30 P.M. Mom just talked to Karen (Priscilla's daughter-in-law) and Greg. They aren't doing well. We don't know many details as they are kind of in a mess. Mom is going to call them tomorrow. They were driving home (from Boston). Mom will write you more tomorrow. Love you so much. Night."

If Priscilla's unexpected departure wasn't shocking enough, I heard just a few days later of the passing of an old ice fishing friend, Buster Ingles. I had seen Buster just before I left for India and found him in great shape despite being in his 90s. Still living alone in his own home, Buster was number two. Just a short time later I heard of Randy Knox's death. Randy was a cousin of my wife's only sister's husband. We had been praying for Randy as he was in poor health, but death? Another unexpected departure!

Whether individually, by twos or threes or more, death is a reality of life in India or America? Paul wrote, "And as it is appointed unto men once to die . . . " (Hebrews 9:27) James wrote, "Whereas ye know not what shall be on the morrow. For what is your life? It is even a vapour that appeareth for a little time, and then vanisheth away." (James 4:14) I was not surprised by death; if there was any surprise it was who died, not because I believed they wouldn't die, but when they would die. A church member, a family member, and a friend reminding me again that at any time whether I am around or not when Jesus puts the key in the door of death (Revelation 1:18) those you know are going to go. It is also another reminder that we all need to be ready for our call because death can call at any time, even when your pastor is halfway around the world and not on call.

26

THREE WEEKS AS A COLLEGE PROFESSOR

> II Timothy 2:2 "And the things that thou hast heard of me among many witnesses, THE SAME COMMIT THOU TO FAITHFUL MEN, WHO SHALL BE ABLE TO TEACH OTHERS ALSO."

I WOULD GET A chance to share again with the students of Kerala Baptist Bible College after my return from Orissa, but on Friday, October 19, 2012 the bulk of my teaching at KBBC was over. All told, I had fifteen classes with the senior class in my Prison Epistles course; I had fourteen classes with the junior class in my Historical Books of the Old Testament course; I had seven classes with the entire student body teaching on the Tabernacle, Herod's Temple, Jesus' Jerusalem, and Jesus seen in the Old Testament and New Testament books, and finally, I was able to share fourteen chapel messages with the students and staff about my 2010 trip to Israel. My first three weeks in Kerala were a whirlwind of classes and activities, but I throughly enjoyed every minute teaching God's precious Word.

    I woke that last morning as a professor to an odd sighting: fog outside my second story bedroom windows. In over one hundred days I had never seen fog. It had rained all night, the ninth straight day of monsoon storms, and the combination of water and heat left a heavy fog over the forest. It was a pleasant sight as the sun tried to break through the mist. The rays of light through the water-soaked air were heavenly, as I breathed in the moist breeze blowing into my room. It was one of the best mornings I rose to in India, but my first thought was on my last official day of teaching at KBBC. My fifteenth day of instruction and, before it would be over, I would have four classes with my beloved students. This was also the day I would determine the final test, how I would grade my students. I would give them their final exams when I returned from Orissa, but I was determined to have it all settled before Shibu and I left on Monday. I had changed my mind on the percentages of outlines versus readings versus quizzes versus the final. Today I would make it official to the students. One of the requirements of my classes was a grading of the students. I was actually taking class time from Shibu and others, so the three weeks of instruction were supplemental instruction to their other classes. A grade was required for graduation and the completion of the students' course study. In the end, I felt the students did well, but I could have done better as a teacher. I always think how I could have done it differently. This is what the final totals looked like. Eleven students scored 90 or above, twelve students scored 80 or above, and four students scored 70 or above.

For years I have been inspired by II Timothy 2:2, one of the many responsibilities I feel I have been given as a pastor-teacher (Ephesians 4:11). My three weeks at KBBC was another opportunity for me to pass on what I had been taught by others and have witnessed in my own life. The Word of God is a sacred trust, passed down from generation to generation, and but for the sharing, teaching, commitment of each generation the Word will be lost. One of the tasks I have been entrusted with is to seek out faithful men (men is the generic word for men and women) to pass this knowledge on to, but we are not just talking about men in general but faithful teachers who will also pass on to others what they have learned. I have spent most of my adult life teaching people who never teach others. This is the reality of the Church of God today. Most Church members listen and enjoy and feed on the Word, but basically keep it to themselves. One of the joys of being a professor at a Bible College is the realization that you are teaching and training young people who want to learn the Word so they can pass it on to others.

II Timothy was my guidebook when I first started in the ministry. I saw within its pages the instruction book for my ministry, just as the elder Paul instructed the younger Timothy in what he was to be as a pastor-teacher. Three books (I Timothy, II Timothy, and Titus) in total were written for men like me and ultimately our responsibility was to be "perfect, throughly furnished unto all good works." (II Timothy 3:17) For me, the key phrase that summarizes this concept is "meet for the Master's use" (II Timothy 2:21). It is this phrase that helps me best explain II Timothy 2:2. My ministry at KBBC was to equip each student to be the best they could be for the Master's use, whatever use that was. In my first trip to Kerala, I taught the students a simple prayer chorus, "Vessels for the Master's Use", based on II Timothy 2:21 that I had learned in a Christian camp in Canada. These are the words to that chorus.

> "Filled to overflowing, hearts aglow and showing
> Christ to those who do not know Him;
> Sanctified and holy, yielded to Him only,

Vessels for the Master's use.
O make my life a blessing, Lord.
May it stand Thy testing, Lord.
Filled to overflowing, hearts aglow and showing
Christ to those who do not know Him;
Sanctified and holy, yielding to Him only,
Vessels for the Master's use.

Such is the responsibility of the teacher of faithful men and women; to help shape and mold young people into the instrument God wants them to be. One of my favorite writers, F. B. Meyer, puts it this way in his commentary on "Meet for the Master's Use."

"This I would be, O Lord, clay though I am. Be Thou my potter. Make me what Thou canst and by what process Thou wilt, only let me be what Thou canst use . . . .By Thy grace I am able. Let me die with Thee; lie in the grave of obscurity and neglect; be counted as the off-scouring of all things; be broken on the edge of Thy wheel; pass through the fire of Thy hottest kiln-only let me be one whom Thou chooses and usest, constantly in Thy hand; dipped down often into the brimming well, and back to Thy dear lips, or the lips of whom Thou lovest . . . . .I understand Thee, Master. Thou wouldst winnow my heart, and rid me of all that is proud and selfish. It is true that in the time past I have sought great things for myself: but that is gone now: I am a weaned babe: my only desire is for Thee, for Thy glory, for the magnifying of Thy name: my one cry to be often, always, in Thy hand!"

Such was my desire for the students of KBBC during my stay with them.

Three short weeks, fifteen quick days, fifty simple lessons to help mold and shape a group of Indian students from nine different States in India. Granted, the time was small compared to four to six years in their KBBC career, but my prayer is that eternal precepts were revealed, lasting concepts were taught, and rewarding principles were conveyed to the sixty-nine students I had to teach. My prayer is that each of them will be faithful men WHO WILL BE ABLE TO TEACH OTHERS ALSO. If they are faithful, how many more will there be in a few years?

27

WHAT IT TAKES TO BE A GOOD SUNDAY SCHOOL TEACHER

Ephesians 4:11-12 "And He gave some, apostles; and some, prophets; and some, evangelists; and some, pastors and TEACHERS; for the perfecting of the saints, for the work of the ministry, for the edifying of the body of Christ."

My fourth Saturday and the beginning of my fourth week in Kerala began like the others Saturdays of my trip to India. That first Saturday was spent in a Thanksgiving Service as I was welcomed back to Kerala as a favorite son. My second Saturday was spent in the mountains of Munnar enjoying a corner of God's great creation. The Saturday before was the stirring, moving Testimonial Service where I shared in the greatest outpouring of praise I had ever experienced in my life. My fourth Saturday would see me speaking at a Sunday school teachers' convention for the IGBC churches.

I woke to a cool eighty degrees. Our tenth day in a row of rain had cooled Kerala down tremendously. The animal life and the local population seemed to be enjoying the falling temperatures because Edayappara seemed abnormally noisy that fourth Saturday in India. As usual during the monsoon, the power was out, but as I learned that had little effect on early morning activities at the Simon home. Using her gas stove, Julie had a great breakfast prepared, including the pineapple I had returned with the day before. The field next to the Simon house was a pineapple grove. Just before the rain, I had taken my late afternoon walk to watch a crew of men and women harvest the lower part of the field. As a reward, they gave me a ripe pineapple. Although I am not a big fan of pineapple, I did enjoy the fruit the next morning for breakfast. Perhaps that is why I never enjoyed pineapple before, not fresh enough! I also had more of the papaya off the Simons' tree, and Julie's eggs and toast finished the menu. The convention started at 10:00 A.M. at the Kangazha Church, so Shibu and I were soon off to participate.

The convention started with opening remarks from Pastor Robin, the president of the organization. There were eighteen men teachers and sixteen women teachers from the area churches in attendance. The senior class girls from KBBC were there, and they taught a couple of action choruses to the group. One of the choruses I had never heard before was called "Take My Hand". With a catchy tune we sang, "Take my hand, led me on, down the road. I am driving on, take my heart, I am yours Blessed Jesus lead me on, keep on following you." Then the words were repeated as the girls taught us motions with the words. After a prayer and a bit of singing, it was my turn to address the teachers. Other workshops would follow my message including, of course, a noontime meal. This is the outline of the sermon I shared that day on "What Makes A Good Sunday School Teacher?"

I started by sharing with them that I had been a Sunday school teacher myself for nearly forty years. At the writing of this chapter, I have conducted nearly seventeen hundred Sunday school classes. I am blessed! I shared with my fellow-teachers in India what I felt the Bible taught about the characteristics and qualifications of a good teacher. I also shared with them that it was the first time I had actually spoken to a group of Sunday school teachers. I had addressed AWANA teachers, Good News Club teachers, and future teachers before, but this was actually my first Sunday school teacher convention. My address to them that morning in Edayappara was around this outline:

1. GOOD TEACHERS MUST BE SPIRIT-LED I Corinthians 12:4, 28. In Ephesians 4:11, the teacher is listed fifth, but in Romans 12:7 the teacher is listed third. As with all other divinely appointed positions in the Church, the teacher must be called of God first, gifted by the Spirit second, and recognized by the Church third. Teaching the Word of God is a sacred responsibility given by Christ to His Church.

2. GOOD TEACHERS MUST BE SCRIPTURALLY SOUND II Timothy 2:15. You must know the Word yourself before you can share the Word with others. Every teacher is a student first, and a teacher second, and every Sunday school teacher's TEACHER is the Holy Spirit (I John 2:27). We are challenged to search the Scriptures (John 5:3) and study the Scriptures (II Timothy 2:15) and then pass on what we know to the students the Lord places in our charge.

3. GOOD TEACHERS MUST BE SERVANTS Matthew 23:4. Jesus rebuked the Pharisaical teachers because they were acting more like

masters than teachers. A good teacher stands along-side the student and helps and guides, not as an over-ruler or taskmaster. A good teacher never acts superior, nor do they lord it over their students (I Peter 5:3), but they are to be the example of a humble servant as Jesus was (Philippians 2:7). Our responsibility as teachers is to direct our students through the Scriptures as Jesus did (Matthew 23:11). Stewards make the best teachers (I Corinthians 4:2).

4. GOOD TEACHERS MUST BE SENSITIVE TO THE NEEDS OF THEIR STUDENTS Mark 4:2. Without a doubt, Jesus was the Teacher's teacher, the best of the best, and the reason was He knew all men (John 2:24-25). The advantage Jesus had made Him the greatest teacher ever, but we must develop this skill as well. Even though we will never know the mind of our students, we can be sensitive to the needs of our students as we listen and watch their lives. A classic New Testament example of this is how Aquila and Priscilla taught Apollo the Word of God about the Spirit of God. (Acts 18:24-28)

5. GOOD TEACHERS MUST BE SOWERS II Timothy 2:2. It is all about sowing the good seed of the Word of God into the minds of others (Matthew 13:1-8). As with Jesus' parable on sowing, we won't always find good ground, but our responsibility is to sow as much of the Word as we can and let God take care of the rest (Isaiah 55:11). Ultimately, good teachers produce teachers, for this is the goal of all teachers: to teach themselves out of a job.

I closed my exhortation with this final challenge and illustration. MAKE SURE YOUR TEACHING IS MIRRORED IN YOUR LIFE. Then I shared the most stirring Sunday school teacher story I have ever heard. A man in my second church, Calvary Baptist Church of Westfield, Maine, shared with me the reason it took him fifty years to get saved. Taken to Sunday school at an early age, his Sunday school teacher was also a man who worked for his father. After many years of Sunday school lessons from the man, one day he witnessed that same man stealing gas from his father's tank. He never went back to Sunday school again as a child and used that Sunday school teacher as an excuse for why he would never be a Christian well into adulthood. Eventually, God's Spirit broke through, but not until after many long years of resisting the Spirit's conviction. All because of the bad example of a Sunday school teacher.

28

RAINY DAYS AND SUNDAYS IN KERALA

Proverbs 27:15 "A continual dropping in A VERY RAINY DAY ..."

COASTAL KERALA IS, AS I found out in 2010, world renowned for its splendid sunshine. Its beautiful beaches and warm weather are a mecca for countless tourists from all over the world who love the sea and enjoy the tropical climate. Few travel inland to places like Edayappara, but on the coastal plain from Trivandrum to Kochi, the attractions draw scores of sun-worshippers annually, including many of the locals that have time to play. The only time this pilgrimage to the shore is interrupted is during monsoon season when the rainy period descends on Kerala, a period I was experiencing as I ministered into my fourth weekend.

After my message to the Sunday school teachers of the IGBC, I was off through the raindrops to visit an old friend, Johnson Matthews my first interrupter in 2006, who leads Agape Ministries in Kumpantham. Starting on Friday, the rain continued. The afternoon thunder and lightning storms were diminishing in intensity, and the volume of water was also slacking, but now it seemed to rain off and on most of the day versus a few hours of downpours. I actually liked the cloud-cover and showers because it kept the temperature lower, and I thought the humidity was even less. As we travelled the five miles to Matthew's place, we could see the effects of the rain over the last week and a half. There were puddles everywhere, and the foliage and flowers were brilliant. Nature had gotten a drink from God and was blooming. The few meadows in the hill country were green with new grass; the wildflowers that flourished during the rainy season were budding. Even the stately rubber trees and tall coconut trees seemed to take on a fresh look as we drove through the forest-lined lanes that led to Johnson's home.

I was visiting Johnson's ministry for a second time. I had met him in 2006 as he translated for me at the annual convention of the IGBC. Shibu was just back from America and his Malayalam was rusty, so he asked Shaju's best friend to translate for the rookie. We hit it off immediately because his English was the best I had heard at the time. His style was like mine, so we were a good team. I promised him that if I ever returned to India I would visit his independent work, which I did in 2007. It was then I met his dear wife Lynda, his parents, on whose property Johnson had built a church, and the twelve orphans he was caring for. Over the years, Johnson's dream was to build a building to house the church. Currently the church folks met in his home, and the orphans were scattered between his house and his parents' home. That dream was becoming a reality in 2012, and I wanted to see it. Shaju promised to take me in a spare moment, and on that Saturday weekend of the Annual SS Teachers Convention we had time. The rain wasn't going to stop us.

As we drove into the Matthews' yard, the entire family was waiting for us. This is the typical protocol when a guest visits. The rain had let up which gave us a chance to walk behind Johnson's house to see the new building, a typical concrete structure that was fully enclosed and ready for the final touches. The one story building, with the option for a second story, contained a large room that would be the sanctuary for the Kumpantham Baptist Church, plenty of small rooms for bedrooms for the orphans, and extra rooms for a kitchen and dining room. I could see that Johnson was excited with the prospects of what he could do with the building. As I climbed onto the roof and looked around, I was moved again with the paradise that was Kerala after a rain. The new building was set in a working rubber tree grove surrounded by a thick tropical forest. A hedge of rocks ran along the boundary line between the properties, but also along these lines were beautiful shrubs and colorful bushes with flowers seemingly everywhere. So it was with the flowering saints in Johnson's yard, beautiful people with the colors of Christian character that inspire me each and every time I get a chance to visit. I learned that Johnson hadn't begun to rest on his laurels, but had started his own Bible Institute in the eastern mountains of Kerala to train up believers to reach the unreached people groups of the region. Planting Christian roots in the regions beyond, in the uttermost place, Johnson Matthews had enlarged his coast since I last called.

By the time we drove back to Edayappara, another shower had come and gone and the roadway was awash with the run-off. As the rain refreshed the land, I was refreshed by the shower of hospitality I had received at the Agape Mission, and that was only the beginning of a weekend of blessings that continued the next day as I drove for the fourth time to the Poovanmala Baptist Church. I had visited this church early in my

2006 trip and had returned again in 2007 and 2010. It was like revisiting a favorite flower garden and, like at Kumpantham, I found new foliage and a flowery welcome that would rival the greatest botanical gardens in the world. The colorful saris of the ladies were like the yellows, reds, purples, pinks, browns, whites, and every variation in between of a flower garden. The hues and shades bursting forth in blooming smiles as I entered the sanctuary were not only pleasant to the eyes, but their singing was like the dropping of rain in a forest soothing to the ears. I will never get tired of a Sunday service in Kerala, despite the fact I understand few words. The thrill is equal to walking through a park not knowing the species of tree or plant by name but still enjoying the fragrance, the beauty, and the myriad of sounds coming from the residents. As we left the service, the morning rains had stopped, but off in the distance I could hear the building of another storm coming off the sea. I knew before I entered the garden at Kerala Baptist Bible College that evening the rain would return, but now after twelve days of rain I was beginning to enjoy the spectacle just like I was enjoying each and every chance I had to come into the presence of the Christians of Kerala.

Sure enough by evening time, great, dark banks of clouds were moving in off the sea to our west. They were being pushed by strong breezes from the water. As darkness descended in Edayappara, I went to the window in my room to watch the gathering. I felt the first drops of rain falling on my face. Within minutes the lightning was overhead and the thunder was less than a second behind. Then the rain fell in torrents; little did I know this would be my last storm. Shibu and I would leave for Orissa the next morning, and there would be no such storms there. By the time I returned, the monsoon would be over. But I relished my last Kerala downpour. What a sweet noise! What a refreshing sound! What a renewal to my soul!

By the time my evening service at KBBC was over, so was the storm. The black clouds had crossed over Edayappara, but, as with every storm, it had left its best behind: the water. So it was for me on my weekends in Kerala. They were busy, but there were showers of blessings each and every time you visit old spiritual friends in their gardens of ministry and discover that God has showered (Ezekiel 34:26) His work with mercy-drops, and there shall be seasons of refreshing, sent from the Saviour above just as I experienced that weekend in Kerala.

29

I'LL FLY AWAY IN THE MORNING

Job 20:8 "HE SHALL FLY AWAY AS A DREAM..."

For over twenty days, I had been pulling details of our secret mission into Orissa from Shibu. I had learned that our six-day trip to visit twenty churches would take us into three districts of the State of Orissa: Puri, Kalahandi, and Phulbani. The air flight distance there and back would be nearly one thousand miles each way. Once on land, we would take two train trips, one of three hundred seven miles and the other of three hundred ninety-one miles, and two taxi rides totaling another two hundred fifty miles. It would be a world-wind journey, and, on the night before departure, it still felt like a dream.

My dream of Orissa had begun in 2006 when I met what I first called "the baker's dozen of Orissa", thirteen men and their incredible, indomitable leader, Joy Thomas. Only the Good Lord knows why I was drawn to this group of pastors, evangelists, missionaries, and lay workers, but I was. I felt an immediate connection, a kindred-spirit, and a comradeship with these simple, small (in statue only) men from an uttermost place. I had heard the word Orissa for the first time in the 1990s, but it was only a place, a small spot on a world-wide map, a destination for someone else, not a farmer's son from Maine. Ranjan changed that for me. Once I connected a face to the place, everything changed for me. Once I realized I was in the presence of the persecuted church, my prayers and petitions and pleas to the throne of God to visit Orissa began to ascend on high. Because writing has always been a way for me to keep things current in my mind, shortly after hearing of a renewed persecution in Orissa in 2008, I wrote this.

> I sit before my old computer this morning with a heavy heart. Some very dear Christian friends of mine on the other side of the world are living through a great persecution. We in America know very little of this reality for so many of our brothers and sisters in Christ. I will be honest that I hadn't known of it and had chosen, for most of my life, to be ignorant of the daily

persecution afflicted on so much of the universal Church. It wasn't until 2006 that my head was finally removed from the sand, and the persecuted Church had a face.

Don't get me wrong. Like any good Christian, I had read John Foxe's famous work on the *Christian Martyrs Of The World* at Bible school. I still have an old copy of that work resting in a bookshelf beside my computer desk. At the time, reading it was simply an intellectual exercise and once completed, I placed persecution into the historical corner of my brain and forgot about it! Surely, persecution against Christians had ceased long ago. That is how ignorant I was about the plight of native churches in distant places. I went on with my spiritual education totally unaware of what my fellow-believers were facing from a hostile world. Isn't ignorance bliss?

To this day, I still remember the next time persecution was placed before my face. I had almost finished Bob Jones University when in a class on Hebrew History my professor had the gall to bring it up again. I have never forgotten the statement he made while expounding on Exodus 1. "The best thing that could ever happen to the American Church would be a nation-wide persecution!" Using the example of the persecution of the Israelites by the Egyptians as his soap-box, my teacher went on to explain that the more the Egyptians persecuted the Israelites the more God blessed them, and they multiplied. He went on to demonstrate that this truth was repeated in the life of the early Church at Jerusalem. He even quoted Foxe, "only differing in being upheld by a fiery zeal and fervent faith which grew stronger with persecution!"

I left that classroom troubled by what I heard, but, once again, I allowed the truth of the matter to find a deserted section of my brain to rest. Over the years that followed, I was so wrapped up in my own calling that I cared little for those who were facing persecution on a daily basis. I had a local fellowship to start and three local assemblies to pastor; I couldn't think or even pray for people I had never met or even questioned whether or not they were facing real persecution. Oh, I became as all good pastors do. Familiar with the classic verses on persecution like Matthew 5:10-12, but I had no meaning or understanding to what I read or studied.

Over those ignorant years in the pastorate, I would periodically pick up a book like Elisabeth Elliot's *Through Gates Of Splendor*, the story of the martyrdom of the five young American missionaries in Ecuador. I was shocked into the reality that someone had died for his faith in my lifetime. In an old record book, I still have the pictures of Ed McCully, Pete Fleming, Jim Elliot, Nate Saint, and Rogar Youderian, as they were when they launched Operation Auca. It was my first visible reminder that persecution of the Church was still a factor that many have had to deal with in the modern world, my world! I then read of John and Betty Stam of China and their martyrdom during the early days of the establishment of Communism in China. Though they died before my birth in 1951, I began to realize that the persecution of Christians was as much a twentieth century event as a first century happening. Here we are in the twenty-first century, and persecution is still going on in an uttermost part like Orissa.

As I settled into a restless sleep that Sunday night, I couldn't get off my mind the place where I was going. It was not because I feared going but because I regretted all those years for not praying for and being concerned for the persecuted Church. I can honestly say I never once felt a pang of fear before, during, or after this trip. I would return this minute if I could. Regret plagued my mind.

On October 22, 2012, Shibu and I were driven to Kochi Airport for a flight to Orissa by way of Hyderabad. Within miles of Edayappara, we came across an elephant walking down the road ahead of us. For me, it was a blessed sign that our journey would be like spotting an elephant - joyous! Before we left, the thermometer in Julie's garden read 72 degrees, a sign for me that the trip would be – pleasant! The send-off from the students the night before was as if I was their missionary traveling to a distant land – called! Raju Sagar was especially happy I would visit his home state, and though I wouldn't be going to his village, I would be passing it on my first train ride in Orissa. Our three-hour car ride to Kochi was uneventful as Sijin carefully drove the hilly lanes to the new Kochi Airport. Shibu's grandfather George, a man who came to Christ after a message I preached in 2006 and a man I was given the privilege to baptize the next day, was along for the ride because he had never seen the new sky port. The time had come. The dreaming was over. Reality was now here, and I was actually going to a place where fellow Christians had been killed for their faith; where church sanctuaries had been burned and believers scattered because of persecution. I was ready to sense persecution, even if I wouldn't face persecution. I was heading for holy ground to pay my respect for and honor to a people who had faced persecution, endured persecution, and beaten persecution!

30

SEEING INDIA FROM THE AIR

> Psalms 65:8 "THEY ALSO THAT DWELL IN THE UTTERMOST PARTS ARE AFRAID AT THY TOKENS: Thou makest the outgoings of the morning and evening to rejoice."

THIS BOOK, UP TO this point, has been a collection of simple observations drawn from my days teaching at Kerala Baptist Bible College and preaching in the area churches of the Independent Gospel Baptist Churches of India in and around Edayappara, Kerala. From now on, I will see India through the eyes of a missionary on an adventure to an uttermost place and the profound parables that touched my soul. These spiritual insights began the moment I boarded Indigo Flight #314 for Hyderabad, Andhra Pradesh.

Despite flying in and out of India four times, I had never really seen India from the air. All my fights to and from India had taken place very early, before dawn early, in the morning. The only observation I have ever had looking down on India was how dark the country was. Flying over the west coast of Kerala, either to Trivandrum or Kochi, from the Arabian Sea in the dark is unimpressive. The black coast with dimly lit towns and villages reveals little. Even the big cities of Trivandrum and Kochi are dark compared to their American counterparts. The wattage is not there, so to turn the night into day, as do most American cities, is impossible in India. That is why my first flight over India in the daylight was so wonderful; I was going to see my adopted land as I had never seen her.

Shibu let me sit next to the window. As the 360 AirBus took off, I was excited as we circled around Kochi before heading northeast toward central India. I had taken a train from Kottayam, Kerala to Guntakel, Andrah Pradesh in 2010, a twenty-four hour trip. Our flight time to Hyderabad, the capital of Andrah Pradesh just north of Guntakel, was just over an hour. The train ride took us further east than the plane ride, but now I saw as the eagle sees, from above. What a flight! From the cheerful comfort of that airplane window, a splendid landscape emerged. I learned after I got back to the States that we flew over Silent Valley National Park, a vista of rugged ranges. I saw, for the first time, the three regions of Kerala that I had traveled: coastal plain, low hills, and mountains. Kerala isn't very wide, and from my ten thousand foot seat, I could see all three. Kerala's landscape is much like Israel: rugged mountains, rolling hills, flat plains with each region distinct from the other. Kochi is located next to the ocean on the coastal plain; Edayappara is located in the foothills, and Munnar in the mountains. I had travelled through each region on this trip by car. Now I was seeing it all from the edge of the sky.

The clouds were few and far between as we winged our way towards Hyderabad. My aerial show continued as we passed a great lake. Feeding that lake was a massive, twisting river with what looked like class-four rapids. The view was clear enough to make out waterfalls on the river as well as a great forestland along its shores. The wilderness went on for miles without sight of a village, a hamlet, or a town of any kind. The first part of our flight seemed to be over a remote and inaccessible section of Northern Kerala. I knew from my travels in Andhra Pradesh in 2010 the minute we had crossed the state line. From rugged terrain to flat desert happened about half-way through our flight. The ground turned brown and the hills disappeared. On occasion, you would see a small blue patch where water was found, but rare was the sighting of a stream or brook. I never saw anything that looked like a river. I remember looking out our train window as we crossed what might be considered great rivers, but most were dry riverbeds when I passed over them. The same seemed to be the case from the air. After seventy minutes, my National Geographic Special was over as we made our descent into the airport where I would experience my first shock of the trip.

Our Indigo flight landed smoothly around 2:50 P.M. We had a two hour and a half layover before our next flight to Bhubaneshwar, Orissa. The minute I entered the air terminal I thought I had taken a wrong flight back to America. I thought the new airport in Kochi was quite American, but it was nothing compared to the new Hyderabad Airport. I think I can honestly say I have never been in an American airport any better! I learned that the Indian government had built the transportation hub to draw business from overseas, and it had worked. Everywhere I saw signs of American companies and British organizations. As a matter of fact, I have a deacon in my church whose son makes regular business trips to Hyderabad because his company has a division in India. The accommodations were super-sized, and the only thing I could find wrong was the fact that the local McDonalds didn't sell hamburgers! Our stay was short enough, so I didn't care, but I would care when Shibu and I returned through Hyderabad Airport on Saturday and our wait was seven hours.

I was excited when our next Indigo flight left before sunset. Once again I got to see another piece of India from the air as we circled. I never saw the city of Hyderabad itself, for like the Charles De Gaulle Aero port outside Paris, France, they had built the Hyderabad Airport miles from the city. We flew over the modern airport once before heading northeast toward Orissa at fifteen thousand feet, a little over an hour away. I was getting closer to the State that had invaded my dreams for nearly six years. The territory I saw before darkness occurred was similar to the country south of Hyderabad: flat and dry. But just as the sun began to set, I did notice we were flying into a greener land. The sunlight of the next day would reveal that Orissa had the best characteristics of both Kerala and Andhra Pardesh: gentle rolling hills with plenty of water, a land full of bounty and colorful with an autumn harvest. At 6:40 P.M. on October 22, 2012, I landed at the Bhubaneshwar Airport near the eastern coast of Orissa. Our day's journey had taken us from coast to coast and from southwest India to northeast India.

Waiting at the gate to pick us up was my dear friend Joy Thomas, the director of the Orissa Outreach Mission, and our primary driver for the week Moses, Pastor John's only son. I had meet Pastor John, the former police officer turned pastor, in 2010 in Kanekel, Andrah Pardesh. Moses was a construction site supervisor, but he still lived with and took care of his father and three sisters. In order to keep a low profile, Joy had hired an auto, the three-wheel carts of India, to take us into the city. Bhubaneshwar is a city of two million people and the capital of Orissa. We had arrived in Orissa at the height of the most important Hindu festival of the year. The streets were crowded, and if I didn't know better, it looked like Christmas. There were light displays everywhere as people went from one Hindu temple and shrine to another seeking a blessing for the year ahead. I would soon learn just how pagan and terrified this place of the uttermost part was!

As I prepared this chapter, I came across the psalm I have printed at the head of this chapter. I learned very quickly how the people of Orissa live in constant fear of offending the gods. What the Creator God gave to be enjoyed, they live in terror of, and although the verse is a good description of Orissa, it is also a perfect description of how I felt on my first day going to Orissa. My outgoing morning and my incoming evening was full of joy and rejoicing beyond description!

31

SIDEWAYS ON A SCOOTER

Galatians 3:28 "There is neither Jew nor Greek, there is neither bond or free, there is neither male NOR FEMALE: FOR YE ARE ALL ONE IN CHRIST JESUS."

Each time I sit down to record my memoirs of an Indian, spiritual adventure, I realize that each sequel is really a combination of the current trip blending together with the past trips. Even though this is my fourth memoir, my mind naturally goes back to previous trips as I remember details of the trip I am actually writing about. A case in point is the subject of this chapter and the unique title I have given it. I will not take credit for this title because I understand it is the title of a book written about women in India. I have not read the book, nor do I know its author, but when I heard the title for the first time, I knew I too had to write on the subject suggested by the unusual phrase. In four trips to the subcontinent of India, I have observed the plight of Indian women and their difficult place in Indian culture. That truth was dramatically underlined and highlighted in my first morning in Orissa. Remember before you read on, these are the observations of a Westerner on an Eastern culture that is thousands of years older than ours, yet the precept from the Bible that I have printed at the beginning of this chapter should, at least for the Christian, take precedence over anything that Indian society might deem appropriate.

After sneaking into Orissa, we entered Bhubaneshwar in the backseat of an auto cart before slipping into the Hotel Pushpak in the darkness that had fallen just before our flight landed from Hyderabad. I felt like a spy invading a hostile country, cloak and dagger and all that stuff. I was going along with the wishes of my companions who felt that an American would stand out in the crowd and bring unwanted attention. We even stayed in for dinner that first night walking upstairs to a restaurant on the third floor. It didn't take long for me to sense what Joy and Shibu feared; the looks and stares were enough to make you wonder, but I never did. You see, I have had nothing but positive experiences in India, and I am not one, by my very nature, to fret or fear over something that has never yet happened. This might all change one day in India, but as for now, I felt no hostility that night. I was a curiosity, plain and simple! The trial run into a public place seemed to put my friends at ease because the next morning Shibu did something that he didn't allow me to do in Andhra Pardesh, walk openly in the streets.

I had lived nearly a week in Kanekel but was no allowed once to explore the town. I stayed either at the church compound or was in a car. My roaming feet were shackled, and I was unable to explore the world through the gate. I imagined that the same restrictions would be forced on me in Orissa, but I was in for a pleasant surprise when Shibu said before breakfast, "Let's go to a local market and pick up some supplies for our overnight train ride to Titiagarh." I was shocked, but I didn't once question the statement in fear Shibu might be kidding. We exited the Pushpak Hotel, which was located just off a very busy boulevard in downtown Bhubaneshwar, around 7 A.M. The massive city was just waking up. Perhaps this was the reason Shibu chose this time and place to give me a taste of freedom. As we strolled down the inner street, a wide sidewalk that parallels the main street where people and animals can roam and motorcycles and autos can be parked, to a small market about a block from our hotel, I saw them immediately. Despite the fact that traffic was light and there were very few people out, the women were. My attention was first drawn to a frail-looking, elderly-appearing woman sitting in a mound of sand. Cross-legged, she sat at the foot of a pile of coconuts with a heavy, machete-like knife in her hand. I had seen it countless times before in my travels around Kerala, Andhra Pardesh, Tamil Nadu, and now Orissa. I knew what she was doing. She was doing the same thing the two ladies in the street were doing. I noticed them as I looked up from the old lady. If it is dirty, disgusting, and degrading, there is a woman around somewhere. Women in India are not even second-class citizens. Animals have a better lot in India than do most women. A case in point was the small world I was seeing on my first morning exploring Orissa. Just to the right of the coconut lady was a huge Brahma bull resting before he started his morning wandering the streets of Bhubaneshwar looking for a handout. Most animals don't work in India, but women work like animals. The ladies in the street, each dressed in a colorful sari, were street sweepers. As they swept yesterday's dust into small piles, a man with a tractor and trailer came along and shoveled up the piles of dirt they created by the side of the road. I watched them during my entire time to the market and back. I stopped to watch the lady split her coconuts for sale. I asked to take a picture; she allowed me to, a rare approval. I looked at the image at the back of my digital camera and a flood of similar images from my past visits to Kerala came flashing before my face.

As I sit before my laptop computer screen, those Indian women seem to flash on the screen. A little girl of five that reminded me so much of my daughter Marnie at that age begging on a train platform in southern Andhra Pardesh. She was dressed in rags, dirt on her face, working for someone who was only exploiting her youth and looks. A young lady sitting beside a dusty, hot rural lane trying to pick grains of rice out of the dirt lest she starve! A middle-aged lady sitting sideways on a scooter as I passed by in Shibu's car going to Kottayam. I could tell by the expression on her face that she was probably one of countless women whose marriage was prearranged, caught in a loveless relationship going on with the sham that is accepted, practiced and exploited in every corner of India. Another girl that still haunts me is the only female member of a road crew filling potholes and re-tarring a stretch of highway south of Edayappara. Oh, she had a beautiful smile on her face, but all I could think about was, "Is this any job for a lady? Elbow deep in black, sticky, hot tar under a hot tropical sun surrounded by men who see women as objects not human? The recent gang rape of a girl from northern India is still fresh in my mind. Then there was again before me that coconut lady of Bhubaneshwar trying to make a living out of a few rotten coconuts to get enough profit to buy a few more for tomorrow so that she could return to that same pile of sand and repeat the process. It is at times like this that I ponder again the only hope for such women, the Gospel of Jesus Christ and the truth of Galatians 3:28.

I left the three women of Bhubaneshwar that morning, but as you can see, they have not left me. I still see their lot, but is this the fate God wants for them? I never went to India for the women of India. I never imagined that their circumstances would have such an impact on my life. I pray for them, think of them, and desire God to do more for them than even the children of India, another topic in and of itself. When I see the liberation and freedom that has been allotted to those women who have found Christ, I want it for all. Oh, I know there are still pockets of discrimination of women in America and even in the American Church, but nothing on the scale of India. Even Julie and Annamma and Mary, fine Christian ladies, loved by wonderful Christian men have a sad existence when you consider the magnitude of Paul's statement. Only heaven will equal the genders as they ought, but we should at least try to live in such a godly relationship.

32

A WEALTHY PLACE: BENGAL AND ANA

Psalms 66:12 " . . . Thou broughtest us out into A WEALTHY PLACE."

Little did I know, until the morning of my first day in Orissa, that unlike my other three visits to India I would get a second tourist day in the country! I have already shared the thrilling days I spent at Periyar National Park watching wild elephants and other wild animals of India in their natural habitat; the day I spent with the Simon family and Marnie at the Kodanadu Elephant Rescue Center playing with ana (Malayalam for elephant); the houseboat ride on Kerala's Lake Venbamad, southern India's largest body of fresh water, and my recent trip to the mountains of Munnar. Now it is time to share with you another exciting day visiting more of India's original residents, a variety of creatures the Eternal God created for the subcontinent of Asia.

Shibu and I got back from our market run in time to get breakfast at the hotel restaurant and in time for Joy Thomas to arrive from Pastor John's house. Shibu and I had been put up in a nice room at the Pushpak Hotel while Joy stayed the night with Moses at his father's house. What I thought was going to be a day visiting the various congregations of Bhubaneshwar, which we would do on Friday and Saturday just before our return to Kerala, turned out to be a wonderful tour of Orissa's capital. We would be on a train for western Orissa by 7:30 that evening, so what did the boys have in store to surprise and delight their American friend?

By 8:30 A.M., Moses had picked us up for a day of exploring, even though at the time I didn't know where we were going. Moses had borrowed his boss's car (he only owns a motorcycle) to transport us around the congested city. Once again I was given the front seat beside Moses as Shibu and Joy got into the back seat. My first impression of Bhubaneshwar was only positive. Unlike Kerala, Bhubaneshwar was a well laid-out city that reminded me of the streets of London or the broad boulevards of Los Angeles. Its long, wide lanes and an impressive road system were the best

I had seen in India. I was told the British had originally established the city, and you could see it in the buildings and the divided highways. Oh, it was still India with animals everywhere and plenty of congestion, but the overall feel was much different than the narrow roads and twisting highways of Kerala. Bhubaneshwar sits on a flat plain, and there seemed to be room everywhere, unlike Kerala. Within minutes of leaving the Pushpak Hotel, we encountered crowd after crowd celebrating the Hindu's holiest day of the year. Temporary, portable temples were here and there with throngs of people in front of each, people paying to get a blessing. As we worked our way through the mass, we criss-crossed the city up this street, over that bypass, through that lane, until we eventually got free of the city. I was surprised how quickly we left a relatively modern city for the primitive countryside with rice fields, bullock herds, goats and sheep, chickens and dogs, and simple shacks for homes. The road was still paved, but the care and maintenance was missing. I imagined we were heading for a small congregation outside of the city, when to my surprise after twelve miles we drove into the Nandankanan Zoo. I turned around to the boys and asked, "You're taking me to an Indian zoo?" Both Shibu and Joy had broad smiles on their faces as they said in unison, "Yes!"

My first shock was that they were taking me to such a public place; I thought we were going to keep a low profile during this trip. Shibu and Joy's original worries had been put to rest the night before in the hotel; I was a tourist visiting Orissa with a few Indian friends. What happened at the hotel happened again at the zoo; if anything, I was treated as a celebrity instead of a missionary. I began to feel like it must have felt like for the tent-maker missionaries that go into places like China. I was the only white man I saw that day in the zoo, but I didn't feel any hostility nor did I feel out of place my entire morning at the Nandankanan Zoo. My first purchase of the trip to Orissa was a hat with the zoo's name on it. A perfect cover for the rest of my trip; just a tourist!

Little did I know what Joy and Shibu had planned for me. They knew on our first, full day in Orissa we had just a few short hours before we had to catch a train for Kalahandi. They also knew of my love of Indian animals, and I had yet to visit an Indian zoo. Outside Bhubaneshwar was one of the top zoos in all of India, a world-class menagerie that housed some of the rarest creatures on the planet. The entrance fee was twenty rupees for Indians (55 cents), but the entrance fee for me was one hundred rupees ($2); I also had to pay ten rupees to take pictures, but that was fine. We were early enough to be among the few that entered the gate before the celebrating crowd finished their morning temple-hopping. Immediately upon our entrance, we were confronted with a man who wanted to be our guide, who would take us through the park, show us all the shortcuts, and point out all the important animals. For a fee, of course. We rejected his offer, but he continued to follow us around; it was the only negative aspect of my pleasant day at the Nandankanan Zoo!

From enclosure to enclosure we saw the birds of India including the beautiful eagle of India. We saw the different species of deer that inhabit India, many I had seen in Periyar in 2006. Monkeys and an Indian emu led us to the snake section and my hope of seeing the cobra, up close and personal, but my hopes were dashed when the cobra failed to appear. I still want to see one in the wild! We saw plenty of crocodiles, Indian black bears (not to be compared to our Maine Black Bear), an Indian leopard and lion, an Indian hippopotamus bathing in its own private pool, a very shy (only its hind end) rhinoceros, a fat baboon, the biggest long-nose alligator I have ever seen, and some of the biggest tree spiders imaginable! Despite these fine sightings, I was pushing my companions and our self-appointed guide to take me to the tiger and elephant section of the park. By now you know my love of elephants, but any elephant is a treat for me, even ones in a zoo. The last three elephants I would see (#39, #40, and #41) on my 2012 trip to India I saw in the Nandankanan Zoo. What a disappointment it was! Not because of the elephants, but because of where I saw the elephants; a distant observation platform nearly a quarter of a mile away. Even my telephoto lens couldn't make them big. After you have ridden on an elephant, walked under an elephant, and touched an elephant, a distant elephant just won't do!

The highlight of our morning nature walk was the tigers: both white and royal Bengal tigers. I can honestly say these are the most magnificent animals I have ever seen in person. Oh, I had seen them on television and in pictures in books and magazines, but nothing is to be compared to seeing them up close and personal. I wanted to get in the enclosures with them. I snapped some wonderful photographs, but nothing is like sitting and watching them, which I did. My companions and our self-proclaimed guide couldn't understand why I wanted to linger by the tiger cages. Just to watch them drink, move around, and sleep was a wonderful view for me into the creative mind of God. Despite the fact that the word tiger or cat is not found in the Bible, I felt, on that tourist day in Orissa, I had been taken to a wealthy place!

33

THE BEGGAR AT NANDANKANAN

Luke 16:20 "AND THERE WAS A CERTAIN BEGGAR..."

IT TOOK US ABOUT an hour and a half to circle the compounds of the Nandankanan Zoo, taking a look at all the myriad of animals caged there. Just a thought on zoos! For what it is worth, I still prefer looking at God's creatures in the wild, but on that rare occasion I will venture into a zoo to see something I have never seen before, like the Bengal tiger. By the time we got back to the gate, there was a line as far as the eye could see waiting to enter. Remember, it was a statewide festival day; the schools were closed as well as most businesses. Once the sacrifice at the temple or shrine was over the rest of the day was for partying, visiting places like the Bhubaneshwar zoo, or maybe a Buddhist shrine. We had come at exactly the right time or had the boys planned it that way? Less chance of somebody being offended with the American that had invaded his space?

I must admit that I dragged my feet, not wanting the morning to end. The weather was pleasant, much cooler than Kerala with less humidity. The sun was shining and the air was country air, if you know what I mean. There is a very distinct difference between the aroma of the city and the fragrance of the country and what is true in America is true in India. Bhubaneshwar is a typical large, polluted city, but outside that metropolis, the air was clean with a slight fragrance of flowers, trees, and soil. I have now lived more years in the towns and cities of this world, but I am still a village and hamlet guy with a taste for fresh air and open spaces. Nandankanan had both in abundance the day I visited the zoo. I knew we were heading back to the city, and I wanted to enjoy the country for a few extra minutes. It was then my eyes looked downward, off the animals, the beautiful flowerbeds that lined the entrance to the zoo, and the tall trees that surround the park, and I saw her!

If I didn't know better, I thought she could be the sister of the coconut lady I had met earlier that morning. She was small, frail, bent-over sitting cross-legged on the ground under a small tree by the exit to the park. There was no pile of coconuts at her feet, no flowers, nothing I could see for sale, and then it hit me: a beggar! I am still touched by every beggar I meet. Granted, there have been relatively few in my American experience, but India is different. Beggars are a common sight in India. I still remember my first: a little girl outside a Hindu temple less than five miles from Shibu's house. It was at that crossroad place I was first instructed not to give to beggars. I took the advice then, but have broken the rule many times since, as I did that day at Nandankanan. I have such a hard time passing by a beggar when I have money in my pocket. This beggar moved me to reach for a few rupee coins that I certainly could spare. I know why Shibu taught me the India beggar rule early in my visits to his country. Beggars in India are like the fable about the man who wished to feeds the birds of the world. He thought he could do it because he was the richest man in the world. The moral to the story is that at the end of the first day of feeding the man was broke!

As with most beggars I have stopped to help, it has been the eyes that have drawn me to them. Whether Israeli eyes on the Mount of Olives, British eyes on the streets of London, American eyes near the Washington Monument, or Indian eyes at the Nandankanan Zoo. It was the eyes of that little girl at the Hindi Temple that caused my compassionate heart to break. Like the elderly lady of Orissa, the Kerala lass had dirt on her face, clothed in rags, with that all too familiar out-stretched hand. That out-stretched hand is the second thing, after the eyes, which breaks my heart. Unable to understand their cry, I know the universal meaning of the out-stretched arm. "I am hungry! Do you have anything that could help me? Won't you be gracious to me and meet the need I have?" Don't get me wrong. I have bypassed many a Wal-Mart beggar. You know them, the ones that stand at the end of the road to the Wal-Mart parking lot with a sign that reads: "Hungry need food!" For years I was bothered by them, but not after India. An American beggar is a millionaire compared to their Indian counterpart. If you want to see need, witness despair, look on hunger, you need to spend a few days in India. Whether on the streets, on the trains, by the temples, at the exit to a zoo, they are there, everywhere, anywhere you look down. Few have I seen standing. That is why you can overlook them. I hadn't seen this certain beggar of Nandankanan when I entered the park, despite the fact that the exit and entrance are side by side. I had missed her because I was looking up, over her, to the animals of the zoo. Tragic isn't it that the animals of India are better serviced and fed than many of its citizens? In a previous chapter, I wrote about the plight of women. May I add another note to that observation? I have seen more female beggars in India than male beggars.

A few coins came out of my pocket as I lingered by the beggar of Nandankanan. My companions had already exited the park. Moses was heading to the parking lot to get the car. Shibu and Joy had gotten so comfortable with the crowd they left me for a few minutes, unaware I had stopped. I tried to ask the lady if I could take her picture, but her head had dropped the minute I drew near. Her hand remained upward and outward expecting a donation. It was then I got out my camera and decided to take a final shot at Nandankanan. As I took the picture, I placed the rupees into the palm of that out-stretched hand. Instantly the palm turned upward and outward trying to stop the picture from being taken. I was moved by that act. Was she doing it because she still had a spark of pride left in her feeble body? Was she doing it because most Hindu do not like their picture taken because it is wrong to make such images? Was she doing it because she wanted to hide her face from me? As I left the park, I looked at the picture I took. It is now nearly five months since I left India, and I still don't need to check my India photographs to tell you what that image revealed. It is imprinted on my memory as clear as the day I took it.

The eyes are gone because the outstretched hand it now a mask. All you see is the outline of a little woman sitting on the ground. The palm of her hand it now the focal point of the picture. I have pondered this since and have come to the conclusion that therein lies the lesson of the beggar of Nandankanan. The only hope for any certain beggar isn't the rupees dropped into those palms, but the outstretched palms of another. One who was willing to receive nails, not rupees. One who was willing to give His life, even for the beggars of India. This is the offering we must give them, and I was reminded again why I was in Orissa. Not to see elephants and tigers, but to share Christ with the unreached. To give Christ to those lost, beggaring, hoping for a hand-out, but needing a hand-up! Only the Gospel of Christ can repair the unraveled lives of the lost; only the Gospel of Christ can reverse the rebellious heart of the sinner, and only the Gospel of Christ can rekindle the fire that has been put out by the satanic religions of the world.

34

BLESSED BY A BUDDHIST PRIEST AT DHAUL

> Exodus 32:29 "For Moses had said, Consecrate yourselves today to the Lord . . . THAT HE MAY BESTOW UPON YOU A BLESSING THIS DAY."

WE LEFT THE NANDANKANAN Zoo shortly after noontime heading back into the city. We did stop for a cool drink at one of the many roadside markets along the highway back into Bhubaneshwar. Our conversation was of the morning's experiences with the Indian animals I saw. I thanked the boys, who are slightly older than my son Scott, for taking me and tried to get out of them where we were going next, but, as with Nandankanan, they were tight lipped. I couldn't make out whether or not we were just winging it or they did have a master plan for my day in Bhubaneshwar. I was hoping they were taking me to the oldest Hindu Temple in the capital, a world-recognized, tourist landmark. As we pulled back into the congested streets and roads, we passed the Lingaraja Temple just off the highway. I had seen pictures and recognized the ruins as we sped past. I asked, "Are we going there?" "Maybe," answered Joy, "when we come back from Phulabani." I caught a slight hesitation in Thomas' voice wondering if we would or not. As it turned out we didn't stop there; I think they thought it was too dangerous. I decided not to ask any more questions and just wait for what was before me.

As we weaved our way through narrow lanes and broad boulevards, I sensed we were heading across town. The sights out the car window were fascinating as usual. Numerous times we had to stop to allow a Braham bull to cross the street. At other times, traffic cops in the middle of an intersection stopped us. There were very few traffic lights in that massive city. The cops all had on white gloves and a white, Australia-style hat, and some of them were even women. I had seen this in New York before, but was amazed we didn't see one accident. Every stop was like the beginning of a Grand Prix car race. Motorcycles, autos, trucks, and cars lined up, sometimes twelve wide, ready for the traffic cop with the white gloves to flag them on. You could hear the engines racing in anticipation. We passed large tracks of land enclosed with high walls. Some were military bases, police stations, and governmental buildings, and, mingled throughout, were the Hindu temples and shrines with scores of people in front of them all. Eventually we arrived at a very busy street corner where Moses pulled the car to the side of the road. Shibu and Joy got out and headed into a large compound through a massive gate complex, as I waited with Moses by the car. My eye was immediately drawn back to the street where a cow was trying to make its way across tight, afternoon traffic. We have all heard the question, "Why did the chicken cross the road?" Have you ever considered why the cow wanted to get across the street? Can you imagine a Braham bull on Time Square in New York? Yet, there he was inching his way out into thick traffic. To my utter amazement, the traffic stopped as if he was one of those traffic policemen. From both directions, three lanes on each side, the flow of cars, trucks, motorcycles, and autos simply came to a halt. For the nearly two minutes it took the slowing moving beast to cross, life came to a standstill on that corner of Bhubaneshwar. And why did he cross? He crossed to stand beside a roadside vegetable stand, I think, hoping for lunch.

My bull watching was interrupted a few minutes later when Joy and Shibu returned to tell me the next stop in my tour wasn't happening. They had hoped to take me into the Orissa State Museum to see the artifacts collected through hundreds of years of history. They hoped it would help me to better understand the culture and customs of Orissa, but because it was a holiday, the museum was closed, as were all other state offices and parks. I was thankful that Nandankanan Zoo was a private park. My only entertainment at the Orissa State Museum was the bull that crossed the road. However, instead of heading back to the motel to pack for our night train ride to Titiagarh, we headed out of town, but this time to the west of the city. Fifteen miles later, we drove up a steep hill to the Dhaul Shant Stupa.

As with Nandankanan, Dhaul Shant Stupa was located in a rural setting. As with our morning ride to Nandankanan, our afternoon ride to Dhaul Shant Stupa was through narrow country lanes. The modern Orissa ended at the city line, and the primitive Orissa began. Once again, there was mile after mile of rice fields yellow unto harvest. Countless herds of bullock, cows, goats, and sheep slowed our journey as they, like the bulls of Bhubaneshwar, had the right-of-way, no matter the way we took. Small collections of poor buildings marked a village or two along the way, and eventually we turned into what looked like a long driveway.

Before us we could make out a small rise, a couple hundred feet high, in the landscape. Most of the land around Bhubaneshwar is very flat with an occasional rise of a few feet, but, because this hill was rare, it was impressive compared to the surrounding terrain. It was an ideal spot, a tranquil place for a famous Buddhist temple to be built on its summit. It was the largest and most important Buddhist temple in all of Orissa.

Working our way to the top, we encountered tour buses and many private cars and motorcycles. An auto or two pushed their way through the narrow gaps in the crowd of vehicles and in-between were scores of walkers. I asked who all these people were and the stunning rely, "Hindus!" I asked, "What are Hindus doing coming to a Buddhist temple?" It seems the Hindus believe that any religion has its benefits, and a blessing from a Buddhist priest is just as noteworthy as from a Hindu priest. I was beginning to understand that the people of Orissa were like the people of Athens in Paul's day; they were terrified lest they offend a god, even an unknown god. (Acts 17:23) Eventually we made our way to the small parking lot near the summit. I still couldn't see what all the fuss was about, why there were so many people there, until I climbed a series of steep steps, through and by many merchant stands, to the hilltop. Behind a grove of trees that covered that part of the summit was the most impressive temple I have ever seen.

A massive staircase of at least fifty steps led to a giant statue of Buddha seated in a niche under a huge white temple topped by a massive dome. The rules demanded that on the staircase to the statue, you had to remove your shoes, which I did. On each side of the staircase were gigantic yellow lions, each gazing outward over the landscape as if guarding against intruders. The view from the short rock wall that surrounded the temple was spectacular. The visibility had to have been fifteen miles because we could see back into Bhubaneshwar. It was then I realized why they called it Dhaul Shant 'Stupa' (stupid, my word). The temple was an empty shell, no doors inside, just niches on the outside where you could have your picture taken with Buddha.

Then something unusual happened. A young man with perfect English approached me. No accent, no brogue, no slip of the tongue. It was as if I was talking to a lad from Los Angeles. Before I knew it, he was blessing my children, my wife, and me. His incense, religious words, and hand-signs flowed over me like dirty water. I walked away stunned, saddened, and shocked that so many people have been taken in by this form of faith: impersonal, empty, and fake, as with the moneychangers and merchants of Jesus' day. Dhaul was just a tourist trap!

35

THE WONDER OF ORISSA

> Psalms 105:5 "Remember His marvelous works that He hath done; HIS WONDERS..."

I JUST HAD TO walk away from the young Buddhist priest that wanted to bless me. Little did he know I was already getting a blessing at his shrine, but not from him, and certainly not from Buddha!

Only the person who has spent a season in a pagan land will ever fully comprehend the true wonder of an Orissa landscape. There really is no other physical, turned spiritual, experience on this planet which can quite match the marvel of India rolling out before you as far as the eye can see. It is one of those on-a-clear-day-you-can-see-forever moments. Nothing is so designed to simulate the body, the soul, the spirit, and all your senses like a vista that is God-made and man-kept. As adaptable as man can be, a long stay in a city, the congestion of people, animals, and machines, the unmerciful sounds of the streets, tends to shrink the soul and shrivel the spirit, sicken the senses as if constricted in a prison cell. The gentle, rolling plains of a country scene warmed by a liberating sunshine is the only thing that can unlock a life to wander and wonder again.

This is why I have always needed a trip to the countryside to recharge my spirit. The temple of Dhaul Shant Stupa had dulled my soul for just a few minutes. All I had to do was take a walk to the wall surrounding the temple and look out across the 360-view. There is an aura and an awe to see green fields, yellowing rice, a winding river, the absence of shrines and temples, priests and statues, and Buddha. My spirit soared again, and a song came back to my soul. The tragedy of Dhaul was replaced with the delight of the True and Living God as seen in "the heavens declare the glory of God; AND THE FIRMAMENT SHEWETH HIS HANDYWORK." (Psalms 19:1) I don't know if it was the bitter encounter with the Buddhist priest that highlighted the blessing I got from my walk around the temple of Dhaul Shant Stupa or not. With my back to the temple, the statue of Buddha, the golden lions, my eyes only saw beyond Dhaul. Still for those of us who search out a secluded view, a sun-drenched vista, there can be found spots where the flowers still bloom, the trees still sway in the wind, and the grass is still green, spring-like green. You know it, don't you? Despite the fact it was fall in India, it was spring in Maine in my heart. There before my eyes were hundreds of acres of pristine lands all blanketed in the hue of autumn harvest. It was really my first look at Orissa from above. The view was soothing, the colors calming, the beauty memorable as you can see.

Where there was barrenness in Andhra Pardesh, there in Orissa I found an exquisite beauty; dare I say a Maine beauty? It is the only India I have yet seen that reminds me of my home state. In Andhra Pardesh had been utter severity of scenery, but now in Orissa a softness and splendor existed as if the Almighty Artist had taken His divine brush and painted the scene just that morning and just for me! This was a total transformation from my other India adventure to Andhra Pardesh, a total transfiguration in contrast from the harsh to the heavenly. Oh, don't get me wrong. I knew of the dark nature of man just fifteen miles away in the back alleys of Bhubaneshwar. I knew at my back was the satanic, diabolical nature (Deuteronomy 32:17) of Buddha, but in front of me where I saw no man, just God's marvelous creation where nothing haphazard could be found, I relished in the moment. What a 180-degree transport can do for your spirit: liberate, free, and stimulate! My spirit, now attuned to the Spirit of God, surged with the desire to explore on, climb on, and look on to greater visions afar!

I descended the stairs to find my hiking boots where I had placed them. Shibu, Joy and Moses had already climbed down. At the foot of the staircase was Moses with a man and woman I didn't recognize. Walking up to them I found it was Moses' boss, the man who had lent us his car for our travels. His wife wanted a picture with me in front of the temple, so once again I turned my back on Buddha and smiled for the camera. Moses' boss and wife were Hindus, but Moses and his father had witnessed to them. My prayer is that my encounter with them will add to the testimony already given by those who live daily in the shadow of Buddha and the shade of Hinduism. Until the bright light of the glorious Gospel of Jesus Christ shines into Orissa, the greatest wonder of Orissa will never be realized.

I finished my first, full day in Orissa with another wonder of Orissa, the home of Pastor John. By the time we worked our way back into Bhubaneshwar, the afternoon was nearly over. We were on our way to Pastor John's house for an early supper so that we could be at the train station by 5:30 P.M. I was greeted at the front gate by this dear brother in Christ, a welcome fit for a king. John and I had first met in Andhra Pardesh in 2010, and our reunion was bittersweet. John had lost his wife shortly after I had returned to the States, complications from the stress and strain of having to leave their home in Phulabani for Bhubaneshwar. I found my friend sharing a home with an unbelieving family of four. Shared expenses were the primary reason. I also found a sad man, half a man, struggling to understand his wife's death on top of the persecution that forced him to leave his homeland. The hospitality was perfect; the meal delightful. The conversation was all about Kerala and their desire to move there. At the height of the 2008 persecution, John had moved his wife and three daughters there for protection. Shibu and the churches of the IGBC had taken them in. While there, the girls had fallen in love with the state, mainly the freedom found there compared to Orissa. Yet in the midst of tragedy, heartache, sadness and sorrow, I found a family still in love with Christ and His Church; it was a wonder of wonders.

George Beverly Shea might have best summarized my first day in Orissa when he wrote these words under the title of "The Wonder of it All."

> "There's the wonder of sunset at evening, the wonder as sunrise I see;
> But the wonder of wonders that thrills my soul is the wonder that God loves me.
> There's the wonder of springtime and harvest (my time in Orissa),
> The sky, the stars, the sun; but the wonder of wonders that thrills my soul
> Is the wonder that's only begun.
> O, the wonder of it all! The wonder of it all! Just to think that God loves me.
> O, the wonder of it all! The wonder of it all! Just to think that God loves me."

Though we scarcely seem to realize it, we are also a wonder to God, especially after He has remade us through rebirth. Whether in Orissa or Maine, as we look at His handiwork in nature, He looks at His handiwork in us. I saw that handiwork in the lives of John and his family, and I would be full of anticipation until I returned to Bhubaneshwar to meet the rest of the Church, the wonder seen in the miracle of Gondapather, which I will write about later.

All other human religions and man's philosophies will cheat us of the best blessings unless we turn our back on them and find our blessings in the wonder of God's works!

36

NIGHT TRAIN TO TITIAGARH

> Psalms 16:7 "I will bless the Lord, who hath given me counsel: my reins also instruct me IN THE NIGHT SEASONS."

AFTER A FINE DINNER at John's house, Moses took us to the train station on the edge of Bhubaneshwar. It was similar to the other train stations I had been to in India: congested, noisy, and smelly. Remember, open toilets and trash everywhere, and body-to-body people. We quickly got through security because Joy had already bought our tickets, and we made our way to the lounge near the track where train #18425 would arrive. We had about half an hour to wait for the Puri-Durg Express. Puri was the district where Bhubaneshwar was located, and Durg was the area where we were going. This train would take us from the eastern side of Orissa to the western side of Orissa in a little over ten hours, with very few stops in between. We were scheduled to arrive in Titiagarh by 4:30 the next morning. Despite having taken India's infamous railroad before, I was excited to see, smell, and sense again the unique transport that is an Indian train. This was only the fifth train ride of my life, three in India and two in Australia. We were once again traveling first class so we would have our own sleeping-berths, air-conditioning (though it wasn't that hot or humid in Orissa), and space with no beggars. Beggars were not allowed on first class cars, only on second and third class cars. Darkness had already fallen on the Bhubaneshwar Rail Station, so the sights I would experience would only be of the people and the lights.

As we sat and waited, a young girl approached us. I thought how brave she was. She wanted me to take a picture of us together. Her father wasn't far behind, and a younger brother joined her. I was used to the attention, the novelty of a white man in a brown world. She must have seen my digital camera and knew what it could do or did she just want to meet me? I let her father take the picture, and then I showed it to her. What a smile! It was well worth the waiting. I have never had one problem with a young person in India, few adults, either. They might be shy, as was the brother, but most, like the girl, have been friendly, interested, and happy to meet an American. Give me time and I can probably get a child to warm up to me! After the photo shoot, I walked a bit knowing the cramped quarters on an Indian train. Within the hour of our arrival at the station, Joy was leading Shibu and me to our platform. It was on the way I spotted him, a snow-white, husky pup. The small dog stood out in the crowd flowing by us as they made their way to their train platform. Bhubaneshwar had at least six tracks coming and going through the massive station. Hundreds, if not thousands, passed through daily. Many of the night trains were full. It was a great way to get somewhere in India allowing you to sleep most of your trip. A large Indian woman was carrying the unique dog, and I must admit I stared at her and the cute animal until they disappeared into the gathering crowd. There are few pet dogs in India. As a matter of fact, the first pet dog I had met was at John's house. Winnie was the pet of the family staying with John and his family. I commented to the boys about it as we waited for our train.

Still scanning the passing horde, I was suddenly interrupted by a tug on my shirt. Looking down I saw a little lad with that same white dog in his arms. In perfect English he asked, "Would you like to take a picture of my dog?" I guess the lady and her family had noticed me staring. Instead of being offended, she was delighted that I took notice of the newest member of their family. One of the best train pictures I have is of that boy with his dog, and the memory of another connection I had with the younger generation of India. Despite the warnings of my companions, I was feeling right at home in Orissa; Oh, the terrain was different, the weather was certainly different, the Hindu faith was more in your face, but the people and especially the children were just the same: open, inviting, and drawn to a stranger with a different complexion.

We finally boarded our express for Titiagarh at 6:50 P.M., only twenty minutes behind schedule, which is not unusual. As I learned on my first train trip in India, "We will leave at 6:30 P.M. if it takes all evening!" We quickly found our berth (#2, Seats 35, 37, 38) and discovered we had the eight-passenger space to ourselves, or at least for the start of our trip. This made it nice. We could stretch out a bit, settle our things, and talk. The first thing I asked was how much the ticket was. Joy told me he would give it to me for my journal after the conductor checked it. Within minutes, the conductor came by and stamped the ticket, three in one. As we pulled out of the station I learned some interesting things from that railroad ticket. For example, it had cost 1590 rupees ($31.80) to travel 494 kilometers (307 miles), and that I had saved the boys 25 rupees

(50 cents) because I was considered a senior citizen. Sure enough, there on the ticket were our ages: Shibu-45, Joy-42, and Barry-62. I actually just turned 62 on March 6, 2013. I think it was the first time I had been recognized as a senior citizen on a piece of paper. I was consoled by the memory of when asking John's daughters how old they thought I was their reply was 46, another India first!

My eyes were quickly drawn away from the ticket as the lights of Bhubaneshwar filled the train window. It was like going through a massive Christmas display, but I knew in my heart they were not celebrating the birth of my Christ. It has been at such times, when darkness settles and the world slows, that one has time to ponder the issues of the heart. I had only been in Orissa one full day, and already I was making deductions on what I saw and how I felt. The lights were just the catalysts that started me thinking about the darkness in the lights. Paul said it best when he wrote to the Church at Corinth:

> "In whom the god of this world hath blinded the minds of them which believe not, lest the light of the glorious gospel of Christ, who is the image of God, should shine unto them." (II Corinthians 4:4)

Blinded by the bright lights of a Hindu festival unable to see beyond to a greater light, the citizens of Orissa were as lost as a blind man groping around at night. As our train slowly pulled away from Bhubaneshwar, the Hindu lights gradually went out and all that was left was a black, midnight darkness that revealed the spiritual condition of Orissa. It was then I was reminded the stark warning Paul gave to the Christians of Corinth before he wrote what I have just reprinted, "But if our gospel be hid, it is hid to them that are lost!" (II Corinthians 4:3)

I was now even more determined to let my little light shine in the world I was traveling to on our night train to Titiagarh. I hummed under my breath as I looked through the dark window: "This little light of mine, I'm going to let it shine, let it shine let it shine. I won't let Satan blow it out I'm going to let it shine, let it shine, let it shine. Shine all over Orissa, I'm going to let it shine, let it shine, let it shine!"

37

THOMAS OF INDIA

> Luke 6:13-16 "And when it was day, He called unto him His disciples: and of them He chose twelve, whom also He named apostles; Simon, (whom he also named Peter,) and Andrew his brother, James and John, Philip and Bartholomew, Matthew and THOMAS, James the son of Alphaeus, and Simon called Zelotes, Judas the brother of James, and Judas Iscariot, which also was the traitor."

DESPITE THE FACT WE had eaten at John's house just a few hours before, by the time the train had left Bhubaneshwar for its northern trek through the hills and hollows of upper Orissa, Shibu and Joy pulled out the food they had brought along for an evening snack. This is the same food we brought along with us from Shibu's home, and the food we had purchased that morning at the market by the hotel. It basically consisted of a jar of peanut butter and a jar of strawberry jelly to make sandwiches, Lays potato chips, and a few bottles of orange soda. To my utter amazement, I learned that Joy Thomas had never had a peanut butter and jelly sandwich before! Before we finished, he ate three. As I watched my two dear friends devour nearly a loaf of bread with peanut butter and strawberry jelly between each slice, I thought of another Thomas that had opened up India to the Gospel of Jesus Christ, just like Joy Thomas had done in the region we were heading for. A few years back I wrote this about "Thomas of India".

One of the very first historical names I recognized when I first went to India in the winter of 2006 was the Apostle Thomas. In John Foxe's classic work on Christian persecution, he wrote this about Thomas: "He was called by this name in Syriac, but Didymus in Greek; he was an apostle and martyr, and preached in Parthia and India. After converting many to Christ, he aroused the anger of the pagan priests and was martyred by being thrust through with a spear." Church tradition in India states his martyrdom took place in Kerala, India. I even saw some churches in my first trip to India that claim they can trace their spiritual roots back to Thomas. If this is true then the persecution of the Christians going on in Orissa is twenty centuries old!

In order to understand the patron saint of India, I share with you this simple biographical sketch of the man Thomas. I believe Thomas has gotten a bad rap over the years. Usually, when you read or hear his name mentioned it is always "Thomas the Doubter" or "Doubting Thomas". After the Lord's resurrection, Thomas certainly did question the other disciples' experience when they said, "We have seen the Lord!" (John 20:25) But he was not the only disciple to doubt (Matthew 28:17), and who of us hasn't doubted at times? Often we focus on this one negative event and overlook the wonderful things mentioned in the Gospels about him.

The first three times his name is mentioned is because Jesus had chosen him as a disciple and apostle. Remember all disciples are not apostles, but all apostles were disciples. (Matthew 10:3, Mark 3:18, and Luke 6:15). That, at least, made Thomas a believer, a follower of Jesus, and, though he never fully understood at first how Jesus was going to work it out, he followed. During the Last Supper it was Thomas who asked the Lord, "We know not whither thou goest, and how can we know the way?" (John 14:5) Thomas was a bewildered believer. How could Christ establish an earthly kingdom by going to heaven? The Scriptures, too, have bewildered me. In my logical mind, I, too, have questioned just how God will work things out, but that doesn't make me any less a believer or a follower of Christ. Interestingly, Jesus never rebuked Thomas for his question, but simply gave him the answer to his question, "I am the way, the truth, and the life: no man cometh unto the Father, but by me." (John 14:6) As Jesus answered Thomas' questions you can be assured He will answer yours!

The next time Thomas is mentioned by name in the story of Jesus is when Lazarus is dying. Because Bethany was located a mere two miles from Jerusalem where Jesus has a price on His head, the disciples discouraged Him from going to the funeral of His dear friend. As the others held back, Thomas boldly proclaimed, "Let us also go that we may die with Him." (John 11:16) Little did Thomas know he wouldn't die with Jesus, but for Jesus! A true sign of Christian courage is the bravery to follow Jesus to a dangerous place. Despite the real danger, Thomas was determined to go with and for the Saviour, even at the cost of his life, which happened in India.

I have come to the belief from studying this man's life in the Gospels that he had all the qualities of discipleship to take him to India and to die a martyr in India. There is certainly enough evidence that Christianity did reach India early in the Apostolic Age, and whether or not Thomas was the one might be debated, but there is no argument that men like

Thomas did lead the way. I know this because I have met a man with the same name doing the same work as Thomas and the early apostles in Orissa. He is not an apostle, but he is certainly a disciple, and his name is Joy Thomas!

As I ate my peanut butter and jelly sandwich and enjoyed a bag of Lay's potato chips and sipped on my bottle of orange soda, I looked into the faces of the two men I was travelling with. They were but the tail-end of a very long parade of Christians that have marched their way from Calvary to Orissa. When Jesus gave His disciples the Great Commission (Matthew 28:19-20), little did Thomas know that India was his uttermost part? In Thomas' day, India was as remote a place as there was in the known world. How he got there we know not, probably he took a boat along the trade route of the day, but he could have walked. Whatever the way isn't as important as the fact that he went. The dangers were real, and the prospect of death was also certain, yet he went. That same Spirit and drive is in Joy Thomas and Shibu Simon. I could see it in 2006, witnessed it again in 2010, and now I was a part of the team, the mission, the danger.

I wish I could do poetic justice to the feeling I had that night on a train moving to the uttermost parts of Orissa. I was beginning to understand why the drive to reach the people of Orissa with the Gospel was so intense. It wasn't one man, or two men, but the combined drive of all who had come before. I finally felt I had stepped into the parade and was now marching in step with those who had gone before. Three years ago I wrote these lines to finish my article on the Apostle Thomas.

The same Spirit that led and drove the Apostle Thomas drives and leads another Thomas (Joy) onward and forward into Orissa. Despite the fact that Joy now has a price on his head from the militant Hindus, he continues to venture into that hostile place. Will the day come that I hear of the death of my beloved friend in Orissa? I pray not, but I would not be surprised because he follows the same steps as one with the same name. Perhaps they will share the same destiny.

38

ORISSA IS BURNING

> Matthew 13:21 "Yet hath he not root in himself, but dureth for a while: FOR WHEN TRIBULATION OR PERSEUCTION ARISETH because of the Word, by and by he is offended."

AROUND EIGHT O'CLOCK, I began to feel the effects of forty-eight hours on the move. Shibu and I had travelled nearly eleven hundred miles to date, and the motion of the swaying railway car was beginning to rock me to sleep. As the boys continued to eat peanut butter and jelly sandwiches, I got into my bed. As I drifted off to sleep, did I remember or dream?

It all started with an unexpected phone call early on a Monday morning. I was settling into my office at the Emmanuel Baptist Church in Ellsworth, Maine, for another day of work when the church phone rang. At the end of the line was a familiar voice, but I knew from the tone of that voice something was wrong. Add to the fact I knew the call had originated from Edayappara, Kerala, India, over nine thousand miles away. It was my dear friend Shibu Simon, and despite the fact he at first said everything was "Okay", I knew the call had some bad news connected with it.

I had meet Shibu Simon for the first time in the summer of 2004. I had known his father, Brother Simon, since the early 1980s. With the sudden home going of his dad in January of that year, Shibu and his brother Shagu were now responsible for directing a ministry in the State of Kerala which included an orphanage, a Bible college, a Christian day school, nineteen local churches, and mission works in four other states of India, including Orissa. Those works were under a new mission board called The Associated Missions of India. Actually, in the 1990s, Emmanuel Baptist Church had started supporting the missionary outreach in Orissa through that organization because we wanted to help reach some unreached people groups in the mountains of north-central Orissa. These were the very mountains I was now travelling through by train!

Over the years, I had become a counselor and confidant to Shibu. This was not the first phone call I had gotten from this fellow-labourer in Christ. Shibu was on his way to the monthly meeting of the pastors of the Independent Gospel Baptist Churches of India where he knew what the number one issue would be. As Shibu talked on, I sensed in his voice a continual strain. I had learned in my two trips to Kerala to date not to probe, but simply to wait. It would come out. As if Shibu couldn't stand it any longer it blurted out, "Orissa is burning!" He went on to ask for prayer for our brothers and sisters in Christ facing a renewed persecution in the State of Orissa. He knew that I would understand because I knew many of the pastors in the midst of the tribulation. Shibu went on to tell me of at least five pastors' homes being burned. Believers were escaping into the surrounding woods with only the clothes on their backs. He just wanted me to know so our church could pray, and so I could intercede for my Orissa friends.

That day I also received this e-mail from my friend detailing what he knew was happening to the Church in Orissa after our conversation:

> "We are in much prayer about the situation in Orissa. So far we have heard that many of our believers' homes have been burned and the church building in Dangul (where I was heading the next day) has also been burned. We have not been able to keep in touch with the believers because the attackers have cut the telephone lines and the electricity has also been turned off. Pastor Solomon (a man I had first met in 2006) has reported that the police are nowhere to be seen, even at the police stations. The burnings and killings are continuing. So far ten deaths have been confirmed. Reports say there is not a church building standing in three districts of Orissa!"

I was shocked by the news, but not surprised. Ever since my first trip to southern India in the winter of 2006, I knew of the religious conflicts between the Hindus and the Christians in Orissa. I had met the director of the mission, Joy Thomas, and thirteen of the pastors and evangelists that proclaimed the Gospel in three affected regions of Orissa. One of their church buildings had already been burned down twice, and one fellowship was meeting in secret out of fear.

How bad did it get? About the same time as Shibu's call, this e-mail from another friend of the ministry, Pastor Dave Ryan of Canton, Ohio, arrived. Dave and I had met at a committee meeting of the Friends of the Simon's ministry in Pennsylvania. Dave's report on the persecution in Orissa had come from an article written by Michael Ireland.

"More than 600 churches have been demolished, 4,000 Christians forced to flee from their villages, and at least 25 killed as a result of violent persecution in the State of Orissa in eastern India. Reports from the area say Vishwa Hindu Parishad religious leader Swami Laxmanananda Saraswati and four of his associates were murdered in the Kandhamal District of Orissa on Saturday, August 23, 2008. (In our travels the next day, we would go through the village were the murders took place.) Although a Maoist group claimed responsibility for the murders, supporters of the slain leader claim that Christians were behind the killings. Hindu fundamentalists have launched a series of attacks against Christians in retaliation. Since Sunday, August 24, churches, schools and other institutions, prayer rooms, and homes of Christians have been ransacked, burnt, and destroyed. Christians have been assaulted and some have been burned alive and cut in pieces ......This is not the first time Christians in Orissa have experienced violent attacks. In December 2007 (my daughter and I were in India earlier that year), Hindu militants burned approximately 90 (including an IGBC church building) churches and 600 homes, killing an estimated 10 persons!"

As the history of the persecuted Church in Orissa flashed through my mind, I realized that I was now within a few miles of the epicenter of these periods of persecution. I remembered how I felt after Shibu's phone call. For the first time in my life I felt violated, not because it had happened to me, but because it had happened to people I knew. I saw their faces again. Was that why I had to travel to this uttermost place? To tell my dear brothers and sisters that I was with them, not just in my prayers but in my person as well? I wanted them to know that I agonized with them in their hour of trial. I couldn't be with them then, but I was not afraid to join them now! As I drifted in and out of sleep, I thought again of another article I had written for my dear brothers after that bitter persecution. It was my way of encouraging them in their plight and in their fight against those that would try to rid Orissa of Christ, Christians and Christianity. I hope you will read on because we all need to hear and understand the importance of getting your scars.

39

GETTING YOUR SCARS

II Timothy 3:12 "Yea, and all that will live godly in Christ Jesus SHALL SUFFER PERSECUTION."

I FOUND THIS IN a devotional book by Carl D. Windsor:

"Life leaves us with many scars, only some of which are visible. It is said that when the knights of King Authur's court returned from battle, they were to bear some scar of the fight. If not, the king would send them back out, telling them, 'Go get your scar!' Do you have any scars as a result of your Christian testimony? A story in *Westminster Quarterly* tells of a harried preacher who was so troubled by his church members and so sharply criticized that he went to his superiors to resign. His bishop thought things over for a moment then asked, "Do your people spit in your face?" "No," the preacher replied. "Have they mocked you and belittled you?" "No," he said. "Have they stripped and scourged you, crowned you with thorns?" The minister soberly responded, "No, sir; and God helping me, I'll carry on until they do." When we think of what others, our brothers and sisters in Orissa, and our Saviour, have suffered and endured, we are indeed humbled. All of our persecutions seem suddenly insignificant by comparison."

Jesus warned that persecution would hound and haunt His followers, and Paul confirmed this teaching in the statement printed above. Paul too knew about scars. "From henceforth let no man trouble me: for *I bear in my body the marks* of the Lord Jesus." (Galatians 6:17) A simple reading of II Corinthians 11:23-28 will illustrate the kind of scars Paul carried around in his body. Anybody who gets involved in the service of the Saviour will eventually carry with them scars, either visible or invisible. One of my favorite heroes in John Bunyan's classic allegory, *Pilgrim's Progress,* is Mr. Valiant-for Truth. Just before he crossed the bridgeless river he is reported to have said the following:

"I am going to the Father, and though with great difficulty I am got hither, yet now I do not repent of all the trouble I have been at to arrive where I am. My sword, I give to him that shall succeed me in my pilgrimage, and my courage and skill to him that can get it. My marks and scars I carry with me, to be a witness for me that I have fought His battles, who now will be my rewarder."

To fight is to run the risk of scars, for only he who never gets involved has no scars. I have come to the belief that part of the hardness (II Timothy 2:3) that is required of a soldier for Christ is the ability to be wounded in the cause. One has to be tough to endure the pain and shame that will come when one stands on the battlefield for Christ. I still remember reading the famous book, *The Red Badge of Courage*. I have always been a military buff, even though I have no personal experience in military service, yet I have seen over the years in my reading a similarity between the secular soldier and the spiritual soldier. Paul also makes that connection in a number of his epistles. Often when one speaks to a soldier and he or she has a visible scar, you ask, "Where did you get that wound?" More often than not the soldier is not ashamed to tell you the war, the battle, and the circumstances surrounding the wound that produced the permanent scar. Why then are we ashamed to tell of the difficulty that has resulted in the mark that is on our lives or the scar that is on our soul?

Just this January, my wife and I made the long trip to Southern California, not for the sun and the warmth of that region of America, nor for the joy of escaping a cold Maine winter for a few days, but to visit some missionary friends of ours. The De La Hayes have been special to us because of their willingness, many years ago, to take our daughter Marnie back to the mission field with them so she could experience being a missionary for a summer. Nigeria was their mission and Kent Academy was their mission field. They had already experienced once the heartache of living in a chosen field (Liberia) but having to leave because of persecution. The peaceful compound they lived on in Nigeria seemed well protected and ideal for their service for the Lord among the children of central Nigeria. Their tranquility and solace was scattered one night when a gang of robbers broke into the compound and tried to steal the money that was in the school office safe. Unable to get the safe opened, the men raided the De La Hayes' home knowing that Marcia, the school treasurer, had a key. In the process, they violated Marcia and kidnapped Ray for a few hours but eventually let him go. Three of the De La Hayes' boys were away at the time, but their youngest son Mark was so traumatized that the scars are still visible today. No physical marks remain, but the emotional scars are still clearly visible after nearly five years. (At the writing of this chapter in *The Uttermost Part*, the trauma of that event is now eight years old. Marcia is actually home in Maine visiting her aging and failing mother, and the scars in her life and especially her son's life are still spoken off as a raw open wound.)

I found this just a few years ago:

> Hast thou no scars?
> No hidden scar on foot, or side, or hand?
> O hear thee sung as mighty in the land,
> I hear them hail thy bright ascendant star,
> Hast thou no scar?
> Hast thou no wound?
> Yet I was wounded by archers spent,
> Leaned me against a tree to die; to rent
> By ravening wolves that compassed me, I swooned;
> Hast thou no wound?
> No wound, no scar?
> Yet, as the Master shall the servant be,
> And pierced are the feet that follow Me;
> But thine are whole; can he have followed far
> Who hath no wound nor scar?

To fight for the cause of Christ in dangerous places, often found in an uttermost place like Nigeria or Orissa, is to run the risk of scars. To be scared in the spiritual conflict is to run the risk of wounds: physical, emotional, mental, or spiritual. To be wounded for Christ is to run the risk of some kind of death, perhaps a death of emotion like my friend Mark, a death of family like Pastor John, a daily dying like my son Scott who returned from the battlefield of Afghanistan with the death of four of his battle-buddies on his mind every day. To gain a scar on the field of battle is by far the best a soldier of Christ can ask. However, I ask in closing the question suggested by Isaac Watts in his classic church hymn, "Am I a Soldier of the Cross?"

"Must I be carried to the skies on flowery beds of ease, while others fought to win the prize and sail thru bloody seas?"

No scars?

40

CAR RIDE THROUGH KALAHANDI

I Samuel 27:1 " ... THERE IS NOTHING BETTER FOR ME THAN THAT I SHOULD SPEEDILY ESCAPE INTO THE LAND ... "

My dreaming and remembering continued late into the evening on October 23, 2012. I had settled into my berth around eight and would remain there until five the next morning. As I drifted in and out of a restless sleep, for a six-footer like me, the short, narrow beds on an Indian train leave much to be desired in the category of comfort, I counted three times the conductor came in to check on us. It was either on our third or fourth stop we picked up three more passengers for our eight-passenger berth, but I had already settled into my bed and only heard the commotion and felt someone climb onto my second-level bed to get into the third-level bed above me. The berths had two triple-bunk beds facing each other on one side of the passageway, and a double bunk bed facing the passageway on the other side. I heard talking from the other berths (with an open passageway and only canvas curtains to shut-off the berths, noise is a certain distraction on an Indian train), but I heard no English so it was just noise to me. Shibu and Joy went to bed about nine or so telling me we would be up about four.

I was pleasantly surprise when near four I realized that I had gotten about four hours of uninterrupted rest. I was surprised that Thomas hadn't wakened me because the time of our arrival was near (4:30 A.M.). Thomas was always worried we would miss a stop and usually had us at the door at least half an hour before the train stopped. I looked at my wristwatch to recheck the time, and sure enough it was a little after four. The morning of my biggest day in India, a day I had waited six years for, was finally here. Today I would make the trek into Dangul to see Ranjan. By five, I realized we were already behind schedule as Joy came in to announce the train was an hour late. I must have dozed off between four and five because I don't remember Joy getting out of his bunk. By a little after five, he was hurrying us along because Titiagarh Station was only thirty minutes away. We unlocked our bags, something Joy was religious about, and prepared to disembark. Thieves are very prevalent on India's trains. They get on at one station and, somewhere between the next stop, steal as much as they can and jump from the train. The light from the morning sun could barely be seen on the horizon as we pulled into Titiagarh, a typical Indian railroad town. I could see it was a small town, and the early hour made it a quiet town. Only those waiting the arrival of the train were out, so my entrance into hostile Hindu country was low-profile, but you wouldn't have known it by the speed by which they got me out of town!

Thinking that Titiagarh was our first stop, I was quickly ushered into a waiting taxi and, just as quickly, we were on the road. Waiting to meet us at Titiagarh Station was Pastor Love Lobo from Kesinga, another small village about twenty-five miles due east of Titiagarh. It was then I learned that Kesinga would be the hub for our outreach into western and central Orissa. Pastor Love was the senior pastor in the district of Kalahandi and would be our host for the two days we would be in the area. He had hired a taxi to transport us to our motel for breakfast and a bath before we headed into the outback of Phulabani. Seating in the front seat of the British Land Rover, I quickly realized I wasn't in Kerala anymore. As with the terrain around Bhubaneshwar, the country between Titiagarh and Kesinga was mostly flatland with the occasional low hill. The road was a single asphalt road posing as a two-lane highway. The taxi driver was a Grand Prix racecar driver wannabe. The land might have been flat, but the road was anything but straight. To add to the suspense, a heavy morning fog, rare in Kerala but common in Orissa at that time of the year, was blanketing the area. With visibility barely a few yards in front of us, our driver weaved in and around the obstacles in our way. Don't forget it was semi-dark as well! One would think in that relatively isolated area there would be few on the road, but that wasn't the case. Animals of every kind were constantly crossing the road in front of us. Chickens appeared near every house we passed. Numerous times we had to slow down for animals that had settled onto the road for their nightly nap. We met a number of motorcycles heading for Titiagarh, but it seemed like we always met them on a corner. There were many walkers. Walking where? I couldn't tell, but our driver knew how to use the horn. I noted, in the back of my mind, that the speed was rarely below eighty kilometers. In Kerala, rarely could you get above fifty kilometers because the roads were so full of curves and corners. I, like David, was speedily escaping Titiagarh for another land!

I think the trip from Titiagarh to Kesinga was the fastest twenty-five miles I had ever traveled in India on the ground. We arrived in the sleepy Kalahandi hamlet just as the sun was coming up over the horizon. I was glad to stop because I believed we had already tested fate too many times on the trip, and we hadn't even faced our first hostile Hindu. We took our handbags out of the back of the car and walked upstairs to the lobby of the JK Hotel, a typical, rustic middle-of-the-road Indian motel. A prominent statute of one of the Hindu gods was located at a spot of honor near the front desk. This was something I never saw in Andhra Pardesh or Kerala, but in every motel and public place in Orissa you would find one. When the man behind the desk spotted me, I could feel the change in the room. I hadn't felt it anywhere in Bhubaneshwar, but Kesinga was different. It was then I realized what Joy and Shibu had been warning me about. Quickly I was ushered to a backroom, our place to rest when we got back from Dangul, but our immediate need was a bath and a bite to eat before we got into another taxi for the one hundred twenty-five mile, one-way trip into northern Phulabani.

Despite the cold water, rarely do you bathe in warm water in India, I felt refreshed as I gathered a few things for our estimated five-hour ride into Dangul. We would travel light, in and out, staying only two-hours in Dangul before we travelled another five hours back to Kesinga. It was going to be a long day, but a day I couldn't wait to happen. The last I knew, the people of Dangul knew that Shibu, Joy, and Pastor Love were coming, but to my knowledge I was still a secret. Everybody that knew I was in Orissa had been sworn to secrecy, so the reunion with the Phulabani pastors would be extra special. I had promised them twice in 2006 and 2010 that I would come one day to see them, but they didn't know that it would be on October 24, 2012. After the boys had their pail bath, we ate a quick breakfast with stuff we brought along. Speaking about pail baths, most Indian hotels have showers, but I never saw a tub. The pressure is so light, most just fill a pail with water and wash up that way. We knew if we were to drive into Phulabani in a day we had to get on the road. I was too excited to eat, so I just looked outside the lobby window taking in the poor village that was Kesinga. I did note another rail line into town, but found out that it was just a spur line. I did watch a long, coal car train pass through town while I waited on the boys. Soon we were heading outside where another taxi waited for us with our new taxi driver J R. The minute

I saw his car I knew this day was going to be unique because on the front roof of the car was a swastika outlined by small pink flowers. Before J R picked us up, he had been to the local Hindu temple to have his car blessed by the priest!

41

CANDO FOREST THROUGH EIGHT STICK VALLEY

> Psalms 50:10 "For every beast OF THE FOREST is mine, and the cattle upon A THOUSAND HILLS."

I FELT A BIT uneasy getting into a swastika-marked car, even though I knew that the swastika in India meant something entirely different than in the Western World. Long before Nazism claimed this emblem in the 1920s, for five thousand years the Hindus had adopted the sign as a symbol of peace. Despite knowing the history, I still was uncomfortable getting in beside a visibly devote Hindu. As I settled into the front seat, I noticed a car ornament of the chief Hindu god Brahma swinging from the mirror. All along the dash were other symbols of Hinduism, and, within a few miles of our leaving Kesinga, J R (Jara) was making all kinds of gestures as we passed local shines and objects of worship: sacred trees and animals. I knew I had a chance, despite not knowing J R's language, to interact with a young man who took his religious very seriously.

We actually started out taking the road out of town we had used earlier that morning when we came in from Titiagarh. It was nice to see what I had missed in the fog and darkness. The road was lined with rice fields, and we passed a wide, but nearly empty river. The traffic had picked up, and within a mile of leaving Kesinga, we met more people just walking. I thought there were a lot of walkers in Kerala and Andhra Pardesh, but nothing compared to those in Orissa! Everywhere flocks of animals grazed and moved around, often in the middle of the road. We travelled about two-thirds of the way back to the railhead at Titiagarh before taking a sharp right hand turn toward Phulabani. Phulabani is the name of a district in Orissa, but there is also a city named Phulabani, the ultimate goal and destination for our day excursion into central Orissa.

Once off the main road, the travel really slowed because of the potholes. I recognized immediately the typical Indian rural, road system. Near the centers of population, the roads were maintained quite well, but when you get off the beaten track you are back onto traditional paths. Granted, asphalt had been laid once upon a time, but the rains had washed most of it away sometime in the past and no repairs had been forthcoming. Our day was filled with weaving in and around large holes, and when you came to where there was a stream that crossed the road, you had to literally drive down the pothole and up the other side. I did see a few spots where they were trying to put in a culvert, but I saw no work happening. It may have been because of the national festival going on. The surrounding terrain, however, was breathtaking for natural beauty. The rice fields were yellow just waiting the harvester's sickle. The shepherds were moving their flocks from one green pasture to another, and we saw a lot of still water on the way. The first third of our trip was through open farmland and pastureland with the occasional small village here and there. The road was lined with large trees. It seemed that J R (Jara) bowed to them all, and by the time of our departure (around 9 A.M.), the sun was warm but not hot. I enjoyed the window of the taxi being rolled down; the fresh air was stimulating.

One of the anticipations of this road trip was the fact we were going to travel through the largest forest in Orissa, where Indian elephants and Bengal tigers roam wild. It was my hope to see one or both. I have always loved forestland because I was raised in a region in northern Maine much like the territory I was now travelling through. I have spent some of my finest days driving through woodlands. Like central Orissa, northern Maine still has large tracks of untouched forests. Granted, the wood companies have cut over much of northern Maine, but they have replanted to the point it is hard to tell, in some places, what it virgin forest and what is new forest. The Cando Forest of Orissa is still mostly virgin wood, and the road we were travelling reminded me of a typical fire road in Maine, except in India the road was partly asphalt.

One of the rare and special thrills of life is a ride or walk through a forest. It brings with it a stillness and solitude unmatched. What made the Cando Forest so unique for me was at the same time we were travelling through valley after connecting valley with high hills, a thousand hills it seemed, on each side. They told me that the main valley was called Eight Sticks. Most of the time it was thick forest, but periodically we would break out into small meadows where a few people had settled to raise animals and plant a few paddies of rice. We would also occasionally come to a small village where a few buildings were located; we were nearly half way to our destination before we come to a large city, Baligurha. It was here we thought we might have trouble, but we passed through the busy streets unnoticed and quickly back into the woods. We all need to journey through God's natural cathedrals once and awhile. Like the oasis in a sun-scorched desert, a forest brings renewal and the hope of seeing one of God's great beasts. My eyes were constantly looking from side to side hoping to catch a glimpse of an elephant or a tiger. My companions as usual were not as enthusiastic. I was told a road worker had just been killed in that forest by a Bengal tiger and that elephants were so unpredictable that nobody but me wanted to see one in the wild.

The beauty and serenity of the forest is duplicated by the incredible reflection mirrored in the forest canopy by a bright sun overhead. Every tree, rock, distant ridge and hill was outlined and highlighted by fluffy suspended clouds in the sky above. The combination of a narrow road lined by tall, thick trees only added to the illusion of driving through a tunnel. Add that to the soaring hills to the right and the left beyond the woods, you get the feeling of a tunnel within a tunnel. The forest was also taking on an autumn hue, one of my favorite times of the year, and now you can understand how the five hour, one hundred and twenty-five mile trip was not an ordeal, nor a burden. There was too much to take in, too much to see, too much to experience. Besides, each mile brought me closer to my goal, a face-to-face meeting with the preachers of Phulabani! My pastor friends were right around that next corner, and so might a wild Indian elephant or tiger.

And then it happened! A flash across the road just in front of J R's taxi! I learned later that it wasn't J R's taxi, but that J R was just the taxi driver. Another Hindu man owned the car. My eyes strained to make out the shadow that crossed the road. My excitement showed no bounds as I yelled out to my travelling companions, "Look!" Everybody focused on the shape beside the road. We were still a far distance from the creature when the Land Rover began to rock side to side with laughter. In my great expectation to see a tiger or an elephant, I never thought that of every beast of the forest that God controls the only wild animal that I would see both going through and coming back through the Cando Forest would be a wild boar. A pig, Lord? It was then the Good Lord in His graciousness reminded me that the blessing of this day wasn't going to be found in an animal sighting, but in the smile of a surprised friend at my arrival. Dangul was in sight and just through that Hindu village, by a high rock wall was Ranjan, the lad I had traveled halfway around the world to see.

42

SURPRISING RANJAN

Jeremiah 51:41 "HOW IS THE PRAISE OF THE WHOLE WORLD SURPRISED!"

Eventually, we worked our way through the Cando Forest and the Eight Stick Valley to emerge onto one of the nicest highways I had seen in India. We were still in a well-defined valley, but the villages and the towns were closer together. The roadway was the main thoroughfare through northern Orissa. About ten miles short of the city of Phulabani, we turned off the main road onto a narrow lane that ran between two huge rice fields. At the junction, J R (Jara) stopped the car so that I could move from the front seat to the middle-back seat. Pastor Love got up front while I settled into the passenger's seat between Joy and Shibu. In order to get to where we were going, we had to pass through the Hindu section of the village of Dangul, the very villagers who four years before had burned down the Dangul Baptist Church, Ranjan's home, as well as most of the Christian houses in the area. Not far from where we turned was the burned out shell of the Gondapather Baptist Church. I asked if we might see it, but I was told the residents of that village were still too hostile. I was to be secreted into the village of Dangul without any fanfare, hopefully hidden from view!

    I sensed the rising tension in the car as we neared a rustic Orissa village. We had passed scores of these villages in our five-hour, 125-mile trek from Kesinga to Dangul up Route 217. Grouped together on a small rise in the land were about two dozen small homes. A primitive wall enclosed the hamlet with an open gate area at the front, and I learned later at the back as well. A narrow street, just wide enough for our car to pass through, weaved its way by the closely packed houses, sheds, and animal enclosures. From the car window, I could see the high hills that surrounded the large valley the town was located in. I couldn't see any other villages, just acre upon acre of rice fields for as far as the eye could see. It was a little after one o'clock in the afternoon as we worked our way slowly through Dangul. I saw few people in the street, in the fields, or near their homes. I figured most were resting having gotten up early to do the bulk of their field work before the sun got too high. We had come at the right time, but could we keep my arrival a secret much longer?

Ever since I suggested to Shibu that I wanted to visit the pastors of Phulabani, I dreamed of how to surprise them. I have always loved surprises especially when I am the one doing the surprising. I still remember the expression on my wife's face the day I told her that I had booked a ten-day trip to the British Isles for our 30th wedding anniversary. It is all about the expression that comes over the face when one is totally and completely surprised by a gift, news, or a visit. My trip to Orissa had been over six years in the planning, nearly six months in the execution, and now it was happening. Despite many primitive things in India, communication is not one of them. Most Indians are well connected because of the great advancements in telecommunications, especially in the area of cell phones. How Shibu and Joy had kept my coming a secret and a surprise must have involved a few white lies, stretching the truth a bit, and totally ignoring certain questions, but they had. As I drove up to the front gate of Ranjan's house, there was no indication my arrival was known to anybody but the four men I was travelling with.

The first face I saw as we drove up to Ranjan's home was Ranjan. He was standing near a gate with a group of other men. I quickly recognized Noha, Ranjan's father, Pastor Solomon, and a few others I knew but couldn't think of their names. Ranjan quickly came to the side of the car to instruct J R where to park. As far as he knew, only three guests were arriving for a mid-week praise service. Shibu was going to be the special guest, the leader of the mission on an informational tour checking on the Church of Orissa and how things were progressing since the great persecution of 2008, or so Ranjan thought. I could see that Ranjan still hadn't realized that there were four men in the car besides the driver. J R swung the car into a small driveway across the lane, backing in as if to make a quick getaway if necessary. Pastor Love was the first out of the car followed by Joy, and then I emerged into the light of day. It seemed at first my hosts were stunned by a tall, white stranger that came out of the car just before Shibu. Nobody said anything at first, just long stares with big question marks on their faces. Ranjan seemed focused in getting us all out of sight before the local villagers realized guests from away had arrived. Joy was still a wanted man in the region, and Shibu was also not a welcomed visitor in the area. It was Noha who first came up to me with an open hand and a big smile. I found out later that his first words to Joy were, "How come you didn't tell us Pastor Blackstone was coming with you?"

After Noha's welcome it seemed that everybody, including Ranjan, realized the surprise. I was mobbed by the few at the gate knowing that there were more on the other side of the entrance. I was quickly ushered down a small walkway beside a mud-brick house that led into a small courtyard. I could see that a number of homes surrounded the courtyard as I rushed through. I noticed the entire area was surrounded by a high fence made of bushes and vines and small trees. With each step, more and more people emerged with big smiles and happy chatter. Oriya is the language of Dangul, and despite only knowing one word, "Prosansaa", Praise the Lord, I heard it a lot as I made my way to the church. We left the courtyard by way of a low hanging gate near a wide open well. A group of young ladies were standing beside the well drawing water. We walked around the wide well, nearly ten feet across, to a small concrete building very familiar to me. It was laid out just like the church buildings of Kerala with a small front porch that led to a one-room sanctuary. There were people everywhere, an overflow crowd was already singing as I entered the room with Pastor Love, Pastor Solomon, Pastor Noha, Shibu, and Joy. I will never forget the second song they sung as we settled into the front of the church, "This is the Day the Lord Has Made"!

The simple chorus is taken from Psalms 118:24: "This is the day which the Lord hath made; we will rejoice and be glad in it." Is there a better verse to summarize what was happening as we joined together in praise for the chance to visit with, worship with, and pray with these dear saints? It wasn't long before everybody knew who I was. Unbeknown to me, I had been mentioned often in prayers. My visits with the pastors in 2006 and 2010 had been shared. Not only had I surprised my pastor friends but their parishioners as well. I can honestly say I was treated as both a brother in Christ and a long-lost friend who had finally come for a visit. I felt at home as we celebrated the brotherhood of saints: strangers but friends, unknown, yet well known. But should we be surprised by such a welcome, for is not this how it shall be when we all gather one day before God? The reunion will be sweet, the gathering marked by praise, and the service full of singing. I stood before the congregation and scanned the crowd, and of all the faces I viewed, the one that brought the greatest joy to my heart was Ranjan, standing in the second row of men to my right with the broadest smile I have ever seen in my life!

43

HANNAH'S DEDICATION

John 10:22 "... THE FEAST OF DEDICATION..."

After two songs and a prayer, I was given the privilege of addressing the crowd that had gathered at the Dangul Baptist Church. I only learned after the service that eight of the local assemblies had gathered together to hear from Shibu, or so they thought. Eight pastors and their flocks were there to hear me share a message I called, "My Call to Visit Orissa". I shared my connection to Ranjan in 2006 and spoke about the first time I asked the Lord if He would make it possible for me to visit, claiming Paul's vision of the Macedonia (Acts 16:9) as my inspiration. In 2010, I shared how I had visited their pastors in Andhra Pardesh and had claimed Paul's desire to visit Rome (Acts 19:21) as my desire to visit Orissa, and how I started to pray Romans 1:10-12:

> "Making request, if by any means now at length I might have a prosperous journey by the will of God to come unto you. For I long to see you, that I may impart unto you some spiritual gift, to the end ye may be established; that is, that I may be comforted together with you by the mutual faith both of you and me."

It took nearly seven years for God to answer my prayer, but in the spring of 2012, I got an e-mail from Shibu telling me of a possible trip. We had kept it secret to surprise them so that the gathering would be more meaningful. I shared the scriptures that encouraged me to come to them and the promises I claimed. Acts 10:20: "Arise therefore, and get thee down, and go with them, doubting nothing..." and Acts 18:9-10: "... Be not afraid... I am with thee, and no man shall set on thee to hurt thee ...", and that I had come to them because "... a door was opened unto me of the Lord." (II Corinthians 2:12)

I then went on to share with them the words I believed the Good Lord had sent me to share. I presented a five-fold prayer I had been praying for them, from Paul's classic supplication to the Church at Colosse.

1. THAT THEY MIGHT WANT SPIRITUALLY - Colossians 1:9. That they might seek spiritual wisdom and spiritual knowledge and spiritual understanding as they grew in the Lord (II Peter 3:18). That they might desire to be filled (Ephesians 5:18) with the Spirit, their one great protection from a hostile world.

2. THAT THEY MIGHT WALK FAITHFULLY - Colossians 1:10. That they might walk with God as Enoch walked with God (Genesis 5:24) in a wicked and corrupt world, faithful until the end (Revelation 2:10). That the key to pleasing God is faithfulness (Hebrews 11:5-6 and I Corinthians 4:2).

3. THAT THEY MIGHT WORK FRUITFULLY - Colossians 1:10. That their Father as a Husbandman is seeking fruit (John 15:1-7) from His vineyard, and the fruit that He is seeking is the Fruit of the Spirit (Galatians 5:22-23). Only as we reveal the virtues of love, joy, peace, longsuffering will the Father be pleased.

4. THAT THEY MIGHT WEATHER GLORIOUSLY - Colossians 1:11. That they might continue to look to Jesus for the strength needed to overcome all the obstacles in Orissa (Philippians 4:13). That they had been endued with power (Acts 1:8) from on high and greater is He that was with them then he that is in the world (I John 4:4).

5. THAT THEY MIGHT WITHSTAND JOYFULLY - Colossians 1:11. That there would be a lot to withstand, to overcome (John 16:33) in this present world, but through Christ they could do it with a smile on their faces (Matthew 5:11-12).

I finished my message with the full assurance that my prayers, Paul's classic petitions, had certainly been answered in their lives. I was the one humbled by their testimony in the face of serious and severe persecution!

After I finished, both Joy and Shibu addressed the gathering before Pastor Noha, the senior pastor of the group, closed in prayer and asked a blessing over the feast that would follow. Like Kerala, few gatherings in Orissa happen without a meal at the end. The scattered flocks of Phulabani would head back to their villages after the meal, and we would head back to Kesinga. Our stay in Dangul was scheduled for only two hours, so everything planned had to fall into that narrow time slot. After the final blessing, the crowded began leaving, heading for the courtyard and the feast. Some came forward to greet me, and it was then something that could only happen in India took place. It was a surprise to both Shibu and me, but a blessing we will never forget for the rest of our lives.

One of the pastors I had met in 2010 was a middle-aged man by the name of Sanodo Kohana, the pastor of the Lahauadi Baptist Church. On our way to Dangul, Joy had pointed out the villages where the church works were flourishing. One of those villages was Kohana's village of Lahauadi. Unknown to me, Pastor Sanodo had gotten married since I first met him, and unknown to Shibu, he and his wife had just had a baby. As we gathered in front of the church talking, I noticed that a serious conversation was happening between Sanodo, Joy, and Shibu. Because Shibu can't speak Oriya, Joy was translating. After a few minutes, Shibu came over to me and announced that the service was not over, that there was going to be a child's dedication before the meal. This didn't surprise me because I had witnessed a number of dedications during my previous trips. In India, the family usually waited a few weeks, if not a few months, before a special dedication service is conducted. The interesting aspect of this is the child is not named until that dedication, only on that special occasion is the baby's name revealed. Here in Dangul, however, there was going to be a stunning twist to the Kohana baby's dedication.

Though I had witnessed Indian dedications, I had yet to participate in one myself. Pastor Sanodo asked Shibu if I would do the prayer of dedication and if we would name the baby! I said, "What did he ask?" Shibu confirmed that the family wanted us to come up with the name. I asked Shibu if he had ever experienced that before, to which he replied, "No!" I could tell Shibu was surprised and nervous, but it was clear we couldn't ignore the request. We talked together for a few minutes. I make the suggestion that we could call the baby girl Marnie, my favorite girl's name, but that would be too foreign for them. Shibu knew of their love of Biblical names, and within a short while he asked what I thought of Hannah, Samuel's mother's name. I said, "That is a fine name!" Normally, just before the prayer of dedication, the family informs the pastor of the chosen name, but on October 24, 2012, at the front of the Dangul Baptist Church in upper Orissa, India, a pastor from Maine and a pastor from Kerala stood before a pastor from Orissa and his young family and prayed for a little girl they had just named Hannah.

44

PREACHERS OF PHULABANI

> II Timothy 4:2 "PREACH THE WORD; be instant in season, out of season; reprove, rebuke, exhort with all longsuffering and doctrine."

After baby Hannah's dedication, Shibu and I joined the others in the courtyard for a traditional Orissa feast which included eating on the ground off banana leaves.

It was also there I got to reconnect with my Orissa preacher friends from 2006 and 2010. I learned that besides Pastor Noha from Dangul, Pastor Ugrisah from Kerad, Pastor Rajan from Poda, Pastor Samson from Phulabani, Pastor Solomon from Kenpach, Pastor Sanodo from Lahauadi, and Pastor Rugidisai from Phulabani, they had brought their congregations to Dangul to meet Shibu and Joy and to their surprise a pastor from Maine! Five of the pastors were old friends and three of the pastors became new friends. Ranjan was not a pastor but an evangelist who ministered throughout the region, especially among the youth. It was nice to sit awhile and remember the first time we met. In the year of the great persecution (2008), I wrote this in memory of these persecuted pastors, the preachers of Phulabani:

It was only fitting that my first morning walk into the byways of Edayappara, India resulted in my meeting, for the first time, a group of fellow preachers I named the boys from Orissa. This was mainly because most of them were much younger than I. One of the reasons for my trip to India was to meet the missionaries working in the mission field my church in Maine had been supporting since the 1990s. After losing a number of supporting missionaries, the Emmanuel Baptist Church of Ellsworth, Maine desired to expand its mission outreach to an unreached people group somewhere in the world. The only mission I knew that was doing that kind of work then was the ministry of the IGBC in India. I contacted Brother Simon, Thakadiel, Shibu's father, and he told me about a new outreach into Orissa they had just started under the direction of a man from Kerala by the name of Joy Thomas. It sounded exactly what we were looking for, so the church took on the monthly support of a pastor in Orissa. So for many years before I arrived in India I had supported, prayed for, and taken an interest in the Orissa Outreach. On that first Saturday in India, I got to meet the men I had heard about for over a decade, the preachers of the Phulabani. Only one of the thirteen pastors and evangelists (I also called them the baker's dozen from Orissa) could speak any kind of English, a young man by the name of Ranjan Digal. It was from Ranjan I was able to develop my first impressions of this dedicated group of persecuted preachers. They were a people of small stature, but very big in their love of Christ. Their smiles were appealing, and did they ever love to sing! Many mornings that first week I was brought into my new day by their singing; they were staying in a building just across the front yard from where I would lodge for my entire stay in India.

On that first weekend in January of 2006, I joined up with them as they walked back from a creek, about a mile from the compound, where they had taken their morning bath. It was on that first walk with Ranjan I discovered that it had taken him and his comrades fifty-seven hours to travel from their homes in Phulabani to Edayappara; it had only taken me thirty-nine hours to travel from my home in Maine. I had covered just over nine thousand miles while they had journeyed just over nine hundred miles! I had travelled mostly by airplane while they travelled by bus and train. I was beginning to understand just how difficult it was to minister in India because of the transportation system, but it was then I realized these fellowlabours were willing to endure any hardship to tell others about Jesus Christ and His power to save. It was then I was told they had travelled all that way to meet me. They had been told of my coming and of my church's support of their work, and they wanted to meet in person at least one person that thought enough about their mission field to support them and come to actually meet them. With names like Solomon, Noha, Sugreevan, Binod, Manoj, Krusso, Samanandha, Ugrisah, Samson, Suredra, and of course Ranjan, I now had faces to place next to my prayers for Orissa. Paul exhorts us all, "And we beseech you, brethren, TO KNOW THEM which labour among us . . . " (I Thessalonians 5:12) One of the great joys of India was getting to know my fellow pastors from Orissa. Now that they are in the midst of deep persecution, I can see their smiling faces, and I pray for their ultimate safety and deliverance.

But on that first full day in India, I had yet to meet the individual I most desired to meet: Joy Thomas, the director of the mission outreach in Orissa, the one most responsible for opening up Phulabani and

Kalahandi with the Gospel of Jesus Christ. Sometimes called the Paul of Orissa, I had read his name often in the correspondence we had received over the years from the Simon family. My encounter with the boys from Orissa had taken place in the morning. I would only have to wait until the evening to meet the man who had led all these other men to Christ and through them had started nearly twenty local churches. I had just gotten off the phone with my wife Coleen, my first call home telling my dear ones that I had arrived save and sound, when Shibu called me into the waiting room of the Simon home. There standing in the middle of a long and narrow parlor was a group of men. I recognized some of them from my morning walk, Ranjan and his father Noha were there, and standing beside them was a very short (five feet short) man I had never seen before. He had a glowing face, an infectious smile, and a confident countenance. It was then I was introduced to Joy Thomas. The men from Orissa had come to the Simon house to deliver the offering of the Orissa believers for the up and coming convention: two hundred twenty pounds of homegrown rice! Once the ceremony was over, I got a chance to speak for the first time to the man I had heard so much about. I found Joy to be a well-spoken gentleman with a very good command of the English language. It was then I learned that this man of simple upbringings spoke SEVEN languages. Packed in a very small frame was an amazing man, a gifted evangelist, and an extraordinary missionary.

Over the six weeks I stayed in Kerala, I was able to spend a lot of time getting to know Joy, and I came to understand that God had chosen well the man to lead a persecuted Church. I found him fearless, faithful, and funny. One night I was to speak in a far off church that took us through a Hindu stronghold. Unaware of the danger, I was surprised when Joy Thomas joined Shagu and me in the car. When we got to the church, Joy introduced himself as my bodyguard. I found it funny because like King Saul I am at least a head and a shoulder taller than Joy!

Nearly seven years after that event, I was again in hostile Hindu country and who was still by my side, my good friend and bodyguard Joy Thomas.

Looking back at these memories of the men I was with now, in the very place they had stood firm, a place despite the persecution and suffering where they had stayed and resisted and won their church back. I learned that afternoon in Dangul that to preach the Word in season and out of season sometimes means a season of persecution!

45

OUR DAYS ARE LIKE PASSING SHADOWS

Psalms 144:4 "Man is like to vanity: HIS DAYS ARE AS A SHADOW THAT PASSETH AWAY."

No day in India every felt more like what the Psalmist describes in the verse printed above than my day in Phulabani. The minutes ticked away quickly, despite my attempt to slow them down. Remember, our planned stay in Dangul was just two hours. I wanted to stay longer, but the boys, Shibu and Joy, were anxious to get on the road. We still had to travel back through the region that was at the heart of the 2008 persecution. Because of the festival, there were many people out on the roads increasing our chances of meeting a hostile crowd. News had also gotten around Dangul that a white man was in town. Shibu had even cautioned me to keep my voice down, causing the locals to question why. I felt no danger; I was having such a spiritual high. I haven't been to many places in my life that I felt any more at home, any more blessed. The fellowship with these saints was sweet, a heavenly sweetness!

Four o'clock was nearing as we took a group picture in Pastor Noha's house. I had quickly devoured the simple meal they placed in front of me. I needed no physical food because the spiritual food I was eating was beyond filling. I wanted to mingle more with the saints, so as Shibu and Joy said their farewells, I strolled back into the courtyard. I was immediately met by a group of women that wanted me to follow them. Not knowing where I was going, I still followed them passed Pastor Solomon's home to a simple hut down a side alley off the central courtyard. Unknown to me, Joy had told Ranjan to keep an eye on me because of my tendencies to wander too far afield. As I approached the home, Ranjan was by my side sharing with me the reason the ladies wanted me to come to this particular house. It was then I meet Elizabeth Kruso, the wife of one of the pastor who had just passed away, a man I meet in Andhra in 2010. They wanted me to pray for her. What an honor! The pastor had been a part of the terrible persecution and had to flee with his family into the surrounding hills. Had the stress and strain weakened him? He had suddenly died of a heart attack just weeks before my arrival. His widow was still distraught and weeping as I took her hands and prayed while Ranjan translated. Again the Good Lord had put a face on the sorrows the persecuted church faces even years after the persecution died down.

As Ranjan walked me back to Jara's taxi and our trip back through the Cando Forest, I paused to give my friend a heartfelt handshake and a hug. Ranjan had become an Indian son to me. I don't know if he understands that to its fullest extent, but I know a deep sadness came to my heart the moment I got into the car. How is it possible to be full of joy one minute and in deep sorrow the next? My sadness and sorrow came from so little time to visit, so little time to fellowship, so little time to rejoice in the presence of fellow-believers. As I write these remembrances, my heart still aches. I miss my friend Ranjan; I miss his father Noha and the other saints of Dangul, a Dangul that just a few short years before was in ruins. It was then I recalled a story Marnie told me about Noha and how God had miraculously saved his life, not in the persecution of 2008 but the one that hit Phulabani in December of 2007. My daughter Marnie was in Kerala from late December 2007 to mid-March 2008. She got a chance to meet Pastor Noah and to hear this story firsthand. I pass it on.

"One night late in December, Pastor Noha was returning from visitation in another village. He was warned that a wild band of Hindu militants were looking for him to kill him. Blocked off from getting back home, he sought shelter in the home of a Hindu friend. Telling him about his trouble, the Hindu hid Noah in a back room under some sacks of rice. When the angry crowd arrived at the man's house, they were told that Pastor Noha was not there. Despite a search of the place, they never found the dear pastor. Much like the spies in Rahab's house (Joshua 2), Pastor Noha was delivered from the hands of a blood-thirsty crowd. You talk about something being upside-down. It should have been Noha who died in the uprising, not Laxmanananda, the Hindu leader killed by the Maoist that started the whole 2008 persecution. Surely this was the plan of the Wicked One in Orissa, yet just the reversed happened. It should have been Mordecai, not Haman, to have died on the gallows, yet just the opposite happened. It just shows you who is ultimately in control even during times of persecution!"

The goodbyes were heartfelt, the promises to meet again sincere, and the departure was difficult. Because of the negative news coming from the Hindu side of the village, we secretly left out a back road. Our escape was through a series of dirty roads to the north of Dangul. The scenery was breathtaking. We stopped a couple of times so I could get a few photographs of the terrain. The panoramic pictures reveal a lush valley outlined by dark hills. The patchwork landscape of rice fields was highlighted by a cloudless sky. Despite the lovely portrait of a peaceful place, I now knew of the ugly side of this corner of the world. This uttermost spot is filled with those who hate my Saviour and anyone that claimed Him as Lord and King. I had just left a group of brothers and sisters in Christ that would have to daily live in this threatening paradise. It was then I realized that few in my America understood or cared to understand just how the persecuted Church lives. I wanted to take all my friends with me, back to a safer place, a peaceful spot where threat of attack and assault was unheard of, yet the saints of Dangul were happy to stay. They wanted to stay. Had they not stayed even when they were burned out, chased out, thrown out of their own town? I admired them the more for it.

One of my favorite devotional writers Vance Havner, a man of quick-wit and country-wisdom, once made this observation that might just as well have been a comparison of the Church in America versus the Church in Orissa. Here is what Vance Havner said:

"The modern church member all too often avoids persecution by taking the line of least resistance and living in a truce with this age. The early Christians wore scars, but we wear medals. The Gospel thrives on persecution. It makes better headway against a world that fights it than against a world that trifles with it. Bitter hostility is better than half-hearted endorsement."

In my meeting in Dangul, I found a calm, confident group of believers that seemed untouched by the dangerous land they lived in. Why were they so calm? Why so confident? The answer came that shadowy day I spent a quick afternoon with the church of Phulabani. Their strength was in the Lord; their hope was in the Lord, and their faith was in the Lord. They believed, no matter the foe, the face of the Lord still shone upon them. No matter the adversary, the assault, the attack, they would overcome and be victorious in the end (I John 5:4). I learned that immediately after the great persecution of 2008, Ranjan defied the militants by staging a youth rally to praise and glorify Jesus. I am still humbled by such courage and bravery in the face of open and hostile persecution!

46

HINDU HIGHLIGHTS

Deuteronomy 32:17 "They sacrificed unto devils, not to GOD; TO gods WHOM THEY KNEW NOT, TO NEW gods THAT CAME NEWLY UP, whom your fathers feared not."

BEFORE WE HEADED BACK to Kesinga, the boys wanted me to see Phulabani, the town where two works of the mission were flourishing and where Joy Thomas lived when he was in northern Orissa.

Our trek out of Dangul eventually brought us back to the superhighway we had come in on, but instead of turning southwest, we headed due north for about ten miles. Our plan was just to drive around town and see the sights. It was late afternoon and the preparations for another night of Hindu celebrations were fully underway. The boys knew that we would have to drive through a number of similar villages on our way back to the railhead at Kesinga, so why not test the waters? Would there be interest in a strange vehicle with a few strange passengers? I had read about and heard about Phulabani, so it was nice to get a visual picture of the town in my mind. It was typical of the many cities we had already traveled through in Orissa, and we were in and out without any problems. As we left Phulabani for the Cando Forest and the five hour ride to Kesinga, I began to think about the obstacles Joy and the other pastors were up against in this stronghold of Hinduism. I listened carefully as my companions taught me and Jara demonstrated to me the unique aspects about the Hindu faith.

Sometimes called Brahmanism, Hinduism has been the traditional religion of India for millennium, over 1500 years before Christ. Hindu, from the Sanskrit language, means river in reference to the River Indus, the greatest river on the subcontinent of India. The people that spoke Sanskrit and settled in India probably came from north of the Himalayan Mountains in southern Russia. They brought with them their own religion and over time, the mixture of that religion with the religions of the native people of India merged into the Hinduism of today. The first and greatest of all gods is Brahma, the creator of all life and all other gods. The number of gods has now reached over 330,000,000! They have a holy trinity: Brahma, the creator, Vishnu, the preserver, and Shiva, the destroyer. Each of these three gods can have over a thousand names, and each god is worshipped under a variety of titles. One of the primary beliefs of Hinduism is the sacredness of the soul and all living organisms, trees, and all animals. To a Hindu, even an insect has a soul. That is why most Hindus are vegetarians and why cows are the most sacred of all animals. Close behind are the monkey, the serpent (cobra), the elephant Brahman, not to be confused with Brahma, the creator god, the supreme deity on earth, the bull, the dog, and the mouse.

Hinduism teaches that every living thing has a shared part with Brahman, and the ultimate goal is to unite again the individual soul with the divine essence of Brahman. This comes about in one of three ways: performing good works, living a devoted life, and through divine wisdom. This might take a number of lives to accomplish and, for that reason, Hinduism teaches the transmigration of the soul. This means that when a person or any other living organism dies the soul of that living creature is reincarnated into another body. After going through a series of cycled lives, those who improve their moral condition will come closer to the divine nature of Brahman. The highest moral act is a selfless life, and once achieved, the soul is finally liberated to unity with the supreme deity. Each follower of this religion is encouraged to pick a patron god and follow that god throughout his or her life. This is where devotion comes into Hinduism. Every day the worshipper must pay some kind of tribute to his god: food, flowers, incense, visits to public temples or shrines. Several services a day are conducted at these sacred spots and on special occasions, like what was happening in Orissa when I was there, the gods are uniquely honored with pilgrimages. The greatest of all the pilgrimages is to the Ganges River. To wash in the Ganges is to have your sins washed away. To die on the banks of the Ganges and to have your ashes thrown into its waters will release you from the cycle of life and death, a journey straight to deity with Brahman.

Good deeds and daily devotion are important acts in the life of the Hindu, but the most valuable is divine wisdom. Hinduism teaches that life ought to be in four-parts: the student, the period that one studies under the guidance of a teacher; the householder, the period of marriage and family; the recluse, after one fulfills his duty to family he retires to a life of meditation, and beggar, the individual now breaks all ties with family and friend and wanders for the rest of his life in search of divine wisdom.

This wisdom doesn't come from books or instruction but through earthly experiences with total control of one's passions, keeping one's body pure, and one's mind focused on the meaning of life. Only then can one come into the full meaning of divine wisdom.

Perhaps the best-known aspect of Hinduism is the caste system, where all people are divided up into four main groups. This originated from the Hindu teaching of the eternal cosmic order. There are the Brahmans, the priest-teacher class, the Kshatriyas, the soldier-ruler class, the Vaisyas, the artisan-farmer class, and the Sudras, the servant-slave class. There is however, a fifth class for those who live under the top four, but they are seen as those that have no caste, no class. They are seen as impure, as infamous or untouchable. But, as with the gods who have multiplied over time, even in this subclass over 3,000 sub-castes have developed. Once you are born into a certain caste, you live under the rules and regulations of that caste for the rest of your life. In other words, a practicing Hindu in the traditional sense will live his life performing good acts of service, practicing devotion to his god, and seeking divine wisdom according to his caste.

For ten hours I sat next to a young man trying to live that way. I watched as he bowed to trees and touched the Brahma images hanging from his rear-view mirror. I found a gracious, humble, kind lad. Despite driving a group of Christian pastors all day, I could only conclude from what I observed that Jara was a practicing, devote Hindu. What made me sad was the realization just how legalistic, humanistic, and unrealistic this religion was. How can one choose Hinduism over Christianity when they are compared? One God compared to millions. How can you know so many? "One God and Father of all, who is above all, and through all, and in you all." (Ephesians 4:6) One way to God versus a multitude of ways. How can you be sure you didn't miss one? "Jesus saith unto him, I am the way, the truth, and the life: no man cometh unto the Father, but by me." (John 14:6) One life to live in heaven versus a numerous series of lives. How can you be sure that you will ever make it? "And as it is appointed unto men once to die . . . " (Hebrews 9:27) One lifestyle compared to four and one class versus thousands. How can you live with such limitations? "There is neither Jew nor Greek, there is neither bond nor free, there is neither male nor female: for ye are all one in Christ Jesus." (Galatians 3:28)

47

AN HISTORIC PERSECUTION

> Matthew 10:23 "But when they PERSECUTE YOU IN THIS CITY, flee ye into another...."

OUR ONE HUNDRED TWENTY-FIVE mile trip back to Kesinga took us along the very same path we had traveled that morning, with the exception of our side trip to Phulabani. Within an hour of our leaving Phulabani, we were safe in the easterly end of the Cando Forest. I was still looking for a wild Bengal tiger or a wild Indian elephant, but while my eyes were on the road and the surrounding woodland, my ears were open to the conversations happening in the car. Along the way, Joy kept telling me of the places of the ministry and especially the places the great persecution of 2008 had affected. He told of Gondapather Church as we passed the road leading to the village of the burned-out sanctuary. There were no longer any believers in the town; they had fled according to the instruction of Christ give above. I would meet the real Church of Gondapather in Bhubaneshwar in two days.

As I listened to story after story, what interested me most was the parallel between the saints of Orissa and the historical pattern of persecution as seen in the early Church. When the believers of Phulabani were attacked, they followed the Lord's instruction to flee persecution. There seems to be a popular misconception that we are to stay and fight or be martyred. Granted, there have been situations where the saints have been unable to flee and they have died, but the first commandment in persecution is fleeing! I think it is vital for us to see this precept as taught by Christ and demonstrated by the Church.

When the first great persecution (Acts 8:1) engulfed the Church of Jerusalem after the death of Stephen, the Church was scattered, or they fled from Jerusalem into the regions of Judaea and Samaria. Jesus had made it very clear to His disciples in His instruction concerning the rejection of His Gospel. "And whosoever shall not receive you, nor hear your words, when ye depart (flee) out of that house or city, shake off the dust of your feet." (Matthews10:14) This pattern was followed even by the second generation of believers: "But they (Paul and Barnabas) shook off the dust of their feet against them, and they came (fled or departed) unto Iconium." (Acts 13:51) This would lead to a standard, a pattern of leaving a place versus staying and fighting and maybe dying in a place of rejection or persecution. As I looked through the story of the Church as recorded by Luke in the book of Acts, I found these historic events that verify this precept.

1. When Herod began the second great persecution of the Church in Jerusalem (Acts 12:1), James was martyred, but Peter was rescued and it says, "And he departed, and went into another place." (Acts 12:17) Peter fled!
2. When persecution got heated at Iconium, Paul and Barnabas fled to Lystra. (Acts 14:6)
3. When persecution became deadly in Lystra, Paul and Barnabas departed to Derbe. (Acts 14:20)
4. When persecution intensified at Thessalonica, Paul and Silas were sent away to Berea. (Acts 17:10)
5. When persecution became serious at Berea, Paul was sent away to Athens. (Acts 17:14)
6. When persecution got out of hand in Ephesus, Paul departed to Macedonia. (Acts 20:1)
7. When the third great persecution of the Church in Jerusalem took place and the Romans saved Paul, the Lord oversaw Paul's escape to Caesarea. (Acts 23:23)

One can read the accounts of the martyred saints in such books as the book written by Foxe, but we often forget that not every Christian was martyred. Certainly through the ages thousands upon thousands, yes, millions have made the ultimate sacrifice and laid down their lives for the cause of Christ. I would like to highlight the truth behind the unknown, the unnamed millions that fled, departed, escaped, scattered, and ran away to continue the Faith somewhere else! Granted, the Church has grown because of the blood of the martyrs, but the persecuted Church is not a cemetery, but a living, breathing segment of the universal Church that has chosen on numerous occasions, as in Orissa, to flee instead of fight. Some will and have criticized Pastor John and his flock for fleeing on that fateful Sunday morning in August of 2008, but they were doing just what their Lord had taught: flee, run! I have listened for years to those spiritual, holier-than-thou, Monday-morning quarterbacks who bravely tell how they would have stood their ground and died for the Faith. How easy it is to judge and condemn nine thousand miles away from the front! Even the great chapter on faith (Hebrews 11) reveals clearly the two groups: the martyrs and those that fled. "They were stoned, they were sawn asunder, were tempted, and were slain with the sword (*the martyrs*): they wandered about in sheepskins and goatskins; being destitute, afflicted, tormented; of whom the world is not worthy: they wandered in deserts, and in mountains, and in dens and caves of the earth (*those that fled*)." (Hebrews 11:37–38)

The story is told that when the men who discovered the bodies of the young missionaries on the Curaray River in Ecuador, they recognized they had been fleeing from their persecutors. Interestingly, the Auca five were armed, but not one bullet was fired from any of their guns. The conclusion is that these brave saints would flee, but not fight! Such has been the pattern of the historic Church since the beginning of the Church, and the Church of Orissa was just following that Biblical example.

My observation about these events is this: we are not to seek or provoke persecution, but if persecution comes we are to try to get out of its way. If we can't, then we are instructed to be faithful unto death. (Revelation 2:10) We are not to seek martyrdom, but if God wills it then so be it. Our first duty is to survive to tell the story of Christ to others that will hear. Such has been the testimony of countless unsung heroes in the past, those who have fled to preach another day. The martyrs get all the press, but it is actually those who survive a persecution who actually propagate the Gospel. Dead men preach only one sermon (Hebrews 11:4). And so it was that four preachers fled Phulabani that Wednesday afternoon in late October. We passed through hostile Hindu towns unnoticed, unrecognized, and untouched. We had other Orissa towns to reach, other Hindus to teach, and other messages to preach. Some might ask if I felt like a coward creeping in and out of Phulabani. My answer? I felt honored to be there and to have another day to meet the pastors and the parishioners of Kalahandi. Remember, our job is not to hold onto territory like Gondapather, but to seek the souls of men wherever they may be found because once the soul is reached that is a place the devil or his followers can never capture or reclaim.

48

PROMISED DELIVERANCE

> II Timothy 3:11 "Persecutions, afflictions, which came unto me in Antioch, at Iconium, at Lystra; what persecutions I endured: *BUT OUT OF THEM ALL THE LORD DELIVERED ME."*

JUST BEFORE NINE ON October 24, 2012, we climbed the stairs to our room at the JK Hotel in Kesinga. What an ending to a wonderful day! It had started on a train outside of Titiagarh at four A.M. Now, nearly three hundred miles later, I could rest and record one of the most exciting and meaningful days of my life, a day of shared deliverance in fulfillment of Psalms 34:19:

"Many are the afflictions of the righteous: but the Lord delivereth him out of them all!"

After supper I got out my journal and decided I had to write down the experiences of this extraordinary day before I went to bed. I was still high on the adrenaline that had pumped through my veins for most of the day. I had never been in such a dangerous place before, a hostile land to everything I believe, yet, I had never felt such peace and safety either! As I wrote, I remembered the writings of Paul about his travels through central Turkey in the first century. For him it was Antioch, Iconium, and Lystra. For me it was Phulabani, Sadingia, and Baligurha: these were the main towns we passed through on our way out of central Orissa. Each town was full of Hindu revelers, light displays honoring a god or two, many crowds of potential enemies, people hostile to Christians and Christianity. My companions believed the danger to be very real; they knew it through persecution experiences of their own. Our greatest threat on our trip was the bottleneck of Baligurha. This was the only way in and out of the region because of the massive forest that surrounded this crossroad city. We had passed through this dangerous place around noon when most of its citizens were off the streets and out of sight. Our trip back would take us through town at dark with the streets filled with people celebrating the holiday. One wrong glance or a recognition of Joy, and we would be in trouble, but, as the Lord so often did and still does,

He blinded the eyes of possible militants, and we were never spotted. We passed through Phulabani unnoticed; we drove through Sadingia surrounded by scores of people and animals unrecognized, and by the time we got to Baligurha, the police had blocked off the main street through the city because of the festival and the detour we took was through dark side streets where we saw few people. They were all on the main thoroughfare partying, totally ignorant of the Christian pastors passing through their town.

Dwight L. Moody was a great evangelist, but little known as a good devotional writer. Over the years I have found a number of books he wrote, and one of my favorite is a small work called *Thoughts for the Quiet Hour*. In that book he quotes a G. Bowen:

"All the afflictions of the righteous open out into something glorious. The prisoner is not merely delivered, but finds an angel waiting for him at the door. And with every deliverance comes a specific blessing. One angel is named faith; another, love; another, joy; another, longsuffering; another, meekness; another, temperance; another, peace. Each of these graces says, 'We came out of great tribulation.'"

I know it is easy to write of such deliverance far from the battlefield, and when you travel through a battlefield as I did on October 24 without any conflict, any affliction, any persecution at all, I can write of deliverance!

One only has to go back to the illustrations of Paul used in our key verse above to know that deliverance isn't just deliverance out of actually persecution, but deliverance from potential persecution as well! The greatest deliverance of all is the deliverance from never having to face persecutions or afflictions. What of Antioch? Read carefully Acts 13:14-50 and note that this is not Antioch of Syria but Antioch of Pisidia. What of Iconium? Read carefully Acts 14:1-5. What of Lystra? Read carefully Acts 14:6-20. These were three cities on Paul's first missionary tour, and at the height of the persecution, Paul was stoned and left for dead (Acts 14:19). What deliverance! Perhaps, the best every recorded, yet on more occasions than this, Paul was taken out of the way, delivered not through death, but through departure, getting out of the way. Such was our deliverance that autumn day in October as we traveled through central Orissa.

We should never forget that no matter how hopeless the situation, how grave the circumstance or dangerous the place, we serve the God of deliverance. Deliverance out of and deliverance from are both deliverances. How many accidents have you had? How many accidents could you have been involved in if God hadn't intervened?

Last night was the mid-week prayer meeting of the Emmanuel Baptist Church where I pastor. Besides sharing prayer requests, we also share answers to prayer. That is one of the most thrilling aspects of prayer for me. One of the faithful prayer warriors of Emmanuel is a bus driver named Joe Grover. Rarely does Joe miss the prayer meeting and even rarer is the prayer meeting that he doesn't pray this prayer, "Lord, as I drive the bus keep me alert so I can keep the kids safe!" How many miles has Joe driven the school bus for Gouldsboro? I know not. He has only had one accident, a sliding off the road on a snow day! We praised the Lord that day for safety and no harm coming to Joe's kids, but we also praise the Lord weekly for the deliverances of the days when nothing happened, could have happened, but didn't happen because of God's gracious deliverance. Such was my day as I travelled in and out of central Orissa, a deliverance from not having to experience persecution and affliction instead deliverance out of persecution.

I might never have an experience in persecution like Pastor Noha Digal, or Joy Thomas, or Pastor John Naick, but that doesn't mean I have never been delivered! I have never had cancer like my wife, and certainly her deliverance from the dreaded disease was a wonderful deliverance, but I will praise my Lord for His deliverance from never having to even experience cancer for myself. As I tell people, when a loved one is not cured but instead dies after complications from some form of affliction, they were still delivered. Sometimes God delivers people by taking them home to heaven. During the persecution of 2008, there were plenty of people delivered by this form of deliverance, but there were even more people delivered through persecution, and, yes, there were some who didn't have to face physical persecution at all, but they were still delivered. One of the greatest lessons I learned on my trek into and out of Phulabani was the ways in which God delivers his saints from all things. Just because we have never faced the angry crowd that has come to burn our church or kill our pastor doesn't mean we have never been delivered. I have come to believe that every day of my life my Lord probably delivers me from something. It is about time we start thanking Him for His deliverance, seen and unseen, experienced and not experienced!

49

PASTOR LOVE AND HIS PREACHER BOYS

Titus 1:5 "FOR THIS CAUSE I LEFT THEE in Crete, that thou shouldest set in order the things that are wanting, AND ORDAIN ELDERS IN EVERY CITY, as I have appointed thee."

My fourth day in Orissa began earlier than expected. The adrenaline and excitement from the day before had worn off, and I woke very tired. After a thrilling but exhausting day traveling into the district of Phulabani, we were unexpectedly kicked out of our room before seven the next morning. Unbeknown to us, there was a policy at the JK Hotel that a guest could only stay in his room for twenty-four hours. Because we had registered at 7 A.M. on Wednesday, we had to be out at 7 A.M. on Thursday or pay for an extra day. We were leaving by train for Bhubaneshwar that evening, so an extra day wasn't necessary and only meant wasting scarce mission funds. Our first meeting of the day wasn't scheduled until 9:30, so what to do? These are the notes I put into my journal on the twenty-ninth day of my Indian trip.

"7:03 A.M. Sitting in the lobby of the JK Hotel by an ugly Hindu god starting my fourth day in Orissa! We have been kicked out of our room, and I am now waiting Jara's arrival to take me to the first meeting of seven meetings planned for the day. Before me is a huge picture window looking out of a second-story lobby onto the primitive village of Kesinga. Before my eyes are rows of dilapidated houses along a railroad track. I hear the whistle of a passing train. I get up from my comfortable couch to watch a long coal train slowly pass through town. I can see the Hindu temple on the other side of the track getting ready for another day of worshippers. I wish I could make a visit myself, but it is off-limits to me. Joy's rule. I am restricted to what I can see through the window. The boys seem on edge again today, despite the fact that yesterday was flawless in its execution, without incident. We are out of Phulabani, but according to Joy and Shibu, Kalahandi can be just as dangerous and difficult. Joy has just told me that Pastor Love has moved my meeting with the Kalahandi pastors up to eight o'clock."

The Orissa Outreach Mission is divided into three parts. Joy Thomas leads the overall ministry, but he has a key man in each of the three districts of Orissa now under evangelism: Pastor John in Puri District, Pastor Noha in Phulabani District, and Pastor Love in Kalahandi District. Each section of the work has a key town that is the hub of the wheel to the reaching of the surrounding towns: Pastor Noha in Dangul, Pastor John in Bhubaneshwar, and Pastor Love in Kesinga. Wednesday was my day visiting the seven churches of Phulabani; Thursday would be my day for visiting the eleven churches of Kalahandi, and on Friday I would visit the three churches in Puri. The object of my visit was to first meet the pastors and encourage them, and, if possible, have services with their congregations. My time in Kalahandi would be by far the most productive in this plan, and it all started with a mid-morning meeting with eight of the pastors in the Kalahandi District of Orissa.

Right on time, Jara pulled up to the JK Hotel with his swastika-covered car. The flowers that created the swastika were a bit faded and the car was a bit dirty from our trip inland, but his bright smile and hospitable nature were still there. We piled into J R's taxi with all of our belongings. Our day would be spent in and out of that car until Jara dropped us off at the train station in Bhawanipatna, twenty-five miles south of Kesinga. Our first stop was a small house on the outskirts of Kesinga where Pastor Love sometimes met with the pastors and a place Joy sometimes stayed when he was in town.

All eleven churches in the Kalahandi District were house churches, and the pastors of all those churches were lay-pastors. Only Pastor Love had any kind of formal pastoral training. Because of this, Pastor Love and Joy Thomas spent a lot of their time training these young men in the ways of pastoring. That morning, my purpose was to share something with them that might help them in performing their calling. One of the great needs and desires of men like Raju Sagar of KBBC and Joy Thomas of Orissa Outreach and Shibu Simon of the IGBC is the starting of a Bible Institute in Orissa itself. Perhaps, it could be an extension of KBBC or an independent work that can help train these young pastors.

There to greet us when we arrived were seven very young men. I was surprised by how young they looked, yet their enthusiasm was exceptional. They were already singing when I walked through the low-hanging door. The room was barely large enough to hold all eleven of us. I sat in one of only three chairs. After a period of singing and scripture reading, I was introduced and delivered a message I called "True Evangelism". At the heart of the lesson was the need to get away from emotional evangelism and superficial evangelism and get back to Biblical evangelism based on the calling work of the Father (John 6:37), the convicting work of the Spirit (John 16:7-8), and the converting work of the Son (John 14:6). We need to be about our part of the work of an evangelist (II Timothy 4:5) and that being the preaching of the Gospel (Mark 16:15), and leaving the results up to God (Acts 4:27). I went on to give them this:

1. THE FALSE VIEW OF MAN CONCERNING EVANGELISM - Ephesians 4:8. Evangelism has very little to do with us and mostly to do with God. The false view is that it is all our responsibility to evangelize. We are often found trying to do the Spirit's job by our emotional appeals, and we are often found trying to do the Father's job by calling people, but only "The Lord knoweth them that are His." (II Timothy 2:19) Do your part and get out of the way and let God do His part!

2. THE FALSE VIEW OF THE METHODS OF EVANGELISM - Romans 10:14-17. Man has developed crusades, rallies, revivals, and special meetings. Man's methods of salvation include raising your hand, walking an aisle, and signing a card. All these methods are outward expressions of what might include salvation, but they are not salvation. Confession does not provide a reason for salvation, but a reality of salvation. Once again share the Word and get out of God's way!

3. THE FALSE VIEW OF THE MESSAGE AND EVANGELISM - I Corinthians 1:18. Only the Spirit can convict when the message of Christ is shared (John 21:31). It is by the foolishness of preaching that some will be saved, but that preaching must be the Gospel (I Corinthians 15:3-4). It has become our message, the popular evangelist's message. We must determine like Paul, "For I determined not to know anything among you, SAVE JESUS CHRIST, AND HIM CRUCIFIED." (I Corinthians 2:2) Give the Word and let God save His children!

I spent a wonderful hour and a half with these young preacher boys, and afterwards I had the honor and privilege to visit six of their works and meet their congregations!

50

NANA THE DOORKEEPER

I Corinthians 12:22 "Nay, much more those members of the body, WHICH SEEM TO BE THE MORE FEEBLE, ARE NECESSARY."

WE LEFT THE PASTOR'S sanctuary in Kesinga for our first church service of the day at Ghatpada, a small village about five miles west of Kesinga. A young pastor named Sisira had invited us to his house church for a 9:30 A.M. meeting. Leaving Kesinga, we once again saw only the yellowing fields of rice and numerous flocks of animals as we travelled on the road to Titiagarh. The path into the hamlet of Ghatpada was a dusty lane filled with potholes. The village itself contained about twenty-five small mud huts with straw roofs. The village was in even poorer shape than Kesinga and that is saying a lot. Yet what greeted me was one of the highlights of my day surveying the churches of Kalahandi and one of the great joys of my entire India trip. Definitely worthy of a chapter!

In 2003, long before I thought of India, I wrote a book I entitled *Small Things* based on Zechariah's classic question: *"For who hath despised the day of small things?"* (Zechariah 4:10) I had been fascinated and fixed on this topic for years. Over the years, I had collected numerous examples of small things recorded in the Bible. I put the book together around five major divisions: *small people* - Daniel 11:23, *small projects* - Numbers 16:9, *small places* - Numbers 32:41, *small props* - Exodus 16:14, and *small precepts* - Proverbs 24:10. In all I wrote one hundred fifty-seven devotionals on the topic and thirty-one of them were dedicated to small people. Little did I know that one of my best encounters with small people would happen in a little village in Orissa!

Years before I wrote my book and years before I meet Nana, I found this saying:

"Even today God is looking for little people with little talents, not big shots with big plans!"

About the same time I found this poem by Orson R. Palmer written in 1912:

> "One stitch dropped as the weaver drove his nimble shuttle to and fro,
> In and out, beneath, above, till the pattern seemed to bud and grow.
> As if the fairies had helping been;
> One small stitch, which could scarce be seen,
> But the one stitch dropped pulled the next stitch out,
> And a weak place grew in the fabric stout:
> And the perfect pattern was marred for aye
> By the one small stitch that was dropped that day.
> One small life in God's great plan, how futile it seems as the ages roll.
> Do what it may, or strive how it can to alter the sweep of the infinite whole!
> A single stitch in an infinite web
> A drop in the ocean's flow and ebb!
> But the pattern is rent where the stitch is lost,
> Or marred where the tangled threads have crossed,
> And each life that fails of its true intent,
> Mars the perfect plan that the Master meant."

I was also motivated to write this book because of this true story I once read:

An elderly widow was restricted in what she could do, but was eager to serve the Lord despite her shortcomings. After praying much about her situation, she decided that the only thing she could do was to play the piano, but who would come to her home seeing she was so isolated. Praying more about her dilemma, she finally determined to place a small ad in her local newspaper, *The Oakland Tribune*. The tiny ad read: "Pianist will play hymns by phone daily for those who are sick and despondent. The service is free!" The little notice included the number to dial. Soon people began to call, and the widow would say, "What hymn would you like to hear?" Within a few weeks the shut-in saint had played hundreds of songs for depressed and lonely individuals. Often they would pour out their heart and the little widow was able to help and encourage them with Scripture. After a few months, the widow concluded that her simple service over the phone line was "the most rewarding thing I ever did in my life!"

Have you ever asked yourself, what can a child do for the Lord? In the life of Samuel and Nana, we have at least one answer to the question, door keeping. As I walked up to a fenced in section of Ghatpada that contained the home of Pastor Sisira, there to greet me at the gate was one of the cutest little girl of five or six I have ever seen. Her smile and outstretched hand drew me to her immediately, and all I could think, "Another Samuel!" When it says that the child Samuel ministered unto the Lord before Eli, (I Samuel 3:1) we know from verse fifteen of that same chapter that Samuel opened the doors of the house of the Lord, just like Nana. A little lad and a little lady doing a little job, but an important job. I am thankful that as a child I was encouraged to work in the Church of God. I, like Samuel, might have been ministering before Pastor Clark, my childhood pastor, and Nana might be ministering before Pastor Sisira, but ultimately we all minister unto the Lord! Whether helping the pastor read the Scripture in an evening service or helping the pastor take the offering during a Sunday service or greeting a visiting American in a morning service, a child can work for the Lord even if it is as simple as opening the gate to the courtyard to the house church at Ghatpada!

Door keeping would eventually become a well-respected occupation in the service of the Temple of God (I Chronicles 15:23-24), and the Psalmist would write, "For a day in thy courts is better than a thousand, I had rather be a doorkeeper in the house of my God, than to dwell in the tents of wickedness." (Psalms 84:10) One day gate keeping in Ghatpada is better than a thousand days somewhere else doing who knows what. Being a doorkeeper is an honorable and noteworthy profession even for a little girl named Nana, far better than owning and dwelling in a fancy, decorative palace of wickedness. I remembered the elaborate temples in Bhubaneshwar and the countless temple greeters and, at that moment, the moment I looked into Nana's eyes, I knew I had come to the better place. The little gatekeeper of Shiloh (I Samuel 1:3) would eventually grow up to be a mighty prophet of Israel (I Samuel 3:20). It is yet to be seen what Nana will grow up to be, but she has started in the right place. Oh, that we might be doorkeepers at the house of God, whether a house church or a sanctuary church, setting the right example for the future doorkeepers.

My time with Nana and the other members of the Ghatpada House Church would last about an hour. Besides being my gatekeeper, Nana was also the one the church chose to give me a bouquet of flowers during my official greeting in the home. Two of my cherished photographs of my 2012 India trip are of Nana at the gate just before she let me into the courtyard of the Ghatpada Church and Nana with her arms filled with flowers just before she gave them to me. I shared with the congregation of about twenty a message I called "Practical Precepts for Christian Living" taken from Colossians 4:2-6. As I preached, I thought to myself that Nana was the perfect example of the believer and a perfect demonstration of the truth behind Paul's admonishment printed at the head of this chapter. How necessary are little people like Nana to the Church? They are not only necessary but also vital. They are the future church! Feeble, yes, faithful certainly; little, yes, largely important, of course; small, yes, but needed and necessary. Amen.

51

SIX HOUSE CHURCHES IN EIGHT HOURS

> Philemon 2 "And to our beloved Apphia, and Archippus our fellowsoldier, AND TO THE CHURCH IN THY HOUSE."

MY ONE FULL DAY in the district of Kalahandi was spent traveling sixty miles to visit the house churches overseen by Pastor Love. Even though I met the pastors at the pastors' meeting, I was not able to visit the house churches of Simanchal of Mangapangr, Chitrasen of Paria, Nrupamani of Dastippada, Sujaxa of Kurluppada, and Kambupani of Titamana. Early in the morning, we also took time to visit Pastor Love's home, the church sanctuary of the Kesinga Baptist Church, to meet his lovely wife. I took from the expression on her face our visit was unexpected. Oh, how we pastors take the dear ones the Good Lord gives us for granted at times, especially in the category of surprised guests. Whether in America or India, a pastor's wife loves a little advance warning when a special visitor is going to be brought into their home, even if it is the church! We also made a quick stop to see Pastor Paul, a young pastor I had met earlier that morning in Kesinga, in the village of Kantesir along with his wife and new baby girl. Again, this was just a social call, no service, but what I remember best about this visit was the pride of the pastor and his wife as they showed me around their new home, the church sanctuary of the Kantesir Baptist Church. You could see the newness of the structure, but what a structure! The roof was made of woven flax, the walls of red mud, and the floor and foundation of animal dung. My companions told me that this was the nicest dwelling in the village, and that animal dung was a wonderful building material when prepared correctly. I thought the home would smell and be dirty, but I found it just the opposite. It was clean and refreshing. I could smell no odor at all in the windowless sanctuary. Also according to my traveling companions, the structure was made to keep it cool in the oppressive heat of summer, but warm in the colder seasons. It was easily cleaned and very durable. I have been to the impressive National Cathedral in Washington DC and ornate churches and chapels too numerous to write about, but the church house at Kantesir might just be the best house of worship I have ever step foot in for its simplicity and spirituality. I hated to leave. I felt the Spirit so strongly there!

The bulk of the rest of our day in Kalahandi was filled with four house church services. I have already shared with you the blessings I received while visiting with the people of the Ghatpada Baptist Church and Sisira their pastor and Nana their wonderful little gatekeeper and official greeter. Our second house church service was in the village of Tahansir where Pastor Labanik labors for the Lord. I never quite figured out whether or not it was his home we gathered in or one of the homes of one of his parishioners. What I remembered best about the small concrete structure was all the pictures and drawings of angels on the walls. I never got the significance of the angels because it was a quick stop. We had a few songs and scripture reading followed by a prayer then I shared a message on "What Christ's Strength Gives" taken from Philippians 4:1–7. Our time with these dear folks was so short that many other questions remained unasked and unanswered. Our service at Tahansir finished our morning schedule where we had three services. One service was with the pastors and their two house churches. I also visited two of the pastors in their homes. It was time to head south to have meetings in two other house churches before catching the night train back to Bhubaneswar.

After traveling about ten miles over a now very familiar country road, we took a right turn off the highway for a narrow dusty country lane into the village of Emtha. This now familiar country road is the main highway between the railhead in Titiagarh, where we left the train two days before and the major railhead at Bhawanipatna, where we would catch the night train south and then northeast along the ocean-side of Orissa to Bhubaneswar. I thought the other towns I had already visited were poor, but they looked like wealthy communities compared to this desolate hamlet. We were heading for the home of Pastor Pradeep's parents. I had also met this young man in the pastors' meeting that morning. The village was surrounded by a stick fence outlining the dozen or more huts. By any standard, the people were dirt poor. They seemed to be herdsmen by trade, for we saw goats and other domesticated animals everywhere. I did notice a few fields of rice, but the region didn't seem to be as well-watered as other regions I had been through. I was also struck by how short the door into the simple dwelling was. I am nearly six feet tall and Joy Thomas barely five feet tall, but he had to duck! We entered a primitive living room with an open fire kitchen to our right. Already gathered in the house were about two dozen people, a few cats, some chickens, and I think I saw a dog. I was greeted warmly by the pastor's father. I could tell by the conversation between Shibu, translated by Pastor Love that the father was extremely proud of his younger son and the church he had begun. This was the only Gospel outreach in the entire area. Once again a few songs, a few prayers, and then I preached on "Saintly Standards for Saints" taken from Colossians 3:1–15. The time went quickly, but the afternoon was also slipping by. We still had a few miles to travel for our last meeting of the day. We did take a few pictures together outside the home, and what sticks with me is the fact that Shibu and I were taller than the roof line. They were simple folks surviving on simple things, but with a great faith in their Lord.

By the middle of the afternoon, we were in Bhawanipatna for our last meeting at the home of Pastor Subash. Compared to the other towns I had been to in western Orissa, this was a city of 300,000 in population. We gathered in the city home of Subash's parents. I learned they were well to do by Orissa standards. They owned an eleven-acre rice farm about fifteen miles outside of town where they also had a home. They had moved into town so their son could start a church. There were nearly twenty people who gathered to hear me speak on "The Christian's Ability to Learn" taken from Philippians 4:8-12. The fellowship was sweet, but the time too short. We said our goodbyes, probably the last until eternity, but I will never forget the day I spent with the house churches of the Kalahandi. Each congregation was small, but their enthusiasm was inspiring. Each group was poor, but rich in the things that really matter. Each sanctuary was primitive by Western standards, but they had everything and more of what counts. They, like the Psalmist, were taught to come into each meeting with God with singing (Psalms 100:2). They, like Paul, were taught to always give attendance to reading (I Timothy 4:13). They, like the Hebrew writer, were taught not to forsake the assembling of themselves together (Hebrews 10:25) even when it was in the middle of the morning or the middle of the afternoon when an unexpected visiting pastor from Maine showed up. I have voiced my opinion on the virtues of house churches before, but my eight hours with six of them and meeting the pastors of five more only verified what I already believed. I think when we get to heaven there will be no more churches, chapels, cathedrals, or temples (Revelation 21:22). I think our worship gatherings will be more like what I experienced in Kalahandi that Thursday in October 2012.

52

SUNSET AND SUNRISE IN ORISSA

> Psalms 50:1 "The mighty God, even the Lord, hath spoken, and called the earth FROM THE RISING OF THE SUN UNTO THE GOING DOWN THEREOF."

BY THE TIME OUR last meeting in Kalahandi was over, the shadows were lengthening as the sun began to set on another day in Orissa. One of the pleasures I have enjoyed in India are the sunsets and sunrises, the memorable interludes of the day. Little did I know that the signature event of my entire trip to Orissa, and maybe India itself, would happen in Bhawanipatna before sunset!

After leaving Pastor Subash's parents' home, we headed into town for a bite to eat before heading off to the train station outside of town. We were scheduled to leave before seven, but before that I would relish again those hushed hours around sunset that bring such a stillness and splendor to the soul. These are the moments in which time seems to stop replaced by the wonder of the Hand of God on nature and on the life of a young Hindu man named Jara. This is especially true when that sunset takes place over a pagan city dedicated to the worship of countless gods and goddesses.

The city was busy, but we discovered that the local restaurants were not quite ready for supper. People eat late in Bhawanipatna it seems, so the first two places we tried hadn't even fired up the stoves for cooking. It was after stopping at one of those unprepared restaurants that something quite extraordinary was pointed out to me. I couldn't believe that I hadn't noticed it on my own, but I hadn't. Still looking around at the strange sights of Bhawanipatna and the beautiful sunset that was forming over the hills west of town, I had failed to recognize a major change in the vehicle we were riding in. Remember, nearly forty-eight hours before, Jara had picked us up in Kesinga with a car covered in Hindu symbols, including a huge swastika outlined by orange flowers on the hood of the Landrover. He had been to the local Hindu temple for a blessing before he took the Christians on their tour of central and western Orissa. For all that time, Jara had faithfully carted us from service to service. He had either attended the meetings or stayed by the car. I still remember noticing that with each service he came a bit closer to what we were doing. I was surprised at Emtha that he actually came inside and sat with us as we sang and worshiped the True and Living God. We had no way of knowing something was happening in the heart of this superstitious young man! It was Shibu who first asked me, "Have you noticed the front of the car lately?" As I looked back on the front of the Landrover, I couldn't believe my eyes. Sometime during the day, Jara had changed the arrangement of the flowers from the shape of a swastika to the shape of a CROSS! Yes, from a symbol of Hinduism to the symbol of Christianity.

As the western sky turned from blue to gold, I rejoiced in what the testimony of two days had done to Jara. The swastika was something we never debated or argued or demanded its removal. I learned from Joy that Jara had made the decision to change the symbol without any challenge from any of my companions. Joy told me that he would follow up on this declaration to see just what Jara meant by it. For me, it was a fitting sunset on a memorable two days with a follower of Hinduism. From a third-story restaurant window, I watched the last of the sun's light cast the surrounding area in dark silhouettes. Yet, all I could see was the CROSS on the front of Jara's car. How easily the lines of a swastika could be altered into the pattern of my Faith. Was Jara telling us that he heard us as we proclaimed the Gospel of Jesus from Dangul to Emtha? After the brittle blackness of Hinduism had the rays of the SON cast a shadow upon this single soul? What affect did it have? The long slender fingers of the last rays of this day had reached the center of Bhawanipatna, but the finger of God's grace was reaching further afar into the mind of a taxi driver from Kesinga. It seemed to me the entire ridgeline west of the city was wrapped in a golden glow as my friends eat their supper. All I could think about was the young man eating with Pastor Subash by the fish tank. I glanced over at him a couple of times and prayed a short request to my heavenly Father for his soul. As with the truth that no two sunsets are the same, neither are two souls. Each bears a beauty unique in itself. Each comes with freshness, a newness that carries with it a capacity for untold adventure and reward. What would the dawning of Jara's simple act result in? As I write this chapter, I have heard nothing from Joy about Jara, but I pray for his soul with the hope that the simple act of rearranging of a pattern of flowers was the sunrise of a faith in the Lord Jesus Christ.

By 6:45 P.M. we were on the express train for Bhubaneswar. We paid Jara 6150 rupees or $125 for the three hundred twenty-five miles and the two days he drove us around. Our night travels would cover three hundred ninety-one miles and take us nearly fourteen hours to complete, but it was my fifth sunrise in Orissa that I would remember best about my second train-ride in Orissa.

The train on which I returned to Bhubaneswar was newer and, to my pleasant surprise, the bed was bigger. It was a bit longer and wider, so I had a wonderful night's rest. I got up around six to go to the bathroom, and as I returned to the sleeper car, I stopped for a moment to look out the side-door window. A brilliant sun was just coming up over the horizon at the same time the train was crawling alongside a body of water. I thought at first I was getting my first look at the Bay of Bengal, the sea between eastern India and Bangladesh. It wasn't until later I learned that we were actually traveling by Orissa's largest lake, Chilika. I could make out fishing boats and fishing nets galore, but it was the sunrise over the water that drew me back to the wonderful truth that is a sunrise, the unfolding of a new day, a fresh page, a new scroll, on my last full day in Orissa.

Gradually as the sun moved up, I saw the grandeur that makes a sunrise so special. Like with a sunset, there are no two alike. I would well remember my Thursday in Orissa, but what of my Friday? I wondered and my mind wandered as the warmth of that sun set my heart dreaming of what the day would hold. Morning tide and evening tide have such similarities when it comes to mediation. As I reflected on the afterglow of Thursday and the hope and expectation of Jara's simple act of change, I was relishing in the anticipation of what would happen when I had a chance to preach at the churches of Bhubaneswar. I still don't understand how the skeptics, atheists, and agnostics watch sunrises and sunsets, the splendor of their beauty, the glory and intensity of their colors, and not understand that they are the handiwork of the Divine Designer. No wonder the world of such people is so black; no wonder they love darkness more than light. (John 3:19-20)

As for me, a Child of God, a sunrise and a sunset is filled with amazing possibilities. What will happen in the life of a young Hindu after coming face to face with the reality of one God, and what will happen in Bhubaneswar today? As the train rattled on toward an early morning arrival in Orissa's capital, I enjoyed another glorious sunrise, a special gift from my Father made extra special because of where I was, who I was with, and what I would be doing on this day. I had no way of knowing that a long offered up prayer would be answered and that two names would be added to the Lamb's Book. (Revelation 21:27)

53

THREE FISHER-BOYS AT ATRI STREAM

John 21:3 "Simon Peter saith unto them, I GO A FISHING...."

I HAVE BEEN AN avid fisherman for most of my life, and a fisher-of-men for over half my life. I wasn't long into the ministry before the two began to merge into one area: the theology of why the Lord Jesus first called fishermen to be His apostles. I have come to believe that at least seven of the first twelve apostles were fishermen by occupation (John 21:2). Over the years I have recognized the practical application between fishing for fish and fishing for men. In 2001, I compiled a series of one hundred fifty devotionals that I called "Angling Admonitions". The devotionals talked about what I had learned between my hobby of fishing and the ministry of soulwinning. In the prelude to that book I wrote the following in my very first admonition:

I was on a trout fishing day trip with my father, Wendell E. Blackstone, his cousin Hartson Blackstone, and my cousin and his son, Bob Blackstone. We were heading for our fathers' favorite fishing hole, Beaver Brook. Our goal was the elusive Eastern Brook trout, a Maine native. Bob and I were excited because we had heard for years the legendary fish tales of the huge trout that could be caught in that Great North Wood's stream. After an hour and a half riding in Hartson's pickup, we still had a forty-five minute hike down an old winding wood's road to the secret stream. Those were the days when Beaver Brook was only accessible by daring and determination. Eventually, we arrived at the brook, but instead of waiting patiently for our fathers to catch up and instruct us how to fish and where to fish, Bob and I immediately jumped in and began wading and fishing with our chicken-coup worms. However, as soon as my dad made the bank of the brook, I heard my first angling admonition. "I hate to tell you boys, but you are standing in the middle of one of the best fishing pools in the brook!" I learned then and there that excitement and enthusiasm aren't enough to be a successful fisherman, and neither are they sufficient to be a successful fisher-of-men. As I needed my father's leading and instruction then, so, too, we need the Father's leading (John 6:37) and the Spirit conviction (John 16:8) in our fishing for the souls of men.

Ever since my first trip to India in 2006, I had been praying a secret prayer, a petition only known to my heavenly Father. The request was simple: that I would be able to fish in India. I discovered very early that I was ministering with fishers-of-men, but there wasn't a fisherman among them. Besides, most of the places I visited contained no opportunities to fish for fish. The rare occasion that did come along was quickly ignored because there was no interest whatsoever on the part of my companions. A case in point was my visit to Perumbramavu, Joy's hometown. I had been to his village during my first weekend in India. A beautiful stream literally cuts the town in two, and I learned on our walk to the quarry that is contained fish, but nobody liked to fish, including Joy. I kept my secret desire to myself, asking the Lord when I would get a chance to fish in India.

Our train arrived in Bhubaneswar at 8:30 A.M. about an hour behind schedule. There waiting at the station was our faithful driver, Moses. Within the hour, we were settling into our hotel in downtown Bhubaneswar. A nice shower and clean clothes felt great after our nearly three-day marathon, nearly a thousand miles by train and car, in and out of central and western Orissa. It was after breakfast that I learned that we had a few hours before our first church meeting. Joy wanted to take us to one of his favorite spots around Bhubaneswar. I was still hoping for the Lingaraja Temple, but I knew that wasn't going to be when we headed directly out of town on a superhighway, a toll road that runs eight hundred miles from Bhubaneswar to Chennai. We had traveled about twenty miles when we got off the paved road for a dirt road heading into the countryside. We traveled through small villages, by countless rice fields and grazing animals. My only excitement came when we crossed over a small stream, and I noticed a group of men fishing with a net and a few boys fishing with poles. I had seen net fishermen on Kerala's largest lake, and ocean fishermen on Kerala's coast, but these were the first Indians I had seen fishing like I like to fish. I pointed them out, but got no response from my companions.

After traveling thirty-one miles that took us well over an hour and a half, we finally stopped in front of a concrete structure that led to what appeared to be an empty plaza. I was then informed that we had arrived at Orissa's only hot springs. Hot springs? I must admit for one of the few times in India I was disappointed, actually upset, we had wasted a morning to see hot water bubbling up from under the ground. I had been too hot springs in Israel and there was no comparison. Oh, there were a few Buddhist priests there to bless us, but I had enough of that at Dhaul. I must admit as we walked around the area, I actually got angry, no outwardly, but inwardly. I knew my time in Orissa was short, and I was wasting the few precious hours I had left here? It is in such times we need to recognize that though Joy Thomas was my earthly guide, it is the heavenly Father that orders our steps (Psalms 37:23). Little did I know just why God had directed Joy to bring me out into a no-man's land to visit a hot spring!

We lingered maybe fifteen minutes at the hot springs before getting back into Moses' boss's car and heading back for Bhubaneswar. I will admit the spring water in Orissa was hotter than the springs in Israel. On the way, we passed the stream where the men were fishing, but no one remained. I felt a bit disappointed again because I was determined to have Moses stop and see what the men were catching, but we traveled on. However, we hadn't traveled another hundred feet when I noticed to my right three small boys fishing under a new bridge being put in on the road we were traveling. It was then that a still small voice spoke to me in accent clear, "You wanted to fish in India? Here is your chance!" I shouted for Moses to stop the car. My companions were surprised by my outburst, and Moses drove another one hundred yards before realizing I was serious. Joy and Shibu protested, but as the car stopped, I jumped out and started walking back to where the three lads were fishing. The shock eventually wore off my companions, and Moses was quickly on my heels, to protect the crazy American from himself! By the time Moses caught up with me, I had managed by hand-signals and a bribe of ten rupees to persuade one of the boys to lend me his rod, a four foot bamboo twig with a small white cord tied to the end. A tiny hook was attached to the line, and a bit of bait, which looked like gum, on the tip of the hook. The fishing hole was barely ten feet across, a small eddy created by the current flowing around a piling of the new bridge. The fish the lads were catching looked like small whitefish, the biggest maybe three inches. I have caught Atlantic Salmon forty-six inches long, but I can tell you in all honesty that one of the best times fishing I have ever had was the fifteen minutes I shared with those three little boys (Peter, James, and John-my names for them) at Atri Stream outside of Bhubaneswar, Orissa.

I caught nothing, no time to get the hang of hooking the small fish. I did get a few bites, but catching fish isn't what fishing is all about. The same with fishing for men!

54

A PERSECUTED LAND

Matthew 23:34 "Wherefore, behold, I send unto you prophets and wise men . . . and some of them ye scourge in your synagogues, and PERSECUTE THEM FROM CITY TO CITY."

WE GOT BACK FROM our sixty-two mile round trip mini-expedition into the hinterlands of Orissa around one in the afternoon of my last full day in state. Our remaining schedule called for a house church meeting at four at Moonda and another at six in Bhubaneswar. This gave me enough time for a much needed afternoon nap. I was getting tired, and a good rest was in order before the whirlwind of activities that would underline my last four days in India. I still had another thousand miles in country to go!

My wonderful sleep lasted about two hours. When I woke I found that I had our room to myself. Shibu and Joy had ventured off, so I finished reading a book Shibu lent me called *The Marks of the Messenger*. I made a series of notes to expand upon when I returned to my prophet's chamber in Kerala. Shortly after finishing reading, the boys returned with some bad news. Our first service of the afternoon was being cancelled because of a death in the congregation at the Moonda Baptist Church. As was still the custom and tradition of these mountain people turned city dwellers, the individual was being prepared as we spoke by Pastor Dasrath's people for transport back to the Phulbani for burial. There was no time for a gathering, so my last chance to meet the persecuted church of Phulbani that had moved to Bhubaneswar would be at Pastor John's house church early that evening. I had met Pastor Dasrath in Andrah Pardesh in 2010 and was looking forward to reconnecting. I knew his flock had suffered great loses in the 2008 persecution, and I wanted to hear their stories and see how they had recovered. Our cancelled meeting allowed Joy Thomas to fill me in on the persecuted land of Orissa.

Orissa's western border is the thick forest hills of the Eastern Ghats Mountains, the boundary between the States of Orissa and Chhattisgarh. On the eastern side of Orissa is the Bay of Bengal, three hundred eleven miles of coastline. To the north of Orissa are the States of Jharkhand and

West Bengal and to the south the State of Andrah Pardesh. Within the land mass of over sixty thousand square miles is a population of over thirty-five million. To put this in perspective, Kerala has half the landmass but the same population!

Joy gave me this example of what the Christians of Orissa are up against. In the capital of Bhubaneswar alone there are four hundred Hindu temples and the ruins of seven thousand more scattered around the city limits, earning it the name of "the city of temples". Buddhism began to wane in Orissa in the seventh century when a revival of Hinduism began. It remains today the strongest religion in Orissa and is very militant. Religious tolerance that has been attained in most of the States of India is still lacking in Orissa. The 2008 persecution was an embarrassment to the Orissa government, but the rural nature of the state has allowed pockets of hatred and anger to remain. Assault, murder, and burnings still happen, but not at the same intensity as in 2008. Those who monitor such activities still list Orissa as a persecuted land.

As Joy talked about the challenges for the Christian that still linger in Orissa, I was reminded of a book I had read during my first trip to India in 2006 called *Burnt Alive* by Vishel Mangalwadi. This book tells the story of the martyrdom of the Stain boys in 1999 in the State of Orissa. On January 23, 1999, Graham Stain, a native of Australia whose name caught my eye because of my mission's trip to that land in 1972, was burnt alive with his two sons, Timothy and Philip, by militant Hindus. I was actually in India on the seventh anniversary of that tragic event in Indian Church history: Gladys Stain and her daughter Esther, who were not with the boys at the time of the attack, still minister in Orissa today. Like Elizabeth Elliot and Rachael Saint before them, Gladys and Esther Stain are wonderful examples of why the militant Hindus will never win and why they will never drive Christianity from their shores. Persecution has only made the Church stronger and persecution has only made the Christians more determined to share the Gospel with the unsaved of Orissa.

As Jesus prophesied, from city to city, from Phulbani to Bhubaneswar, the persecution will continue. How long Orissa will be a land of persecution only God knows. Perhaps, until He returns? As Joy talked about the persecuted churches he leads, it became very clear to me that unlike the Churches of Orissa, the Churches of America are not ready for such persecution, but why? Many years ago, after a ten-year study of the Psalms, I came to the conclusion that one of the major subjects taught in that classic collection is persecution. The sweet psalmist of

Israel (II Samuel 23:1) reveals many faces. Here are the broad categories I discovered:

1. The Psalmist in the pulpit preaching - Psalms 40:9
2. The Psalmist in prayer petitioning - Psalms 102:1
3. The Psalmist in prophecy prophesying - Psalms 22:1
4. The Psalmist in praise proclaiming - Psalms 146:1
5. The Psalmist in the pits pleading - Psalms 28:1
6. The Psalmist in peril praying - Psalms 59:1
7. The Psalmist in the past pondering - Psalm 78
8. The Psalmist in peace protected - Psalms 4:8
9. The Psalmist in persecution persecuted

I believe at least twenty of the one hundred fifty psalms deal with persecution. Note that over thirteen percent of the time, the Psalmist writes about persecution starting with the seventh psalm. It became an eye-opener to me that our Lord, far in advance, has prepared us to face persecution. Whether or not we have faced it or will face it doesn't mean that God has left us unprepared. One of my conclusions, after meeting the persecuted church in Orissa and seeing how they have marvelously handled persecution, is that their knowledge of the Word sustained them. They know the songs of persecution, and they know the meaning of Annie Johnson Flint wonderful poem "What God Hath Promised".

> God hath not promised skies always blue,
> Flower-strewn pathways, all our lives through;
> God hath not promised sun without rain,
> Joy without sorrow, peace without pain;
> But God hath promised, strength for the day,
> Rest for the labor, light for the way;
> Grace for the trials, help from above,
> Unfailing sympathy, undying love!

55

HAPPY IN PERSECUTION

Matthew 5:11 "BLESSED ARE YE, WHEN MEN SHALL . . . PERSECUTE YOU . . . FOR MY SAKE."

The Devil seemed to have won the first round that last afternoon in Bhubaneswar with the death of the saint from the Moonda Church that cancelled my meeting with Pastor Dasrath, who is Pastor Love from Kesinga's brother, and his flock. Pastor Dasrath and many of his people had moved out of Phulbani during the 2008 persecution but found fertile ground among the Moonda people that had left their tribal homelands in the mountains of northern Orissa for a better life in the sprawling suburbs of Bhubaneswar. Despite the setback, I knew from my theology the only power the Devil had over death is the fear of it (Hebrews 2:14-15). These people had faced fear on numerous occasions, and the death of a saint wasn't something to fear, dread, or be sad about. Actually the Biblical word is blessed (Revelation 14:13), the same word that is connected with persecution!

Bhubaneswar Baptist is the ministry of Pastor John Naick. It is the twentieth ministry I had either visited or met the pastor of in my tour of Orissa. I still have in my possession the first e-mail I ever received from Shibu Simon with Pastor Naick's name on it. As a matter of fact, the topic of the e-mail was "Please Pray for John Naick". Shibu wrote this:

"Some of you remember me mentioning about a retired policeman who is working as an evangelist in Orissa. With his dedication, he has been able to reach a lot of villagers with the Gospel of Christ. Since he is a retired policeman, he can get to places and people that others cannot. In the last wave of attacks, he has lost his home with all his earthly possessions. On top of this, he has three single daughters from the ages of twenty-five to thirty. He has tried his very best to find suitable husbands for them but has not been able to. This adds extra burden to the Indian parents. Yesterday morning his wife died of a heart attack. Due to the stress related with the burning and all, we think. Please pray for this family as they are going through a very difficult time. I have talked with the third daughter Pushpalatha this morning who I know is a strong believer and now doubts about God and thinks that God has abandoned them. She said, 'What have we done against this people but bring them the good news, but look what they have done to us and God is not taking revenge upon this injustice!' Julie and I and Joy Thomas spoke to her for a long time. This family needs our prayer as do all the families in Orissa."

That was in 2008. In 2010, I got a chance to meet John face to face in Andrah Pardesh, and my first stop in Orissa was at his home in Bhubaneswar. Now it was time to join him with his congregation at the home of one of his parishioners in a slum area on the outskirts of the city.

As we drove off the street, I noticed we were in a very poor region of Bhubaneswar. Before me was a row of shacks, and that is a polite description. We were heading for the home of a bus driver, the house church of the Bhubaneswar Baptist Church. As we walked through the area, I realized I was back in the village of Emtha, but I wasn't in the country but a city. Pastor John who had arrived before us greeted me and as we talked outside I learned more about where I was. The owner of the home had built it himself in twenty days, out of mud and discarded timber. He actually owned the forty by fifty foot lot the hut rested on, a rare situation according to John. The man's job gave him an above average income, and most of the people in the church were actually better off after the persecution than before the persecution. What impressed me most was when the man of the house said through Joy, "THE PERSECUTION WAS THE BEST THING THAT HAD EVER HAPPENED TO US!"

The first thought that came to my mind was the realization that I had met someone that had actually suffered persecution and believes in Matthew 5:11. When Jesus proclaimed His great list of beatitudes, He was trying to tell us what would make us happy. The word blessed is the old King James way of saying happy. If we place this concept before our eyes in relationship to persecution, we come up with a very hard doctrine to understand and apply - happy in persecution?

One of the very first precepts Jesus tried to teach His followers was the reality of persecution. But He didn't want persecution to be something His followers dreaded or feared, but something in which they could find happiness. I have met happy Christians wherever I have traveled, but the happiest must be the saints of Orissa because of the kind of happiness they possess: happiness in persecution. As I talked to the owner of the sanctuary of the Bhubaneswar church, I sensed a joy I never witnessed before in any believer. This group of brothers and sisters in Christ had come to an understanding of Jesus' beatitude: happy are you when you are persecuted!

That must bring us to the $64,000 question. How is this possible? I have come to believe the answer revolves around two phrases found in Matthew 5:10–12: 'righteousness sake' and 'my sake'. How can man, with his human nature, be happy when he is beaten, burned-out, battered, and belittled? It is natural to be sad when you hurt, are hunted, hounded, and harassed. The feelings that plagued Pushpalatha in Shibu's e-mail were completely different when I visited their home in Bhubaneswar. I found a different daughter who was so like her father. There must be something else in the character of the Christian that turns this sadness into gladness. The early church had it (Acts 5:40-41), and the Church of Orissa has it. I found this explanation in the writings of Oswald Chambers:

"Our Lord says that His disciples are to rejoice when they are reviled, persecuted, or slandered for His sake. So many times we are told that if we suffer for conviction sake or conscience sake we have suffered painfully. Not so. We are supposed to suffer for Jesus' sake. Our whole motive in suffering is to be well-pleasing to God. The true blessedness of the saint rests in determining to make and keep God first. The disadvantage of a saint in our present world is that he must make confession of Jesus, not in secret, but glaringly in public. The tendency to be holy and say nothing about it is right from every standpoint but God's. It is the greatest need of this world. Be faithful to share the good news of Christ, even if sharing it brings ridicule."

Could I add even when it brings persecution? The reason that persecution went on in Orissa is the very reason Chamber gives: witness! The Church is not a secret organization, and when it acts on righteous living and proclaims the Gospel in Jesus' name and for His sake, persecution will be the result. Vance Havner wrote: "The trend today is to try to make the Saviour, the Sect, and the Saint popular. But such is not the Scriptural reputation they bear. When the persecuted become popular they are powerless!"

The last word goes to Pastor Naick. When I asked why the persecution was the best thing that ever happened, he replied: "*We learned to trust God!*"

56

TWO NEW NAMES IN GLORY

> Revelation 21:27 " . . . they are WRITTEN IN THE LAMB'S BOOK OF LIFE."

Since childhood I have loved C. Austin Miles church hymn, "A New Name In Glory." Since boyhood I have understood the theology behind that song (Revelation 3:5 and Philippians 4:3), a heavenly registry containing the names of every person from the beginning that has put his or her faith in the redemptive work of Christ. Since adulthood I have shared in the moments when individuals have placed their faith in Jesus and experienced with Miles the joy that comes from knowing that their names are written down in glory. I am excited each and every time I learn of a new name written in that listing, like I did on my last night in Bhubaneswar, Orissa. Before I reveal those names, sing with me the words of this grand song.

> "I was once a sinner, but I came pardon to receive from my Lord:
> This was freely given and I found that He always kept His word.
> I was humbly kneeling at the cross, fearing naught but God's angry frown.
> When the heavens opened and I saw that my name was written down.
> In the Book 'tis written 'saved by grace', O the joy that came to my soul!
> Now I am forgiven, and I know by the Blood I am made whole.
> There's a new name written down in glory, and it's mine, O yes, it's mine!
> (Mine was on June 4, 1958 at the Perham Baptist Church.)
> And the white-robed angels sing the story, 'A sinner has come home.'
> For there's a new name written down in glory, and it's mine, O yes, it's mine! With my sins forgiven I am bound for heaven, nevermore to roam."

Over thirty people were crammed into the small structure that served as the sanctuary for the Bhubaneswar Baptist Church. Because it was after six before we started the service, the only light in the small home came from a few florescent lamps. A ceiling fan hung in the middle of the largest room. I remembered I had to be careful with my hand gestures lest I hit one of the blades and my head least I walk into the blades. The two-room house contained only three chairs: one for Shibu, one for Joy, and one for me. The congregation either sat on the floor or stood. Pastor John Naick introduced us, and the singing and praying began. As I listened to the transplanted Phulabani Church rejoice in the Lord, I recalled a story I once read written by a man named Carl Windsor.

A story in the *Presbyterian Survey* points up the reality of persecution for Christ's sake that we don't often see. The writer reported he had a dream in which he was in heaven and met saints who had been there for years. A saint said, "I was a Roman Christian who lived in the days of the Apostle Paul. I was burned at the stake by Nero." "How awful," I exclaimed. "Oh, no," he replied, "I was glad to do something for Jesus because He died for me."

Then another man spoke. He came from a South Seas Island and had been converted because of the faithful missionary John Williams. When asked how he had died, the islander said, "I was beaten unconscious, then cooked, and eaten by cannibals." "How terrible," I said. "No, as a Christian I was glad to die because Jesus wore a crown of thorns and was scourged for me."

Then these saints asked me, "How did you suffer for Him, or did you sell what you had and use the money to send missionaries like John Williams to tell others about Jesus?" Just then I woke and with sorrowful eyes lying on my soft bed thinking of the money I had wasted on my own pleasures and had not shared with those truly in need!

As I listened to the joyful voices of these persecuted saints, I knew that none of them had died for their faith, even though some of their group had, and cannibals had eaten none, but I realized they had suffered, and I hadn't. It was a humbling experience to sit in that primitive dwelling with those people.

When I got to speak, I shared a message from the title of another old hymn I have sung all my life, "Is Your Name Written There?" Mary A. Kidder wrote these words and I used them to explain the way of salvation and the heavenly registry.

"Lord, I care not for riches, neither silver nor gold;
I would make sure of heaven; I would enter the fold.
In the book of Thy kingdom, with its pages so fair,
Tell me, Jesus, my Saviour, is my name written there?
Lord, my sins they are many, like the sands of the sea,
But Thy blood, O my Saviour, is sufficient for me.
For Thy promise is written, in bright letters that glow,
Though your sins be as scarlet, I will make them like snow.
Oh! That beautiful city, with its mansions of light,
With its glorified beings, in pure garments of white;
Where no evil thing cometh to despoil what is fair;
Where the angels are watching, yes, my name's written there.
Is your name written there, on the page white and fair?
In the book of Thy kingdom, is your name written there?"

I shared the doctrine and asked the question and invited any who didn't know Christ to add his or her name to the list. I left the service thinking that there had been no response.

After the meeting, it was difficult to departure for John's home for supper. The people didn't want us to go. We took a group picture in the courtyard of the bus driver's home in complete darkness. Praise the Lord for a powerful flash on my digital camera! This would be my last church service in Orissa, and I hated to leave. There is something special about being around people that have few earthly possessions, but possess huge heavenly treasures. They know something about real spiritual happiness. The car ride back to the Naick house was solemn. We arrived a little after eight and were greeted by the three Naick daughters. The oldest prepared the evening meal while the two younger daughters entertained us. We had met on my first day in Orissa, so our second meeting was more open and free. I asked the girls what they desired most, their unison reply, "To move to Kerala!" We talked of husbands; I suggested my friend Binu, and marriage and the difficulty of both in Orissa. After about half an hour, John arrived home after staying to talk to some of his flock. He had fantastic news! Following my message and Joy's invitation, two people responded to the Gospel call. Our dinner took on the atmosphere of the prodigal's first meal after returning home: " . . . and they began to be merry." (Luke 15:24) If the angels of God can rejoice "over one sinner that repenteth" (Luke 15:10), then the servants of God ought to celebrate over two!

On October 26, 2012, two new names were added to the Lamb's Book of Life: Simon Digal and Resmitha Digal. These were the only direct fruits from my days in Orissa, but this I learned: the Lord is still adding to the Orissa Church daily those that will be saved (Acts 2:47), and He is still adding to His Son's Book those names that recognize their sin and acknowledge Jesus as Saviour. My prayer is Jara will be another soul saved by grace. Can you sing, "Yes, my name's written there on the page white and fair; in the book of Thy kingdom, Yes, my name's written there?"

57

SINGING YOUR WAY THROUGH PERSECUTION

> Psalms 7 "Shiggaion of David, which HE SANG UNTO THE LORD, concerning the words of Cush the Benjamite.

WE GOT BACK TO our motel room a little after nine. An amazing five days were over. I still couldn't quiet my mind as a myriad of memories floated through my brain. A thousand miles of images flashed before my eyes, as I tried to recall the faces of the persecuted people I had visited, the collection of churches I had worshipped with, and the soul-stirring situations I had experienced in Orissa. The one truth that kept coming back to me was the rejoicing and exceeding glad saints I had met (Matthew 5:12) and how they were daily living Jesus' clear instruction of Matthew 5:44-45.

> " . . . Love your enemies, bless them that curse you, do good to them that hate you, and pray for them which despitefully use you, and *persecute you*; that ye may be the children of your Father which is in heaven . . . "

I had spent my Orissa hours with the children of God. At every turn and during every stop, I found them singing.

A number of years before Orissa, I wrote a trilogy of books. I love to write in threes! The trilogy was entitled *Trusting Your Way Through Tribulation* (a look at the different kinds of faith described in Hebrews 11), *Loving Your Way Through Life* (a look at the Biblical definition of love described in I Corinthians 13), *and Singing Your Way Through Persecution* (a look at the persecution songs in the Book of Psalms). As I mentioned in a previous chapter, I believe there are at least twenty Psalms that deal with the topic of persecution. David found himself often in a persecuted state. So what did David do? He sang his way through it. I believe the first psalm of this collection is Psalms 7. In the introduction to this chapter, I have recorded the words written about it in the King James Version of the Bible. The key phrase is he sang unto the Lord. I found the persecuted people of Orissa doing the same thing. In my book

Orissa is Burning, a work that is being translated into the Cuie language by my good friend Ragu Sagar, I have a chapter on each of the Persecution Psalms. I share with you now the themes of each of these psalms, these Psalms of Persecution.

1. HYMN - Psalms 7 - How to Handle Persecution
2. HYMN - Psalms 10 - The Persecution of the Poor
3. HYMN - Psalms 31 - From Persecution to Praise
4. HYMN - Psalms 35 - The Enemies That Persecute Us
5. HYMN - Psalms 41 - The Effects on Our Bodies during Persecution
6. HYMN - Psalms 56 - Persecution Made Personal
7. HYMN - Psalms 69 - The Persecution of Christ
8. HYMN - Psalms 70 - Help in Times of Persecution
9. HYMN - Psalms 71 - A Persecution Prayer
10. HYMN - Psalms 83 - Asaph's Persecution Psalm
11. HYMN - Psalms 94 - How Long Persecution?
12. HYMN - Psalms 109 - Petitions under Persecution
13. HYMN - Psalms 119 - The Need of the Bible in Persecution
14. HYMN - Psalms 123 - Waiting Patiently in Times of Persecution
15. HYMN - Psalms 129 - Looking Back on a Former Persecution
16. HYMN - Psalms 137 - The Babylonian Captivity Persecution
17. HYMN - Psalms 140 - A Persecutor in Persecution
18. HYMN - Psalms 142 - Deliverance from Persecution
19. HYMN - Psalms 143 - Persecution That Grinds
20. HYMN - Psalms 144 - Praise and Prayer in Persecution

In a letter, in epistle format, I sent to the Orissa Churches in 2008 through Joy Thomas, I wrote this:

> Brethren of Orissa:
>
> Greetings in the precious name of our Lord and Saviour Jesus Christ! Grace be unto you, and peace from God our Father. We are now thanking God for you because your faith has been proven true in the exceedingly abundant persecution you find

yourself in; that your love for one another has grown, and that your desire upon those that persecute you is only for their salvation. We glory in your patience and perseverance at this difficult time in your history and marvel how you have endured so much, yet continue to rejoice that you are worthy to suffer such things for the cause of Christ. It is a token of grace that you have been able to suffer, yet rejoice in your tribulation as the righteous people you are; that you understand that recompense will one day be judged upon those that trouble you, but that your heart's desire is that they might be forgiven of all they have done to you.

I stand in complete amazement just how you have been able to withstand these trials with such loving affection and gracious resolve; how you have stayed together despite the destruction of your churches, your homes, and your possessions; that the news from your troubled land doesn't contain the phrases falling away and departing from the faith; that your goal is to rebuild, reestablish, and reorganize that which has been destroyed.

It is with a heart-felt prayer that you will be able to do just that and more. So I honor you and glorify your Lord and Saviour that I have had the privilege to witness and know those who have surely given the Church an example to follow when our time of persecution falls upon us. My only hope is that we will be able to endure with patience and faith as you have. Now the God of peace Himself grant you peace always, if not in reality, yet in heart and mind, that by all means you will continue to rejoice in the Lord *and keep on singing!* The Lord Jesus be with you and yours. The salutation of Barry with mine own hand, which is the sign of this epistle; so I write and so I record these thoughts on this day of Our Lord - 2008. The grace of our Lord Jesus Christ be with you all. Amen and Amen.

As I settled into my bed for what I hope would not be my last night in Orissa, I realized that my prayers for the Orissa believers in 2008 were answered. Everything I ask of the Almighty for them in 2008 had been given by 2012. One of the greatest joys of Orissa for me was the eye witness experiences I had over five days that confirmed to me that the persecuted Church in Orissa had survived because they, like David, had learned to sing through persecution and that the grand old psalms were still being sung in the face of great opposition. Maybe, we ought to learn these songs for ourselves because who knows when we will need a song in the night season of persecution? (Job 35:10)

58

A CROSS LESS LIFE?

Luke 14:27 "And whosoever doth not bear HIS CROSS, and come after me, CANNOT BE MY DISCIPLE."

My mind continued to drift as I relived my days in Orissa and sought to go to sleep at our Bhubaneswar hotel. A question kept haunting me. "Was I living a cross less life? I had known the scripture printed above for most of my life, but had never been confronted with its stark meaning until I came face to face with the persecuted saints of Orissa. I wrestled that night with another question. "What does it mean to bear the cross of Christ or my own cross?"

Before Calvary, Jesus told his followers that they too would bear a cross. His Cross has become a symbol of the suffering of Christ, but is there a cross for us as well? He told his disciples that if the world persecuted Him it would persecuted them (John 15:20). Peter learned this lesson and expounded on this truth when he wrote in his epistle these eye-opening words.

> "Beloved, think it not strange concerning the fiery trial which is to try you, as though some strange thing happened unto you: but rejoice, inasmuch as ye are partakers of Christ's sufferings; that, when His glory shall be revealed, ye may be glad also with exceeding joy. If ye be reproached for the name of Christ, happy are ye; for the spirit of glory and of God resteth upon you: on their part He is evil spoken of, but on your part He is glorified." (I Peter 4:12-14)

Where did Peter get this philosophy? From the teaching of Jesus in Matthew 5:10-12?

One day while reading an article by Richard DeHaan in *Our Daily Bread*, these words caught my attention.

One of the best cures for self-pity is to ponder the price other believers have had to pay in their service for Christ. Consider, for example, the following article that appeared in *The Evangel* dealing with the various ways in which the apostles and leaders of the early church were put to death.

> "Matthew is supposed to have suffered martyrdom by being slain with a sword in a city of Ethiopia. Mark was dragged through the streets of Alexandria in Egypt, till he expired. Luke was hanged on an olive tree in Greece. John was put into a cauldron of boiling oil in Rome, but escaped death. He afterward died a natural death at Ephesus. James the great was beheaded in Jerusalem. James the less was thrown from a pinnacle of the Temple, and then beaten to death with a club. Philip was hanged up against a pillar at Hierapolis, a city of Phrygia. Bartholomew was flayed alive at the command of a barbarous king. Andrew was bound to a cross, from whence he preached to the people till he expired. *Thomas was run through the body with a lance at Caromandel in Kerala, India.* (Where the church he founded still exists!) Jude was shot to death with arrows. Simon Zelotes was crucified in Persia. Matthias was first stoned, then beheaded."

And if Church history is right, Peter was crucified upside down in Rome because he didn't think himself worthy to die like his Lord! Each of these early disciples discovered their crosses, as had the saints in Orissa. But have I discovered mine? I am still touched by the saying that was printed at the bottom of DeHaan's devotional:

> "A cross-less life means a crown-less death!"
>   The old hymn writer Isaac Watts wrote of this theme in his classic work, "Am I a Soldier of the Cross?"
> "Am I a soldier of the cross? A follower of the Lamb?
> And shall I fear to own His cause, or blush to speak His name?
> Must I be carried to the skies on flowery beds of ease,
> While others fought to win the prize, and sail through bloody seas?
> Are there no foes for me to face? Must I not stem the flood?
> Is this vile world a friend to grace, to help me on to God?'
>   In answer to his own questions, Isaac Watts ends his amazing poem with this statement.
> "Sure I must fight, if I would reign; increase my courage, Lord;
> I'll bear the toil, endure the pain, supported by Thy Word!

That night in the darkness of an Orissa hotel, I asked myself again. Why am I so blessed and my friends in India so burdened? Why do I face an easy Christianity, and they a difficult Christianity? I am one that seems to be sailing through flowery seas while their journey is through bloody seas. Than it struck me like a thunderbolt. That it is I who is burdened, and they are blessed. I understood for the first time why the believers in Orissa could face such persecution as a-matter-of-fact. They had come to see that carrying the cross was not a burden, but a blessing; that with the cross-life comes an amazing joy, rejoicing if you will, just as Jesus had foretold. Oswald Chambers once wrote this under the title of "Baffled to Fight Better".

> "There is a saying of Bacon's to the affect that if prosperity is the blessing of the Old Testament, adversity is the blessing of the New; and the apostle Paul says that 'all that will live godly in Christ Jesus shall suffer persecution.' (II Timothy 3:12)"

This stands against the modern movement proclaimed by so many television preachers and evangelists that ours is supposed to be a life of blessing in prosperity. That God wants us healthy and wealthy, and when either is not in our lives then we are in the wrong. That God wants us without aliment or attack, and when either or both are in our lives, we must be in some kind of sin. If their philosophy is right, then my friends in Orissa must be some of the worst sinners on this planet. The saints of Orissa must be the most hypocritical believers in the world. To these theological hucksters, a cross life is enduring a church service without air-conditioning on a hot and muggy Sunday or enduring a thirty-minute sermon by a monotone. To face persecution in America is to be ridiculed for the style of church service one attends on Sunday. Let us be honest with ourselves; we know nothing of persecution. I still to this day struggle with whether or not I have yet to take up my cross.

59

A TASTE OF HOME IN HYDERABAD

I Peter 2:3 "If so be YE HAVE TASTED that the Lord is gracious."

MY RESTLESS NIGHT HAD me up before six on my last morning in Bhubaneswar. While the boys slept, I started to prepare two sermons: Jesus and Herod's Temple from John 2:20 and Paul's Prayer Requests for himself from Hebrews 13:18. I would share both messages with the KBBC kids before I headed home. Shibu and Joy got up about seven for breakfast, but I stayed in the hotel room to finish my sermons and prepare for our flight out of Orissa. By eight Moses had arrived to say goodbye, and before eight thirty we were in a taxi headed for the airport where we parted with Joy. He was staying in town to continue his ministry. It was bittersweet to say farewell to this dear brother in Christ, but the aftertaste of my first Orissa adventure would linger with me for a long time; as you can see!

Our trip through the three security checks in the Bhubaneswar Airport went smoothly, like a strawberry milk shake on a hot day smooth. Our flight out of Orissa was right on schedule. I found the flights of the airlines more dependable than the schedules of the train lines. By one we were back again at the Ragi Gandhi Airport outside Hyderabad, Andrah Pardesh where we had flown through on Monday. A first for me at this airport was the fact that the baggage conveyors had television cameras in the tubes leading up to where your bags come out, so you could be prepared when they arrived. I hadn't seen this feature in any American airport I have been in. It was Saturday and our three thousand mile odyssey in six days would be over with one more flight (Hyderabad to Kochi) and a car ride home (Kochi to Kangazha). The only difficulty was a SEVEN-HOUR layover in Hyderabad. Our original plan was to take a taxi into the city, the airport is about a forty-five minute ride outside of town, to see the sights, but a careful check of our finances revealed we were short of cash. Our Orissa expenses were more than we had planned, so about all we had left was enough rupees for a meal. I was upset with myself because I had left a substantial amount of rupees back in the prophet's chamber at Shibu's house. With no ATM machine and no way of getting other funds, ours was to be a sit-and-wait time, or was it?

The first amazing blessing at the Hyderabad Airport came in the form of a former student from KBBC who traveled three hours (one-way) by bus to meet us at the airport. Shibu had e-mailed Suresh that we would be in the area on October 27, 2012. In 2006, Suresh was one of my students, from the state of Assam and a good friend of one of my favorite students Billy Graham Warry, and was also taught by my daughter. He still had pictures of Marnie on his cell-phone from 2008. Since graduating from KBBC, Suresh had taken a job as a Hebrew teacher at Shiloh Bible Baptist College in Toopran, Andrah Pardesh. The small Bible school of twenty-five students was located on the other side of Hyderabad, opposite the airport. Besides teaching Hebrew at the college, Suresh also taught church history and the poetic books of the Old Testament. As we talked, we decided to get a bite to eat. Our first trip through the Hyderabad airport revealed few options, but having more time to look around our second time through revealed a food court on a lower level, and to my surprise a familiar logo was found on the vendor's sign: KFC, not Kerala Fiery Curry, but, Kentucky Fried Chicken!

By the time Suresh, Shibu and I headed down the staircase to the food court, I had been in India over a month. I had eaten nothing really American, despite eating American style foods they were far from American tasting, so the chance to get a taste of home made my mouth water just thinking about it. As Suresh and Shibu looked over the variety of Indian fast-food establishments, I headed directly to the KFC line. Unlike the McDonalds in the upper level, the menu seemed to be like any American KFC. I made the front of the line in a few minutes and asked the young attendant if they served the original recipe. And to my sheer-joy, they did! While my meal was being prepared, I had a chance to talk to the young people behind the counter. They all knew English and were happy to show-off to the American. I told them of my travels, and they seemed happy to given me a taste of home, but would it be?

I paid 216 rupees for a two-piece meal. I only had 300 rupees to my name, a little over four bucks. My meal came with French fries and a Pepsi. After paying my bill, I took my tray to where Suresh and Shibu had found us a place to sit. The court wasn't too busy, but I still got my American fast-food before the boys got their Indian fast-food. Shibu prayed, and I dug into my first taste of home in over a month! The first reality was these were not Purdue chickens. I had a tiny leg and an even smaller thigh. During my first pastorate in the mid-1970s, I worked for a chicken company that supplied most of the KFCs in New Hampshire. For nearly two years, I cut up chickens for KFC, and American poultry is not Indian poultry. I had learned that over the years, but I was hoping KFC India had higher standards. They don't! I finished my two-piece meal in about four bites, very little meat on those bones. As for the taste, I think they left out a few of the original ingredients. It was fried, and it was crispy, but that was about it. The French fries were ok, but too few to satisfy a hungry American. I will concede the Pepsi tasted like Pepsi, a taste of home!

The difference between an American meal in India and an Indian meal in India is the size of the meal. For half the price, Shibu and Suresh had a platter full of food. Granted, I wouldn't have eaten any of it, but they had a banquet while I ate a few mouthfuls. Despite the minor disappointment, the fellowship was sweet, though the time together short. Suresh still had a three-hour bus ride back to the college, so about mid-afternoon we parted. There are more tastes in this world than those that come from food. The sweet taste of Christian friendship is a savor and favor that can be enjoyed even during a layover in the middle of India.

After saying goodbye to Suresh, Shibu and I headed upstairs to the large lobby in the upper level to wait for our departing flight. We had hardly settled into a quiet area when a young lady with a cart full of luggage approached us. Her first sentence revealed an American accent. She was the first American I had met on the trip. She was looking for someone to fly to Mumbai with. She was on her way home to Austin, Texas after attending a wedding of an Indian friend. As we talked, I discovered she was Jewish and she too had been to Israel, another talking point we had together. It was her first time in India, so she also added a vacation to the wedding schedule. She had been in India three weeks, but was ready to head for home. The more I talked to her, the first real lengthy conversation I had in over a month, the more I realized that, despite my love for the land and the grand time I had, I too was ready to return to my family and ministry in Maine. Our conversation lasted about an hour, and the last I saw of my taste of home was her full cart going around a corner. I still had three more hours in Hyderabad and three more days in India, but I had gotten a taste for home, and I was ready to depart. How gracious the Lord is when we need a taste of home.

60

TRAVELING TO MY INDIAN HOME

Acts 21:6 "....AND THEY RETURNED HOME AGAIN."

AFTER THE VISIT AND lunch with Suresh and the conversation with the young lady from Austin, I spent the rest of my Saturday waiting in the Hyderabad Airport reading and walking and napping. Our scheduled SpiceJet Air flight to Kochi was at 6:45 P.M. The massive lobby area held few people, so it was easy to find a place to rest. One of my favorite pictures of the wait is of Shibu with his shoes off, feet on his luggage, and sound asleep. I think I tired the lad out on our six-day adventure! Because the Indian officials frown on anyone taking photos in their airports, I secretly snapped a few pictures of the planes we flew on and a huge mural of a massive Indian elephant outside the Lingaraja Temple in Bhubaneswar. Sorry, I just can't get over not being able to go there!

One of the places that entertained me for a few minutes was a bookstore near Gate 25, where we were to board our final flight home. As I browsed through the books on display, I came across an interesting story about Jesus that I had never heard before. After fifty-five years of Christianity, you would think I had heard every tale and legend, but this one was new to me. It seems that there are some in India who believe that Jesus traveled to India as a boy. This would be during the gap of eighteen years between Luke 2:42 at twelve and before the start of his earthly ministry at thirty along the Silk Road (Luke 3:23). Once he arrived in India, he converted to Buddhism and became a master before returning to Israel to die. After his resurrection, instead of returning to Heaven he returned to India as a grand master and lived out the rest of his life in the State of Kashmir in northwestern India. Eventually he died again and was buried, and his grave can still be visited today. Wow! Now that is quite a story. When I told Shibu about it, he confirmed that he had heard the fable and that the author of the book relating the tale was well respected in the country. All I could think of was Paul exhortation to Timothy.

> "For the time will come when they will not endure sound doctrine; but after their own lusts shall they heap to themselves

teachers, having itching ears; and they shall turn away their ears from the truth, and shall be turned unto fables." (II Timothy 4:3-4)

As it had been with our other Indian flights, SpiceJet Air flight #SG105 left Hyderabad right on schedule. The flight down to Kochi was smooth and uneventful, until we neared the Kochi Airport. Thick clouds greeted us, and we began to circle. A massive thunderhead had moved into the area delaying our landing. Kochi lies on the Malabar Coast of Kerala and, like the rest of Kerala, is often attacked during monsoon season with unending grey skies and merciless sheets of rain. Our scheduled two hour flight lengthened to three hours. We did experience some turbulence and saw some rain on the plane window, but our pilot kept us far from the heart of the storm. My experience with the storms at Edayappara taught me that I didn't want to be in the middle of one in a plane. The landing was eventually smooth, and our faithful driver Sijin and Pastor Shaji Matthews from the Kangazha Church were waiting to take us home. We still had a three-hour car ride ahead and that journey wouldn't end until after midnight.

My eighteen-hour day ended as I climbed the stairs in Shibu's house. I had barely gotten into the prophet's chamber when I heard Shibu calling me from downstairs. The phone had rung, and on the end of the line was my wife Coleen. She had called to see if I had survived Orissa and to warn me about a possible obstacle in my return to the States. It seemed that a mega-storm called Sandy was building over the East Coast of the United States, and they were predicting it would arrive just as I was arriving in New York. I didn't give it a second thought thinking it would surely blow through before I arrived on Wednesday. I was more focused on reliving my great adventures in Orissa to my wife than worrying about potentially bad weather. We talked about fifteen minutes and finished with, "I will see you in four days." Little did I know of the side adventure I would have the next week as I tried to leave India.

Re-climbing the stairs, I took a few minutes to relish in the joy of being home again. Edayappara had become a second home to me and my room in the Simon home a sanctuary as special as my Maine home. I had left that upper room early on Monday morning and here it was after midnight on Saturday into Sunday. In less than six days, Shibu and I had traveled three thousand one hundred and fifty-seven miles by car, plane, and train. My final thought of the trip was remembering how it must have felt like for the first missionaries, Paul, Barnabas, and Silas, as they returned home. Look again at the verse I have printed at the head of this chapter. Part of any trip is returning home. Despite the fact, I was still four days (or so I thought) from returning to my coastal home in Maine, I still felt like I had come home.

I remember the first time I had that feeling. While on a mission's trip in Australia in the summer of 1972, my cousin Bob and I had been adopted by the Kew People's Church in Melbourne. We had stayed with them nearly two weeks before we headed across the country by train to work six weeks with the Aboriginal people of the Gibson Desert in Western Australia under the tutorage of the United Aboriginal Mission. When we returned to Melbourne and the Kew People's Church, we were greeting as one of their own. Oh, we would feel the same affection and excitement when we returned to our home church in Perham, Maine, but that first feeling of accomplishment and achievement was felt in Australia not Maine. I was having the same feeling in India.

As I lay my tired head on my prophet chamber pillow and looked out onto the dark tropical landscape outside my bedroom window, I drifted off into a deep sleep; a tired but contented sleep, a sleep that comes after a hard day's labor but a satisfying day's work. That sleep lasted from 12:30 A.M. to 7:30 A.M. I woke the next morning well after sunrise refreshed and excited to share with my Indian family the memorable events of my great Orissa mission. As Paul of old, I would report back to my brothers and sisters in Kerala my observations and impressions before I would report back to my church in Maine. Part of coming home is the responsibility to report just like Paul taught us nearly two thousand years ago.

> "And thence sailed to Antioch, their home church, from whence that had been recommended to the grace of God for the work which they fulfilled. And when they were come, and had gathered the church together, they rehearsed that entire God had done with them, and how He had opened the door of faith unto the Gentiles." (Acts 14:26-27)

One of the greatest thrills in the service of Christ is the opportunity to repeat actions first performed by those who have ministered before us. Returning home to report on the great and wondrous things the Lord has done through you is one of those special thrills, whether at your church home in India or your church in Maine!

61

CAMPUS PASTOR FOR A DAY

> Jeremiah 17:16 "As for me, I HAVE NOT HASTENED FROM BEING A PASTOR TO FOLLOW THEE: neither have I desired the woeful day; thou knoweth; that which came out of my lips was right from thee."

It was only fitting that my last Sunday in Kerala would be spent with the students of Kerala Baptist Bible College. Even though my mission's trip to Orissa was the highlight of my fourth trip to India, it was with the students of KBBC that I spent the bulk of my time, teaching and mentoring and preaching. I had both church services on the campus that last Sunday in Kerala.

My Sunday began not in the sanctuary preaching the Word, but in the bathroom of the Simon's prophet chamber hunting a gigantic spider. I had seen such spiders before, most recently in the trees at Nandankanan Zoo, but this spider wasn't in a tree but on the mirror in my bathroom, making it appear twice as big. I hadn't even noticed it until I had finished my shower. This shows how unobservant I am in the morning. Oh, the stories my wife could tell you! I am not afraid of spiders, but they do give you a frightful feeling especially when they are as big as your hand and you're standing before them naked. I knew that I couldn't leave it alone, even though I knew it would leave me alone. The very sight of it was enough to make me act. I twisted up my wet towel and attacked. My first swipe only knocked it onto the floor. This wakeup call sent it into instant retreat. Quickly its legs began to move over the tile in rapid motion toward the drain in the far corner of the room. I swiped at it again but missed. I landed my third blow, but my feet went out from under me on the slippery floor recently dampened by my shower. I thought I had broken my arm as I hit the tile floor hard, but my focus was still on the spider now that I was on its level. I soon realized that I had nothing to fear, as it seemed that my last blow had killed my adversary. I turned on the shower and washed the spider down the drain. To my relief my fall chasing the spider resulted in no serious injury, just a sore arm.

After breakfast I was off to the campus, where I rejoiced in the hymns the students had chosen to sing that morning: "Come Thou Almighty King", "Fairest Lord Jesus", "To God Be the Glory", and "As the Deer". One of the young men spoke on the one hundred and nineteenth Psalms and the importance of giving praise for God's Word. Another young man sang a solo in his native tongue, and then I preached on the classic mission's verse found in Jeremiah 8:20.

"The harvest is past, the summer is ended, and we are not saved."

I shared my Orissa experiences with them as I challenged them to go forth into God's harvest field. I knew a group of them were going to go after graduation to Manipur for a month, but I wanted them all to see the need. After the service, Ragu Sagar, the campus pastor from Orissa, came up to me and shared his desire to start a Bible Institute in his native land. I have come to realize that Jesus' prayer for workers for His harvest is being answered, at least in India.

> "Then saith He unto His disciples, The harvest truly is plenteous, but the labourers are few; pray ye therefore the Lord of the harvest, that He will send forth labourers into His harvest." (Matthew 9:37-38)

Is there a more plenteous harvest field than the billion plus souls in India?

The reason I was speaking at the college in the morning instead of at one of the local churches was because this Sunday had been designated Youth Sunday. The young people of the churches were conducting the services in all the IGBC churches. As I walked over to the Kangazha Church, I realized that the young people of Kerala were more long-winded than I was. Their service was still going on well after noontime. I decided to take a walk around town. As I strolled down the main thoroughfare of the village, I was thanking the Lord for getting me back to my Indian town. Something I have not shared with you about our seven-hour layover in Hyderabad, Andrah Pardesh the day before was the last ten minutes. When Shibu and I got to our gate, the last check before boarding our plane to Kochi, the security guard pulled me out of line and told me I couldn't board because my carry-on hadn't been stamped. I had gone through screening, but the bagged agent had failed to stamp the ticket he had put on my bag. That meant I had to rush back through the terminal and get my bag rechecked. Shibu was thankfully behind me and not in front of me. If he had gone through before me I would have been on my own. There was no admittance after you leave the airport. Quickly we got the help of an airline attendant, and he guided us through the maze back to screening. When we got back to our gate, all our fellow-passengers had already boarded, and we were literally the last two to get on the plane. They shut the doors behind us! As I walked the empty lanes, all churches were still in worship, I thanked the Good Lord for His wonderful hand of grace and provision in an Indian airport.

After my walk-about around town, my afternoon would consist of a late lunch, a short nap, and a fight with an invasion of tree ants! I had seen plenty of ants in my days in India, but nothing compared to the ants I found in my room after I woke from a very pleasant and necessary nap. The floor of the prophet's chamber was completely covered with ants. I immediately called Shibu who came running. We traced the source of the invasion to the backdoor on the roof. It seems that when a colony of ants decided to move they send out huge columns of ants searching for a suitable place to make a nest. Because the Simon house is in the woods and the trees hang over the backside of the house, the ants had direct entrance, and they chose my room for a possible nesting site. Shibu had some ant-killer and began to spray, and I began to sweep. I had never swept up ants in such numbers before. I must admit it was worse for me than the huge spider of the morning. It took us awhile, but eventually we stopped the onslaught and put a barrier of ant-repellent to prevent their return.

That evening, I returned to the chapel on the campus of KBBC for their evening service. The music was again inspiring and the testimonies were challenging. My sixth and final sermon to the students was a message I called "Paul's Prayer Petitions for Himself and Us". I shared with them this outline and my hope is that you will take the time and ask these things for yourself and others.

1. RESTORATION - HEBREWS 13:18-19
2. REQUEST - I THESSALONIANS 5:25
3. RECOVERY - ROMANS 15:30-31
4. RECOURSE - II THESSALONIANS 3:1
5. REVELATION - COLOSSIANS 4:3-4
6. REASON - EPHESIANS 6:18-19

62

THE LOST CHURCH OF GONDAPATHER

> Ezekiel 34:16 "I will seek that which was LOST, and BRING AGAIN that which was driven away, and will BIND UP that which was broken, and will STRENGTHEN that which was sick . . . ."

THE PSALMIST ONCE WROTE " . . . joy cometh in the morning." (Psalms 30:5) For me, the greatest joy of my 2012 trip to India came on my last Monday morning in Kerala.

I was eating a breakfast of bananas and coconut with the Simon family when the phone rang. I expected it to my wife, but instead it was our friend Joy Thomas calling from Orissa. As Shibu listened to Joy, I could tell there was some exciting news being delivered. All I could think was had more people gotten saved during our trip than at first been reported or that something wonderful had happened to one of the pastors, a wedding or the birth of a child? The longer the conversation lasted the more I couldn't contain myself. What could it be that caused Joy Thomas to call so early in the morning?

Eventually, Shibu put his cellphone down and began telling me Joy's good news. It seems that Joy stayed in Bhubaneswar after we left with Pastor John for the weekend. He conducted services in the mission's churches in the area, including visiting the congregation we hadn't been able to visit because of a death in the fellowship. After worshipping with the Bhubaneswar churches that Sunday morning, Joy returned to Pastor John's home to spend the night before traveling back to Phulabani. As Pastor John and Joy talked of the work, the phone rang. When it was asked if Joy Thomas was there, the phone was given to Joy. To Joy's surprise and amazement, the voice on the other end of the line was a man he had been trying to find since the persecution of 2008. Perhaps, the best way to understand Joy's excitement is to give you a little history of a place called Gondapather.

When Joy Thomas started the Orissa Outreach Mission in the late 1990s, his primary region of evangelization was the district of Phulabani, and in particular, the northern region of that district. After establishing a number of congregations, he began working on permanent sanctuaries for each of the churches. The first and only two sanctuaries he built before persecution broke out were at Dangul and Gondapather. I remember the first glimpse I ever had of Gondapather was through pictures Shibu sent to me of the dedication service he had at Gondapather with his brother. I still have the video he sent me of the trip they took in 2006, after my first trip to Kerala, and the letters that came shortly afterwards with pictures showing the destruction of that same sanctuary by militant Hindus. I still have the letter Shibu sent me concerning the second burning of the Gondapather church and the scattering of the saints.

> "Dear Prayer Partners: The situation in Orissa is getting worse in many places. More churches are being burned and houses being destroyed by the rebels. Let me point out some things that have directly affected the people that we are working with. Pastor Noha, Pastor Solomon, Pastor Kruso, and Evangelist Suseel lost their houses along with everything in them. They left with what they were wearing. Evangelist Jonah and Evangelist Ugrisan lost their homes also. ALL THE BELIEVERS IN THE VILLAGE OF GONDAPATHER LOST THEIR HOMES AS WELL. IT IS THEIR CHURCH THE REBELS BURNED IN DECEMBER 2007. THIS TIME THEY BURNED THEIR HOUSES. ALL THESE PEOPLE KEEP ONE YEARS SUPPLY OF RICE IN A BAMBOO CONTAINER WITHIN THEIR HOMES, SO THEY HAVE ALSO LOST THAT. Presently, they are in the forest areas. We have not been able to directly get in touch. (Little did Shibu know that for some of the saints of Orissa it would take four years to make contact?) The homes of our believers in the villages of Dangul, Sathanamandi, Gumakattu, Lahavadi, Kenpach, Koyanchar, Pipisajay, Barsigubhu, Hajiriputa, Duburiguda, Thresapather, Phulabani, Lajurumunda, Gondapather, and Sarankadu (in 2012 I only visited Dangul) have been attacked by the same group called VHP (Vishwa Hindu Parishad). We really praise God for protecting their lives. As we talked with Pastor Virendra's wife she said, 'We are ready to face death for the sake of Christ!' We thank God for their courage; please pray for them." Shibu Simon

Before the great outbreak of 2008, there had been isolated attacks, but mostly only on church buildings, not Christians. The flock at Gondapather rebuilt just prior to the great assaults of 2008 when hundreds of churches were burned (including both the church building at Dangul and

Gondapather), and thousands of Christians were driven from their homes as their houses were burned. The churches of Phulabani were scattered, but as I have shared in this book, most, if not, all have returned, rebuilt, and reestablished themselves in the towns of Phulabani. The exception to that rule has been the families that left Phulabani for Bhubaneswar. I have shared their story in other chapters.

What I didn't know until that Monday morning was that there were eight families from Gondapather that Joy had led to Christ himself, but he had lost contact with them at the height of the exodus from the district of Phulabani to the capital of Bhubaneswar. Over the months that followed, he had been able to find the entire Lord's people except that group of eight families from Gondapather. He hadn't given up in four years, but he had exhausted all his leads wondering if they might have been killed in the attack. The first indication they were alive and well came after the church service on Sunday, October 28, 2012.

Over four years had passed, but the voice on the line was the head elder of the group. Why had they taken all that time to contact him? They didn't know that he was still in the area. They had moved into a small village about ten miles outside of Bhubaneswar, but unlike the rest of the flock that had moved into Bhubaneswar, this group kept their location secret in fear of being hunted down. Little do we know the horror of such events in the hearts and lives of the persecuted! The good news was they had kept the faith and had started a small assembly and were looking for the right time to come out of hiding. Their courage returned when they heard that Joy Thomas and Shibu Simon were back in town with an American.

After that afternoon phone call, Joy and Moses made the trek out of town to find the eight families, and that evening they reestablished fellowship. Joy's joy was boundless as he explained to Shibu the excitement of the people to get back into contact with their spiritual father. The celebration lasted well into Monday morning as they sang and prayed and rejoiced together. That is why Joy had waited until we got up to give us a call. The lost segment of the Church of Gondapather had been found physically alive and spiritually well. Joy was even considering whom to place as pastor of this remnant body of believers that were given up as lost, but now were found. Was it the coming of an American, for so long held away, that finally convinced the lost church of Gondapather that the coast was clear, and they could make contact again with their brethren?

63

FINAL EXAMS AND ISRAELI MEMORIES

Proverbs 10:7 "THE MEMORY OF THE JUST IS BLESSED..."

My final two days in Kerala, or so I thought, were spent fulfilling my final obligations as a professor at KBBC and final responsibilities to the IGBC. I had to give my juniors and seniors their final exams. Also, I had two final classes, two final chapels to share at the college, and two final meetings with the pastors. Monday took care of two-thirds of those responsibilities. It was also on Monday I got the first of many e-mails from my wife telling me of the super storm named Sandy. I was unaffected by my wife's warning believing by the time I arrived in New York the storm would have blown through, so I continued on with my schedule.

That Monday included the following:

1. The final exam of The Historical Books of the Old Testament plus a lecture on "Jesus: As Seen in the Old and New Testaments"
2. A PowerPoint in chapel on "Jesus and Herod's Temple"
3. The final exam of The Prison Epistles plus some final remarks on "Did Paul Take a Fourth Missionary Trip to Spain?"
4. Watching a rival volleyball game in the afternoon between the towns of Mundathanam and Edayappara in the churchyard at the Kangazha church. WE WON!
5. E-mailing my two kids concerning their twenty-ninth spiritual birthdays. Both my children got saved on October 30, 1983 after family devotions!
6. Speaking to the monthly meeting of the Kerala pastors of the IGBC on the subject of "The Dangers of a False Salvation"

The highlight of my day was the trip I took back in time after my Israeli presentation at chapel. Whether in India or Maine, it doesn't take much to send me back to those glorious days in May of 2010 when Marnie and I walked the ancient land of Jesus. The other reason I am focused on those Holy Land memories is the fact that I am writing this chapter on the third anniversary of my leaving Israel for the last time?

I am driving again beneath a canopy of blue on the ascending road up to the Holy City that is to this day the heartbeat of three faiths. For nineteen days, we traveled through that land passing signposts, markers of Biblical history. At some signposts, we were able to stop for a while and experience the thrill of being on holy ground, but most of the signposts passed us by in a flash. Within hours I was overwhelmed by the past of the place never more so than in Jerusalem. I had come to immerse myself in the history of its places and found instead the greatest spiritual high of my life. I was not distracted by the dramatic panorama of the new Jerusalem growing up around the ancient walls of the old city. I was not distracted by the ring of concrete walls and watchtowers that surrounded the modern-day fortress to kept Israel's enemies out. I was not distracted nor did I spend much time in the new opulent hotels like the King David, grand museum, except the Yad Vashem, or the Holocaust museum, or the massive governmental buildings, although I did see the Knesset building from across a valley. It was David's city I had come to see and, from a distance, the massive Dome of the Rock reflected a golden sun.

As I told my students of Herod's temple and the times Jesus made the trek up the steep steps to Temple Mount, I relived again my few fleeting moments on the Mount, and my memory was as vivid and as alive today as the day we arrived in the vast plaza that sets before the vast Western Wall. Access was only possible through an impressive checkpoint that would put any airport checkpoint to shame. There were screens to detect weapons and explosives, and an Israeli guard to check all handbags. Even though it was early in the morning, the plaza was filled with people, tourists and locals. The wall towered above as we made our way up a ramp at the southern end of the wall. The bottom stones in the wall still spoke of the glory days of Solomon when he built the first temple, the greatest temple of them all until Jesus returns to build the Millennial Temple. There on that wall where the stones of Herod's massive temple complex and the top of the courtyard he created by leveling off a mountain peak so he could build, perhaps the greatest building of its day, Herod's temple. The great Hebrews historian Flavius Josephus called Herod's supporting wall "the greatest ever heard of". The longest of these four walls, the western wall, was five hundred thirty yards long. Many of the stones used were over five tons in weight, and the temple itself was gilded much like the Dome of the Rock. It was said that one could see the temple from a great distance and even further if the hills didn't block the view. As I described to the students of KBBC my experience of Temple Mount, I was transported back to that place in my memory.

Another memory I wanted these students to experience through my pictures and remembrances was the other walk I took a few days earlier with Marnie to the base of the Western Wall also called the Weeping Wall. I headed for the men's section of the wall as Marnie headed for the women's section. The way was steep that lead to the bare stones at the base. White plastic chairs were placed here allowing people to sit and pray. Men had to cover their heads and provision was made for those who had no head coverings. I was wearing my hat, so I pressed on through those who were in deep contemplation and those simply resting. I looked over the low wall that separated the two sections. This was the first time Marnie had been out of my sight, and I was concerned about that. The women were wearing square pieces of silk as they lined up in front of the wall. Some were, as the men, rocking back and forth holding their arms in front of their chest. Others were pressing their faces into the stones, and still others were weeping. It was then I realized I was weeping, but not for the same reason. The Jews there had come to directly communicate with Jehovah and plead for the Messiah to come and for Jerusalem to be finally out from under the hand of their enemies. I heard sobbing on both side of the curtain and those crying the most were the old orthodox Jews covered from head to toe in black with thick black hats and long beards.

I watched for over a half an hour as they flooded into the area just in front of the wall. Marnie and I had predetermined a time to meet in the plaza, so I was able to spend some time there. Young and old, they came singing and praying and weeping and reading the Torah. Tiny sparrows fluttered overhead as they headed for the cracks and crevices of the wall to feed their young. The lower cracks and crevices were reserved for the written prayers of the worshipper believing that his written prayers would be read by the God of the Wall. My final challenge to the students that day was the reality that we neither need a temple or a wall to be heard. Our direct access to the very throne of God is simply through a name, and that name is Jesus. If I have learned anything from my India and Israel experiences, it is that God hears much clearer from India than from Israel!

64

STRANDED BY HURRICANE SANDY

> Isaiah 28:2 "... AND A DESTROYING STORM, AS A MIGHTY FLOOD WATERS OVERFLOWING...."

I WOKE UP TO a typical Indian sunrise, my last for this trip, or so I thought! Since Coleen's first e-mail about Hurricane Sandy, I had checked the reports on the Internet, but I still thought the storm would pass before I was scheduled to arrive in New York City late on Wednesday night. My last Tuesday in India would be busy until I headed for the Kochi Airport later than evening. Any good day in India starts with a Julie breakfast.

The first change in the routine happened when I sat down at the dining room table. No Shibu! He had left early for a funeral at 504 Colony. That meant I had the Simon children all to myself and would get the privilege of taking them to school before I headed off to the college. It was during our conversation around the breakfast table that I learned just how Indian children study. I learned that both Abigail and Joshua were in the midst of a week of testing, two tests a day for five days. The average school year is divided up into three semesters, and the school year runs from June to March. The second semester was over, so the children would be tested on their ten, yes, 10 courses:

1. English
2. Hindi (the national language)
3. Malayalam (the state language)
4. social studies
5. computer
6. moral science (an ethics course)
7. basic science
8. math
9. general knowledge

10. information technology (another general course to help with modern technologies)

Having given my final exams on Monday, my morning at KBBC was just the daily chapel. I shared with the students a final Israeli PowerPoint on "The Jerusalem Model", a fifty to one scale of Jesus' Jerusalem. Marnie and I had toured this unique exhibition at the Jerusalem Museum. I was able, through my pictures, to take them on a walking tour of the major sites Jesus would have seen in His day; later that afternoon I was invited back to the campus for a farewell program put on by the students. They even had an order of service.

1. Daniel Standhope was the program leader.
2. Presentjith Basumatary opened in prayer.
3. Solomon Rongar led us in singing "More About Jesus" on his guitar.
4. Henmin Kipgen shared what my coming meant to him from a senior perspective.
5. Ashok Kumar Kalum shared what my coming meant to the junior class.
6. I then was able to share my final words with the students of KBBC, and I shared with them the hope of "The New Jerusalem" compared to the old Jerusalem I had shared with them in our last chapel together.
7. Sophy K. Paul presented me a picture of me with the junior class.
8. Romita Devirungbam presented me a picture of me with the senior class.
9. Vikiye S. Awomi then sang "God Be With You Till We Meet Again".
10. Then we all sang, "God Will Make A Way".
11. Vijay Kumar M. closed in prayer.
12. Finally, we had a little social time with plenty of group pictures taken.

After the program I went over to the college office to check on Hurricane Sandy. According to the news reports and the four e-mails I had in my inbox, the storm had hit with devastating results. Once again I believed, because I was still over twenty-four hours before I arrived in New York, the storm would be passed. My final event before I headed for the airport was a Thanksgiving service instead of the regular weekly Pastors' Prayer Meeting. The service was held in the Kangazha Church, and once again the children from the orphanage, the students from the college, and the people I knew in Edayappara showed up to stay farewell. It was determined the last time I was India that there would be no more welcome or goodbye services for me. I would be treated as a member of the fellowship in my comings and goings. My final message was taken from James 1:17 "Every Good and Perfect Gift". I had about three hours to finish packing before Shagu, Sijin, and Shaji took me to the Kochi Airport for my flight home.

My journey home started at 12:30 P.M. Maine time on Tuesday October 30, 2012. Just before I left Shibu's home, I got a surprise call from my good friend Binu, my driver for my first three trips to India. The call was all the way from Qatar City to wish me the best on my trip home. It was a final farewell that I wasn't expecting. The three-hour trip to Kochi from Edayappara was routine for the fourth time on this trip. Little did I know I would travel that route two more times before I finally got out of India!

As is the custom at Indian Airports, I was dropped off at the curb. Only passengers enter Indian airports with bags in hand. I said goodbye to my three friends and entered the maze of security. I glanced at the flight board, and my plane to Kuwait City was on time. The weather was perfect in Kerala, and I was nine thousand miles from Hurricane Sandy, so no worries right? I got through the second level of security checks within minutes and was heading for the Kuwait Air ticket counter when a pretty Indian lady approached me with a simple question, "Are you heading for JFK?" I said, "YES!" And she replied, "Would you please follow me." It was then I had the first taste in my mouth that something wasn't right.

I was escorted to a group of four men standing in the middle of the lobby. The older man standing in the middle of the group informed me that all passengers heading for the East Coast of America were being held at their point of origin; in simple terms, I wouldn't be leaving India today. I tried to explain my situation; I had been left off at the airport by friends that live three-hours away, so not only was I stranded in India, I was stranded in Kochi. The man asked if I could call anybody; my mind was blank. While I was thinking what I would do I asked, "When will I be able to leave; I will stay in the airport till the first available flight comes up." "Impossible," replied the man, "You must leave the airport immediately!"

It seems only people with flights can stay in the airport. What was I going to do?

It was then I remembered I had Shibu's cell phone number. The man let me use his cell phone to call Shibu to call Shagu to turn around and pick up the stranded America. This was another first for Shibu and me. For all the visitors that have come to India to ministry with the IGBC, I was the first ever to miss a flight. It was 1:00 A.M. so I woke Shibu up. He said he would try to get the message to Shagu. Immediately after placing my call, I was ushered back through security and left at the front door of the Kochi Airport. However, for some reason I didn't feel deserted or lonely. Within minutes I knew why. There in the sea of faces outside the terminal were two young men I knew: Sijin and Shaji. It seems that it has been Shagu's practice, when he drops people off at the airport, to wait around for half an hour or more to make sure they make their flights. He had never had to re-pickup anybody until me!

65

WHY 48 EXTRA HOURS?

> II Chronicles 21:19 "And it came to pass, that in the process of time, after THE END OF TWO (DAYS) . . . ."

By five A.M. I was right back where I had started, in the prophet's chamber at the Simon house trying to get a few hours of sleep before I tried to figure out how I was going to get back to the States. My faithful friends hadn't left me in Kochi as I feared, but had waited for my exit from the airport as if they knew I wasn't going to New York that day. It is wonderful to travel with the Lord who knows every delay and tropical storm. Actually the flights out of India hadn't been cancelled just passengers traveling into JFK. The Kuwait Airway's official told me I was just one of thousands being held back at their place of departure. I would have to check with the ticket agent in the morning for the next possible flight. He also warned that it might take days to straighten it all out. Hurricane Sandy had thrown the air travel industry a real curve ball!

Instead of traveling home, the last day of October 2012 was spent e-mailing and telephoning travel agents explaining my dilemma! After four e-mails from home, I discovered that my travel agent Emily in the States couldn't help me; I would have to make my own arrangements out of India. It was then my friend Shibu stepped into the fray and told me to enjoy my day. He would contract the Kuwait agent in Kochi and see what could be done. From all fronts, the best would or might take five days to figure out. Instead of being upset, I was thrilled with the prospect of spending a few extra days in my favorite country. I had a wonderful place to sleep, plenty of food, and opportunities were around every corner in Edayappara. I decided I would compile a list of the blessings I enjoyed that I wouldn't have if I had left Kochi on time.

My first added blessing on my 2012 trip to India was the opportunity to share one more service with the students at KBBC. What a surprise it was for them as I walked into chapel for their regular Wednesday Night Prayer Meeting. That evening they had begun to practice Christmas Carols for the variety of celebrations during the holiday. I had never been to India near Christmas, but I had heard plenty of what the Kerala Christians make of our second holiest day of the year. Easter must be our holiest. As they sang the familiar carols, I couldn't help but join in; surely I wouldn't still be here at Christmas? I was also asked to share one more time, so I preached on "A Picture in the Parable" taken from Matthew 21:33. It was my eighty-fourth and last message. Would I get to preach to them again?

That evening after I got back from the college prayer meeting, I had a chance to borrow a book from Shibu on church history. I was preparing an Evening School class on the subject, and the information I was able to glean from Shibu's book would be helpful in my study. If I had left India on time, I would never have had the chance to get that information. As I read Shibu's book, Elmer the gecko was back in my room catching flying ants. I asked him where he had been during the invasion of the ants, but he seemed to be more concerned about how he was going to get the huge flying ants down his throat. I will miss Elmer; he had given me plenty of entertainment over my month in Kerala. I was glad I got a chance to watch him work again. My next blessing came at the Simon's breakfast table after a wonderful night's rest listening to a gentle rain.

As Shibu and I discussed my options for the day, Joshua asked if I would like to listen to his speech. Joshua had entered a speaking contest and was practicing his speech. I sat and listened to a young man speak in English without an Indian accent. His message about why English is an important language in India was clear and his presentation was excellent for a lad his age. I told Shibu that we had nothing to fear turning over the preaching to him. If I had left the day before I would have missed this glimpse into the future. Right after Joshua's speech, Shibu tried to reach the booking agent for Kuwait Air in Kochi, but the office wasn't open. Shibu was off to a house dedication and promised me he would try again as soon as he got back. After Shibu left, Julie and I were talking about my full suitcase. I had determined to leave most of my clothes behind, but in the busyness of the last two days, I hadn't found a place for them. Julie knew of some needs, so after breakfast I was able to go upstairs and empty my suitcase and carry-on and leave six complete outfits of clothes for people in Orissa. Another gift I wouldn't have been able to give if Sandy hadn't blown through!!

By eleven Shibu was back from his dedication. In India they dedicate everything to the Lord, even their homes, with a dedication service. His second call to the booking agent only revealed that there were a lot of people trying to rebook and that it would take time. It was about that same time I got an e-mail from my Maine booking agent Emily Muise telling me that she saw opportunities for November 2, but she couldn't rebook me from home. The minute I knew of my new flights, it was important I contact her so she could work out how I would get home from JFK. I sat at lunch with Annamma, Julie, Shagu, and Timothy, and by 2:30 P.M. I was back in the Simon's house. Shibu was there to greet me, and I could see by the expression on his face it wasn't good news. The booking agent had called and the earliest flight out of Kochi was on November 5, four days away. It looked like I would be spending another weekend in Kerala. In my heart I accepted the verdict, but, as we were discussing the change of events, the phone rang again. It was the booking agent with information that if I could be in Kochi by 4:30 the next morning, there was a seat on a Qatar flight through Doha then on to JFK. If I caught all my flights I would be home by early Saturday morning. Once again a blessing to watch how my Heavenly travel agent is able to move on the hearts of people. If that booking agent had not looked further into the flights on other airlines, my two-day stay in Kerala would have been extended to five days!

The rest of my day was getting ready for my sixth car ride to Kochi: the trip that brought me first to Edayappara, the trip back to go to Orissa, the trip back from Orissa, the first trip to catch my original flight, the trip back to Edayappara after I learned that Sandy had shutdown JFK, and my final trip after a forty-eight hour delay. There was the normal anticipation that always links a journey home. I did get one more blessing late that afternoon, a blessing I wouldn't have gotten if I hadn't been delayed. With some time on my hands, I was looking through Shibu's library. I saw a book by a favorite author that I had never read, John Philip's book on Jude. It is a simple, short book packed with many blessings. I read it straight through before I headed for Kochi Airport. It was after reading that book I discovered that Shibu had written a book on Jude (a book that was published in 2015), but in Malayalam. Maybe someday I will get the English translation and remember my extra blessing in 2012.

By late that afternoon, I got an e-mail back from Emily confirming my American connections to my trip home. It was time to repack and get back into the car with Sijin, Shaji, and Shagu for that all too familiar road to Kochi. We left at ten o'clock after a series of final goodbyes. By 1:38 A.M., I was at gate #5 in the Kochi Airport waiting my flight out of India. I still had two and a half hours to wait, but I had gotten use to waiting!

66

GOING HOME ANOTHER WAY

> I Kings 18:6 "So they divided the land between them to pass throughout it: Ahab went one way by himself, and Obadiah WENT ANOTHER WAY BY HIMSELF."

I HAD COME TO India by way of Kuwait Air through Kuwait City, Kuwait, and if it hadn't been for Hurricane Sandy I would have returned the same way. My forty-eight extra hours in Kerala had changed my way home. If it hadn't been for a persistent Kuwait Airline agent in Kochi, I would have had to wait five days for my next flight out of India by way of Kuwait Air, but because this unnamed lady had looked at other options on other airlines, she found me a seat on a Qatar Airline flight on November 2, 2012 through Doha, Qatar. I was leaving from the same place and arriving back in America in the same place, but I was going home another way. Even when I got to the States, I would be also going back to Maine from New York another way. This final leg of my 2012 adventure in India had one final spiritual lesson for me. I wrote this in my trip journal:

> This morning as I traveled back from India, I slipped back into my past and strolled again along the path the Good Lord created for me. I returned in my mind to Perham, my boyhood home, and what reminds of old scenes and fond recollections that have been stored and enshrined in the cathedral of my memory for over sixty years. I made my way through the woodland-lined lanes of my youth as I winged my way west over the Arabian Sea. I crossed again the familiar stream from my home in the hills of west Perham to the little church in the wildwood that Sunday morning, as I had every Sunday morning of my youth. To me it seemed no different that dawning, but like my last India experience, I would find a new way home before the morning was through.
>
> As I crossed the Persian Gulf to land in Doha, I thought of all the water that has run through my childhood creek since I made that memorable crossing on June 4, 1958. It was a typical Sunday morning at the Perham Baptist Church. As was the custom then, we had morning worship service first and Sunday

school would follow. Instead of joining my parents in the sanctuary, I went into the basement of the church with my sister Sylvia and the rest of the kids of the Church. Our worship time would be conducted by Lily Harris, our Junior Church leader. I knew only this format all my days in Perham; for until the age of twelve, no child was allowed in the adult service. We didn't know any better; actually when I experienced other forms of Sunday worship I thought them strange! The call for boarding my Doha to JFK flight only interrupted my journey back to Perham for a moment as I settled into my seat near the back of the plane. My thoughts drifted again back to a middle seat in the front row of a series of rows filled from front to back, according to age. Being but seven, I was in the front row with my best friend Morris, a next-door neighbor my family brought to church.

As the Qatar pilot took us to 35,000 feet and pointed the nose of his massive jet towards Eastern Europe, I was taken back as if what I was remembering happened yesterday. I recalled that the little band of country kids who had gathered to learn about Jesus didn't have much. As far as I knew, there were no rich people in Perham; we didn't know much compared to what seven-year-olds know today. We didn't need much because we didn't know about all the stuff that was out there. We were a contented group that enjoyed our simple form of fellowship because the same kids that showed up to church were the same kids I went to school with during the week. Life was wholesome and without the great temptations there are today, both at school and Sunday school. As I gained back the ten and a half hours I lost on my trip to India, I gained back the clear image of that monumental day at the Perham Baptist Church Junior Church. It took hours to clear Europe and Iceland and the southern coast of Greenland before heading over eastern Canada for a northern approach into JFK. Despite the fact the average junior church service was less than an hour, each minute became an hour as if in slow motion that soul-searching statement by Lily penetrated my spirit and electrified my mind:

"If you were the only person living on planet Earth Jesus still would have died for you!"

I still don't remember what Lily's Bible lesson was on, but I have never forgotten that statement. In my thoughts, I debated the truth of the phrase. There was a part of me that doubted, but there was a glimmer of faith that believed it was true. I know now the theology of it all: how the Spirit of God was planting in me the faith to believe, and instead of rejecting the conviction, I grasped it like a drowning man after a stick. It was then I felt the glow of the indwelling of the Spirit of God in my life. I was only seven and I still had much to learn about the Bible, the God of the Bible, and my Lord Jesus Christ, but as of that moment, I knew I was going home another way, another person!

Through my memory, decades have passed, and my landing in New York was flawless. That old gang of mine from the Perham Baptist Church is scattered around this world, and a few have already departed to that other world. I stood quietly in the terminal at JFK and couldn't believe the mess one storm had created in one of America's biggest cities, just how many people were trying to get home another way. It took me two hours to ride a bus to the terminal where I would catch a flight to Boston, which was another way from how I had come. If I had dared fight the congestion, it would have taken only a simple ten-minute walk. My wife had tried to warn me of the disruption Sandy had created, but until one experiences it, one never realizes how vulnerable mankind is. I still didn't know if I would get to my flight on time and catch a bus from Boston to Portland by another way on this trip, but deep in my heart was the wonderful peace that my way to heaven was clear, settled long ago when sitting in a small chair in the front row of a junior church service, I decided to go home another way!

I stood quietly that morning on an airline shuttle bus heading for the JetBlue terminal reflecting how far I had come on my other way home. I came to the conclusion that Jesus was right when He said, "Take my yoke upon you and learn of Me . . . ." (Matthew 11:29) I have been in His school for nearly six decades now, and I know I still have a lot to learn. I am a slow learner at best with few A's to my credit. I only seek at the end of this road a "well done" from Him. But if there is one thing I have learned, it is the way home (John 14:6), so it was only fitting that on the last hours of my 2012 journey to India I was able to find my way home another way. I made my JetBlue flight into Boston, and when I stepped out into the autumn air, the bus to North Station was only a few minutes behind me. There was a seat for me on the Boston to Portland bus, and when I reached Portland, my dear wife Coleen was waiting for me.

Our three-hour car ride home was over familiar ground. I arrived safely home early on Saturday morning November 3, 2012. I had been fifty-two hours without sleep, thirty-eight of them to travel from

Edayappara, India to Ellsworth, Maine, but I was home. I expect nothing less from the spiritual journey I am on. Vance Havner once wrote:

"And I am upheld by that sweetly solemn thought that comes to me o'er and o'er- (like on another way home from India) that I am nearer home than I've ever been before."

——— POSTLUDE ———
MY INDIAN PRAYER LIST

Philippians 4:6 "Be careful for nothing; but in everything BY PRAYER AND SUPPLICATION with thanksgiving LET YOUR REQUESTS be made known to God."

With every trip to India, I come back to my American ministry with a page or two in my travel journal of prayer requests I picked up along the way. One of the first things I share with my wife when I made it safety back home is what is happening among the people she has also learned to love. Despite the fact she has never travelled to India, some of our dear friends from India have travelled here. My wife has entertained at least seven individuals over the years from the ministry that is the Independent Gospel Baptist Churches of India. My trip to that ministry and the information I brought back has only filled in the blanks for her. One of the first things she asks me is what the prayer needs are. My wife is the real prayer warrior of our family, so it wasn't long after I returned in 2010 I share with her requests like this. In 2012 I heard how so many of these requests were answered.

1. That Pastor Lawrence can get the work at Tholady restarted. (He did!)
2. For the marriage of Raju Sagar in March in Orissa. (They were!)
3. For Mary John and the death of her husband. (Got to see her!)
4. That the TorchBearers Ministry in Assam will work with the IGBC. (Not yet!)
5. For the start of another academic year at KBBC in June. (It did!)
6. That the Simon family will be able to get their dual-citizenship in America. (Yes!)
7. For the need of a better water supply for the village of Mukkada. (Still praying!)

8. The difficult situations developing in the mountain churches of the IGBC. (Still!)
9. That Pastor Thanks of Elappara will join the IGBC. (Not yet!)
10. That Pastor Johnson and wife Lydia might have children of their own. (Not yet!)
11. That the newest orphan (Angel) at the orphanage would get saved. (Not yet!)
12. Whether or not Shaju should go back to school for his Masters. (He will!)
13. Whether or not an official church should be started at 58 Colony. (No!)
14. Julie's brother's arranged marriage will overcome problems. (They haven't!)
15. For Joy Thomas as he begins a new work at his mother's house. (Has!)
16. Health concerns for Rachael Simon, Mary's sister. (Got to see her!)
17. The health of PP Mati, former pastor of Kangazha, after a disabling stroke. (Still!)
18. The troubles with the neighbors at Venmony will be resolved. (Still!)
19. That Jaldev and his father will accept help from the IGBC. (Not yet!)
20. That Joy Thomas will be able to move back to Orissa with his family soon. (Yes!)
21. That Julie will get a Visa to come to America the next time Shaju does. (She did!)
22. The needs of Pastor George's family who lives away from Kangazha. (Still!)
23. That Pastor Surendra's (pastor from Orissa) shoulder would get better. (It did!)
24. For all those who made a profession of faith in Andrah Pardesh. (Pray on!)
25. That the Church in Dangul might be able to build another sanctuary. (They did!)

26. For the operation Sake Matthew needs for his bad shoulder (accident). (Yes!)
27. A place can be found for a Pastor's School in Orissa. (Waiting!)
28. That the Simon's cousin Rudy and husband Alex can move to England. (Done!)
29. That Sujin Rai from Tamil Nadu will become a pastor. (Still praying!)
30. That Professor Matthew will find a cure for his battle with gout. (Heaven!)

Paul admonished us best when he wrote the church at Philippi, "Be careful for nothing, but in everything by prayer and thanksgiving let your requests be made know unto God." (Philippians 4:6)

India is a land with many prayer requests, but it is also a land with many prayer warriors. I count it one of my greatest honors to be allowed to pray with them about their prayer needs. So, to add to the requests I already have, I came back to share these requests with my wife and church family:

1. Joy Thomas' mother and wife's health concerns.
2. Mary George fighting breast cancer.
3. That George of Munnar would know Christ better.
4. KJ Thomas fighting blindness.
5. The work in the Punjab will continue.
6. Lalu and the Gospel working in a new village.
7. Four lads from Kunnam, Jobin, Joegin, Kensin, and Sobin, would go to KBBC.
8. Grace for Marie, 93-year-old oldest member of the IGBC.
9. What is Joyce to do after the orphanage?
10. 504 Colony Church needs a new roof.
11. Johnson Matthew able to finish church and orphanage building.
12. Johnson Matthew's Bible Institute in the mountains.
13. Saints able to build a new church sanctuary in Bhubaneshwar.
14. Hannah, the only child I have dedicated in India, grace to grow.
15. Elizabeth, the widow of Pastor Kruso, grace in widowhood.

16. Jara, my Hindu driver, would get saved.
17. Shamus, my Moslem driver, would get saved.
18. Sisters, Prosandy and Suesandy, are able to attend KBBC.
19. Where Pastor John should move his family to Kerala.
20. Safety for Joy Thomas in the dangerous areas of Orissa.
21. Sisters, Silu and Asha, find husbands.
22. Pastor Dasrath and the Moonda Baptist Church.
23. Suresh's sick father.
24. Raju Sagar begin a Bible Institute in Orissa.
25. KBBC mission outreach to Manipur in April 2013.

    For me, one of the greatest obligations I have after visiting the uttermost parts of the world is the prayer requests I return home with. I was so burdened with this responsibility this time that I have set up a time each week (Tuesday at 9:00 A.M. – the same time the pastors in Kerala meet for their weekly prayer meeting) to pray for the requests I have received on my four mission trips to India! The uttermost places are prayerful places and places in need of prayer! At the last edit of this book, three and a half year of such prayer meetings are behind me, and I will prey on until I get to return to the uttermost part.

CONCLUSION
THE UTTERMOST ULTIMATUM

> Hebrews 7:25 "Wherefore He is able also to save them to the UTTERMOST that come unto God by Him, seeing He ever liveth to make intercession for them."

MY TRIP TO THE uttermost part of India and back took thirty-seven days between September 29 through November 3, 2012 and covered 22,999 miles. Despite the Sandy delay, I arrived home safe and sound or so I thought. I only discovered a few days after my journey that I had picked up my first bladder infection, a small price to pay for such a marvelous trip. I have only fond memories of my fourth Indian mission trip. During my travels, I spent twenty-five and a half hours on a train or bus; thirty-two and a half hours on planes; thirty-six and a half hours waiting for a train, a bus, or a plane, and thirty-nine and a half hours in a car. I spent eighteen days at Kerala Baptist Bible College, seven days visiting the churches of India, five days traveling to India and Orissa, three days celebrating special events in the IGBC, two days touring and two days waiting on Hurricane Sandy. I have now travelled eighty-three thousand one hundred and eighteen miles in my four missionary trips to the subcontinent of India. The uttermost part will take you far away from home, but what you find is the uttermost becomes home.

So how does one end a record of a journey to God's uttermost part? What is it about this special part of God's domain that has captured my imagination and has drawn me to its shore all these years? Why am I saving still and praying still to repeat this trip, even if it is to another section of this region far beyond Maine? I believe the answer to these questions and so many more are found in the verse I have printed for you at the beginning of this final chapter: salvation to the uttermost for those living in the uttermost. Is there any doctrine more profound than this when it comes to taking the Gospel to any corner of the world? Even before the missionary arrives, even before the first Gospel message is delivered, the Lord Jesus has already made provision for redemption from sin. John put it this way. "And He (Jesus) is the propitiation for our sins: and not for ours only, but also for the sins of the WHOLE (including the uttermost) world." (I John 2:2)

It was years ago while studying the Psalms that I came upon one of the greatest ignored psalms of the Psalms. Psalm 139, I believe, has one of the best insights into the Person of God described in the Bible. I especially love verses 7-12, but in particular this concept:

"If I take the wings (like plane's wings) of the morning, and dwell in the UTTERMOST parts of the sea" (Psalms 139:9), (but could I expound on this with the uttermost parts of the earth) "Even there shall Thy hand lead me, and Thy right hand shall hold me." (Psalms 139:10)

Not only will Christ save to the uttermost, He will be with you in the uttermost. Where can we go in God's creation that His saving grace and merciful hand is not already there? We often call places like India pagan lands or demonic countries, yet we forget that even in hell we can find the Spirit of God. Read carefully Psalms 139:8. God promised His people Israel that if they would repent and turn back to keep His commandments and do them that even if they were "cast out unto the uttermost part of the heaven" (Nehemiah 1:9), yet He would still gather them back to the Promised Land. If God can do that for them, then He can gather the people of the uttermost part to Himself. He is daily doing that very thing around the world (Acts 2:47).

God can save to the uttermost, gather from the uttermost, but His wrath is also explained by the uttermost.

"For ye, brethren, became followers of the churches of God which in Judaea are in Christ Jesus: for ye also have suffered like things of your own countrymen, even as they have of the Jews: who both killed the Lord Jesus, and their own prophets, and have persecuted us; and they please not God, and are contrary to all men: forbidding us to speak to the Gentiles that they might be saved, to fill up their sins always: FOR THE WRATH IS COME UPON THEM TO THE UTTERMOST." (I Thessalonians 2:14-16)

The doctrine of the uttermost has several layers of interpretation. India, like all lands including America, is like the people Paul was writing about. There are those I found in Orissa that would hinder, block, or bar the Christian from speaking the Gospel. One day these will be cast into utter darkness in the Lake of Fire. There is reserved an uttermost place for those that will not heed the Gospel call. Originally created for the Devil and his angels (Matthew 25:41), this uttermost part of God's creation will also house those who have rejected God's Son. I have met more in India that have rejected Christ than those that have accepted Christ, yet my hope and prayer is as my brothers and sisters in India proclaim the Truth about Christ, others will join them, as the two did in Bhubaneswar the last night I was there.

My final challenge on the uttermost is a verse I just discovered as I prayed and pondered how I would end this book. This concept comes directly from the lips of Christ when He was speaking of the Great Tribulation days (Mark 13:24-26).

"And then shall He send His angels, and shall gather together His elect from the four winds, from the UTTERMOST PART OF THE EARTH to the UTTERMOST PART OF HEAVEN." (Mark 13:27)

It was upon reading this verse that I realized the uttermost is also a heavenly term, from the uttermost corners on this planet to the uttermost parts of heaven. I can honestly write that each of my five trips to the uttermost have been heavenly in nature, so if my sixth is to Heaven, I already know that I have been saved to the uttermost, saved from the uttermost, and gathered from the uttermost to live forever in the uttermost of God. As I write in the beginning of this conclusion, the uttermost is home no matter which way you understand it. That is why I enjoy singing this old gospel song.

> This world is not my home I'm just passing through.
> My treasures are laid up somewhere (it is called the uttermost) beyond the blue.
> The angels beckon me from Heaven's open door,
> And I can't feel at home in this world anymore!

I desire the uttermost, and I am destined for the uttermost. Are you?

—Barry Blackstone